THE CHARLTON STANDARD CATALOGUE OF

ROYAL DOULTON BESWICK STORYBOOK FIGURINES

FOURTH EDITION

BY
JEAN DALE

INTRODUCTION
BY
LOUISE IRVINE

W. K. CROSS
PUBLISHER

The Charlton Press
TORONTO, ONTARIO • BIRMINGHAM, MICHIGAN

Canadian Cataloguing In Publication Data

The Charlton price guide to Royal Doulton and Beswick storybook figurines Annual.
1994-
Issues for 1995-   have title: Charlton price guide
to Royal Doulton Beswick storybook figurines.
Cover title: Charlton standard catalogue of Royal Doulton Beswick storybook figurines, 1995- .
ISSN 1198-1652
ISBN 0-88968-196-1 (1998)

1. Porcelain animals - Catalogs. 2. Royal Doulton figurines - Catalogs. I. Charlton Press.
II. Title: Royal Doulton Beswick storybook figurines. III. Title: Charlton price guide to Royal Doulton Beswick storybook figurines. IV. Title: Royal Doulton and Beswick storybook figures. V. Title: Charlton standard catalogue of Royal Doulton Beswick storybook figurines, 1995- .
NK4660.C5   738.8'2'0294   C94-900402-2

EDITORIAL

Editor	Jean Dale
Editorial Assistant	Nicola Leedham
Graphic Technician	Davina Rowan
Photography	Marilyn and Peter Sweet

ACKNOWLEDGEMENTS

The Charlton Press wishes to thank those who have helped with the fourth edition of *The Charlton Standard Catalogue of Royal Doulton Beswick Storybook Figurines*.

Special Thanks

The publisher would like to thank Louise Irvine for writing the introduction to this edition. Louise is an independent writer and lecturer on Royal Doulton's history and products and is not connected with the pricing in this price guide.

We would also like to thank Carolyn Baker for all the work on the Beatrix Potter series, both for this edition and previous editions.

Our thanks also go to Royal Doulton (U.K.) Limited, which helped with additional technical information, especially Ian Howe; and Christine Tatton, Lawleys By Post.

Contributors to the Fourth Edition

The publisher would also like to thank the following individuals and companies who graciously supplied photographs or information or allowed us access to their collections for photographic purposes: **George and Nora Bagnall**, Precious Memories, Charlottetown, P.E.I.; **Judith Best**, Madoc, Ontario; **John and Diana Callow**, England; **William Cross**, William Cross Antiques and Collectibles, Burnaby, B.C.; **Margery Forester**, Devon, England; **Keith Jones**, Shropshire, England; **Pat O'Brien**, Toronto, Ontario; **Ed Pascoe**, Pascoe & Company, Florida; **M. J. Pearle**, Wiltshire, England; **Jamie Pole**, Seaway China, Michigan; **Annette Power**, The Collector, London, England; **Andrew Reid**, By Dollar, Scotland; **Laura Rock-Smith**, Sayville, N.Y.; **Leah Selig**, Merrylands, Australia; **Marcy Shope**, Kingsport, Tennessee; **Marilyn and Peter Sweet**, Bolton, England; **Gene Truitt**, Tru-Find Collectibles, Virgina; **Nick Tzimas**, U. K. International Ceramics, Suffolk, England; **Loretta Wilson**, Kinsport, Tennessee; **Stan Worrey**, Colonial House, Ohio.

A SPECIAL NOTE TO COLLECTORS

We welcome and appreciate any comments or suggestions in regard to *The Charlton Standard Catalogue of Royal Doulton Beswick Storybook Figurines*. If any errors or omissions come to your attention, please write to us, or if you would like to participate in pricing or supply previously unavailable data or information, please contact Jean Dale at (416) 488-1418, or e-mail us at chpress@charltonpress.com.

**Printed in Canada
in the Province of Manitoba**

The Charlton Press

Editorial Office
2040 Yonge Street, Suite 208
Toronto, Canada. M4S 1Z9
Telephone (416) 488-1418 Fax: (416) 488-4656
Telephone 800-442-6042 Fax: 800-442-1542
www.charltonpress.com

HOW TO USE THIS PRICE GUIDE

THE PURPOSE

The fourth edition of this price guide covers the complete range of children's figures issued by Royal Doulton and Beswick. In the process we have taken liberties with the name of this catalogue, for all figures listed are certainly not derived from storybook characters. However, the great majority are, and thus we have carried the name forward.

As with the other catalogues in Charlton's Royal Doulton reference and pricing library, this publication has been designed to serve two specific purposes. First, to furnish the collector with accurate and detailed listings that provide the essential information needed to build a rewarding collection. Second, to provide collectors and dealers with current market prices for the complete line of Doulton and Beswick storybook figures.

STYLES AND VERSIONS

STYLES: A change in style occurs when a major element of the design is altered or modified as a result of a deliberate mould change. An example of this is *The Duchess With Flowers* (style one) and *The Duchess With a Pie* (style two).

VERSIONS: Versions are modifications in a minor style element, such as the long ears becoming short ears on *Mr. Benjamin Bunny*.

VARIATIONS: A change in colour is a variation; for example, *Mr. Jeremy Fisher*'s change in colourways from spotted to striped leggings.

THE LISTINGS

The Beatrix Potter figures are arranged alphabetically. At the beginning of the Beatrix Potter listings are two pages graphically outlining backstamp variations. Backstamps are illustrated for eleven different varieties covering over fifty years of production. In the Beatrix Potter pricing charts, the reader will see Beswick and Doulton model numbers, backstamp numbers and market prices.

The Brambly Hedge figures are listed by their DBH numbers. There are no backstamp variations known.

The Bunnykins figures are arranged in numerical order by DB numbers, with the exception of the first six, which were issued in the late 1930s. These are *Billy, Farmer, Freddie, Mary, Mother* and *Reggie*, and they are arranged alphabetically. There are six different backstamps used on the Bunnykins figures. Please see the section on backstamp variations at the beginning of the Bunnykins listings.

The Snowman series is listed in numerical order by the DS numbers. There are no backstamp variations.

All of the above listings include the modeller, where known, the name of the animal figure, designer, height, colour, date of issue, varieties and series.

A WORD ON PRICING

The purpose of this catalogue is to give readers the most accurate, up-to-date retail prices for Royal Doulton and Beswick figures in the United States, Canada, the United Kingdom and Australia.

To accomplish this, The Charlton Press continues to access an international pricing panel of experts who submit prices based on both dealer and collector retail-price activity, as well as current auction results in the U.S., Canada, and the U.K. These market prices are carefully averaged to reflect accurate valuations for figures in each of these markets.

The prices published herein are for figures in mint condition. Collectors are cautioned that a repaired or restored piece may be worth as little as 25 percent of the value of the same figure in mint condition.

Current figures are priced according to the manufacturer's suggested retail price in each of the market regions. Please be aware that price or promotional sales discounting is always possible and can result in lower prices than those listed.

One exception, however, occurs in the case of current figures or recent limited editions issued in only one of the three markets. Since such items were priced by Doulton only in the country in which they were to be sold, prices for the other markets are not shown.

A further word on pricing. As mentioned previously, this is a catalogue giving prices for figures in the currency of a particular market (U.S. dollars for the American market and sterling for the U.K. market). The bulk of the prices given herein are not determined by currency exchange calculations, but by actual market activity in the market concerned.

In some case the number of models produced is so small that market activity does not exist. There is no price activity on which to base a price. An example of this is the "Spirit of Whitfield" with only four existing models. The price in this instance is purely between the buyer and the seller. We have therefore listed the last known auction price for this model. If this model was to be offered for sale at a future date the price may be higher or lower than the auction price listed depending on the demand for the model at that time. For models with little or no market data due to the limited number of figures produced, we have reverted to the following rarity table:

Rare	26 - 50 figures known
Very rare	11 - 25 figures known
Extremely rare	5 - 10 figures known
Auction results	1 - 4 figures known

When prices are italicized in the pricing tables, for example, *Duchess*, this indicates that the price is only an indication. The prices are too high and too volatile to establish a solid market price. Once again, the final price determination must be made between buyer and seller.

CONTENTS

INTRODUCTION
By Louise Irvine

THE HISTORY OF STORYBOOK CHARACTERS FROM THE ROYAL DOULTON, JOHN BESWICK AND ROYAL ALBERT STUDIOS

For over a century, the Royal Doulton Studios have entertained us with storybook characters, particularly animals endowed with human personalities. In Victorian times, a group of frogs enacting a well-known fable raised a smile in much the same way as the antics of the BRAMBLY HEDGE™ mice amuse us today. The tales of BEATRIX POTTER™, with lots of different animals acting and conversing as if they were human, are as popular now as when they were first written in the early 1900s. Similarly the BUNNYKINS™ characters, first created in the 1930s, have survived the vagaries of fashion to become the most popular collectables of the 1990s. Obviously the idea of a creature simultaneously human and animal is deep rooted in our literary culture, and it is interesting to trace when it first became apparent in the Doulton world.

A Tinworth mouse group

The Doulton factory was founded in London in 1815, but for the first 50 years production was confined to practical pottery. In the late 1860s, Sir Henry Doulton established an art studio, employing students from the Lambeth School of Art to decorate vases, jugs and plaques in fashionable Victorian styles. Some artists specialised in figurative sculpture, notably George Tinworth, who was the first to seek inspiration from

well-known stories. The Bible provided him with most of his subject matter, but he also enjoyed reading the fables of Aesop and La Fontaine. These moralistic tales feature foxes, mice, lions and other creatures exemplifying human traits, and they fascinated the Victorians, particularly after the publication of Darwin's theory of evolution. Tinworth modelled several fables groups in the 1880s, including *The Fox and the Ape, The Cat and the Cheese* and *The Ox and the Frogs*. Later he produced mice and frog subjects, based on his own observations of human nature, which reflect his perceptive sense of humour.

The potential for dressed-up animals to disguise a deeper message soon led to their widespread use in children's literature, notably *Alice's Adventures in Wonderland* and Lear's nonsense poems. In 1908, Kenneth Grahame wrote *The Wind in the Willows* to comment on the behaviour of the English aristocracy, but the exciting adventures of Mr. Toad subtly conceal the author's critical stance. The dapper toad in his pinstripes and tails was modelled shortly afterwards by Lambeth artist Francis Pope, and a companion piece shows Mr. Toad disguised as a washerwoman in order to escape from prison.

Mr. Toad disguised as a washerwoman

Figures like these probably encouraged Beatrix Potter to approach the Lambeth studio in 1908 with a view to having her own animal characters immortalised in ceramic. Miss Potter published several illustrated stories about her favourite animals after the success of *The Tale* of Peter Rabbit™ in 1902, and some characters had already appeared as cuddly toys and decorative motifs on clothes, etc. Unfortunately an earlier contract with a German china firm made any arrangement with Doulton impossible, but she tried on a later occasion to have figures made of her characters at Grimwade's factory in Stoke-on-Trent. They suggested that Doulton's other factory in Burslem would be the best place to have the figures decorated, but again plans fell through. It was not until after Miss Potter's death that her dream was realised when the John Beswick factory in Longton began making little figures inspired by her books.

The John Beswick factory was founded in 1894 to produce ornamental jugs, vases and other decorative fancies. By the 1940s the Beswick artists had established a reputation for quality animal modelling, particularly portraits of famous horses by Arthur Gredington. In 1947, Gredington demonstrated his versatility when he modelled *Jemima Puddleduck* at the suggestion of Lucy Beswick, the wife of the managing director. She had been inspired by a visit to Beatrix Potter's Lake District home, where many of the tales are set. The success of this first study led to an initial collection of ten Beatrix Potter characters, including *Peter Rabbit*, *Benjamin Bunny* and *Mrs. Tiggy Winkle*.

A group of Beatrix Potter books with the figures beside

Launched in 1948, the new Beatrix Potter figures were welcomed with enthusiasm, and it was not long before Gredington was at work on another collection of character animals, this time from an American animated film. The *Lion* cartoon by David Hand was released in 1948, and Zimmy the Lion became a new star for the Rank Film Organisation. Sequel cartoons introduced Ginger Nutt, Hazel Nutt, Dinkum Platypus, Loopy Hare, Oscar Ostrich, Dusty Mole and Felia Cat, all of which were modelled in 1949 as the *DAVID HAND'S ANIMALAND*™ series. David Hand had formerly worked for the Walt Disney studios, directing Mickey

Mouse shorts, as well as the major films *Snow White* and *Bambi*, and it was not long before these cartoons also inspired a collection of Beswick figures. Arthur Gredington modelled the little figures of *Snow White and the Seven Dwarfs* whilst Jan Granoska, a trainee modeller, was given the task of portraying Mickey Mouse and friends, plus some characters from *Pinocchio* and *Peter Pan*. Although Miss Granoska was only at the Beswick studio for three years, she was responsible for some of their most desirable figures.

Music (of sorts!) is being played by the BEDTIME CHORUS™, a group of enthusiastic children accompanied by a singing cat and dog. These were amongst the first character figures to be modelled by Albert Hallam, who gradually took over responsibility for this area in the 1960s. As head mouldmaker, Hallam had made many of the production moulds for Gredington designs, so he was already familiar with the subject matter. He continued the *Beatrix Potter* collection, adding characters such as *Old Mr. Brown* and *Cecily Parsley*, and in 1968 he launched a new Disney series based on their newest cartoon hit, *Winnie the Pooh and the Blustery Day*.

The late 1960s was a time of transition for the company, as Ewart Beswick was ready to retire but he had no heir for his successful business. Fortunately the Royal Doulton group was in the midst of an expansion programme and they acquired the Beswick factory in 1969. They soon benefited from Beswick's expertise in the field of character animals, as Albert Hallam began modelling little figures inspired by their famous Bunnykins nurseryware.

The Bunnykins characters were originally created in the 1930s by Barbara Vernon, a young nun who taught in an English convent school. She often entertained her pupils with sketches and stories about the Bunnykins characters and their potential as nurseryware decoration was recognised by her father Cuthbert Bailey, who was Doulton's managing director at the time. Bunnykins was launched in 1934 and, more than sixty years later, it is still one of the world's best-selling nurseryware patterns.

Artist Bunnykins with the nurseyware plate

There had been an attempt in 1939 to start a collection of Bunnykins figures, but the Second World War intervened and production was not resumed, making the first six characters very rare indeed. Nine new style figures by Albert Hallam were launched in 1972, followed by three more the following year, and they were all derived from characters in the Bunnykins nurseryware scenes. When Albert Hallam retired in 1975, Graham Tongue became the head modeller at the Beswick Studio under Harry Sales, newly appointed as design manager.

Harry Sales was primarily a graphic artist and he dreamed up many new ideas for Bunnykins figures, which Graham Tongue and others modelled during the 1980s. He created a new adult audience for Bunnykins with his witty sporting subjects, for example *Jogging Bunnykins* and *Bogey Bunnykins*, and as collector interest grew, he began to design special commissions, such as *Uncle Sam* and *Collector Bunnykins*. At the same time, he was responsible for the continued development of the Beatrix Potter range, which was becoming increasingly difficult as the most popular characters had already been modelled. Favourites, such as *Peter Rabbit* and *Jemima Puddleduck*, were introduced in new poses, and he came up with the idea of double figures, for example *Mr Benjamin Bunny and Peter Rabbit* and *Tabitha Twitchet and Miss Moppet*.

As well as developing the established figure collections, Harry Sales delved into lots of other children's books for inspiration. He reinterpreted the timeless characters from classic tales such as *Alice's Adventures in Wonderland* and *The Wind in the Willows*, and he worked from contemporary picture books, notably Joan Walsh Anglund's *A Friend is Someone Who Likes You* and Norman Thelwell's *Angels on Horseback*. Whenever possible, Harry liaised closely with the originators of the characters he portrayed. He spent many happy hours of research at Thelwell's studio, studying his cartoons of shaggy ponies with comical riders, and he also worked with Alfred Bestall, the illustrator of the Rupert Bear adventures in the *Daily Express* newspaper before embarking on this series in 1980.

With their outstanding reputation for developing character animals, it is not surprising that Royal Doulton artists were invited to work on the publishing sensation of the 1980s, the Brambly Hedge stories by Jill Barklem. Within three years of their launch the spring, summer, autumn and winter stories had been reprinted 11 times, translated into ten languages, and had sold in excess of a million copies. Readers young and old were captivated by the enchanting world of the Brambly Hedge mice, as indeed was Harry Sales, whose job it was to recreate the characters in the ceramic medium. In his own words, "The first time I read the books and studied the illustrations I felt that I was experiencing something quite unique. Over a period of many years designing for the pottery industry one develops an awareness, a 'feeling' for that something special. Brambly Hedge had this."

Ideas flowed quickly and eight leading characters were chosen from the seasonal stories for the initial collection, which was launched in 1983. Such was the response that they were soon joined by six more subjects, making a total of 14 by 1986, when Harry left the company. Graham Tongue succeeded him as design manager and continued to add new Brambly Hedge figures from the original stories. Miss Barklem's later titles, *The Secret Staircase*, *The High Hills* and *The Sea Story*, provided inspiration for some of his figures; for example, *Mr and Mrs Saltapple* who supply the Brambly Hedge community with salt in *The Sea Story*.

Encouraged by the amazing success of the Brambly Hedge collection, Royal Doulton's marketing executives were soon considering other new storybook characters. Like millions of TV viewers, they were spellbound by the magical film, *The Snowman*, which was first screened in 1982. Based on the illustrated book of the same name by Raymond Briggs, the animated film about a snowman who comes to life has become traditional Christmas entertainment in many parts of the world. The absence of words gives the tale a haunting quality, and there is hardly a dry eye in the house when the little boy, James, awakes to find his Snowman friend has melted away after an exciting night exploring each other's worlds. Fortunately the SNOWMAN™ lives on in more durable form in the Royal Doulton collection. Again Harry Sales was given the challenge of transforming this amorphous character into ceramic, whilst remaining faithful to Briggs' original soft crayon drawings. He succeeded in this difficult task by adding additional curves to the contours of the figures which gives them a life-like appearance. The first four figures were ready and approved by Raymond Briggs in 1985, and the collection grew steadily until 1990, latterly under the direction of Graham Tongue.

So far the 1990s has seen Graham Tongue and his team of artists developing the Beatrix Potter and Bunnykins collections for two major anniversaries—the 100th birthday of *Peter Rabbit* and the diamond jubilee of Bunnykins in 1994. Also in 1994, the centenary of the Beswick factory was marked with the launch of the *Pig Promenade*, featuring a special commemorative backstamp.

This series is just one of three new collections of novelty figures, and it is refreshing to see this traditional type of Beswick ware being revitalised by a new generation of artists. Amanda Hughes-Lubeck and Warren Platt created the LITTLE LOVABLES™, a series of cute clowns with special messages, such as "Good Luck" and "Congratulations," and they also worked with Martyn Alcock on the collection of ENGLISH COUNTRY FOLK™, which has been very well received.

The collecting of Beatrix Potter and Bunnykins figures has reached epidemic proportions in recent years, and there is now a growing awareness of the desirability of all their storybook cousins, hence the need for this much expanded price guide.

COLLECTING BEATRIX POTTER FIGURES

A number of factors have combined recently to make Beatrix Potter figures the "hottest" collectables of the 1990s. The 100th birthday of *Peter Rabbit* was celebrated amidst a storm of publicity in 1993, and the centenary of the John Beswick factory in 1994 focused a lot of collector attention on its products. 1997 saw more celebrations as Beatrix Potter figures had been in continuous production at Beswick for fifty years.

The market has been stimulated by recent withdrawals from the range—a record 19 figures were withdrawn in 1997, making more than 60 retired figures to find so far. Prices are rocketing for the early discontinued figures, and most collectors will need a bank loan to purchase *Duchess with Flowers*, the first Beatrix Potter figure to be retired, if indeed they are lucky enough to find one for sale.

Ever since the Beswick factory launched their Beatrix Potter collection in 1948, most of the figures have been bought as gifts for children. However, many young fans have grown up to find they have some very valuable figures, with early modelling and backstamp variations, and they have begun collecting in earnest to fill the gaps and find the rarities. Figures marked with a Beswick backstamp are most in demand, as this trademark was replaced with the Royal Albert backstamp in 1989. The Royal Albert factory, another famous name in the Doulton group, produces all the Beatrix Potter tableware, and the change of backstamps was made for distribution reasons. The most desirable Beswick marks are the gold varieties, which predate 1972, and these are often found on early modelling or colour variations, which also attract a premium price, for example, *Mrs Rabbit* with her umbrella sticking out and *Mr Benjamin Bunny* with his pipe protruding.

As well as seeking out discontinued figures and rare variations, it is advisable to keep up to date with new models as they are introduced. A complete Beatrix Potter figure collection will encompass more than 100 of the standard-size models, around three inches tall, and ten large models, which are about twice the size. *Peter Rabbit*, the first of these large size models, was launched in 1993 with a special commemorative backstamp from the John Beswick studio, and it changed in 1994 to the standard Royal Albert mark.

If owning all the Beatrix Potter figures is beyond the realms of possibility, whether for financial or display limitations, then why not focus on particular types of animals or characters from your favourite tales. There are twenty mice figures to find, a dozen cat characters and more than twenty rabbits, including 12 portraits of *Peter Rabbit* to date. There are also discontinued character jugs, relief modelled plaques and a ceramic display stand to look out for, so happy hunting.

COLLECTING BUNNYKINS FIGURES

The diamond jubilee of Bunnykins brought the famous rabbit family into the limelight once again, and a special *60th Anniversary Bunnykins*, proudly carrying a birthday cake, was just one of eight new figures released in 1994. The wide variety of introductions each year is indicative of today's tremendous enthusiasm for collecting Bunnykins. When the DB range was launched in 1972, most of the figures were purchased to amuse young children, but the sporting characters of the 1980s began to appeal to adults and, in many cases, exchanging whimsical gifts developed into serious collecting.

Harry Sales drawing for Collector Bunnykins

The Golden Jubilee celebrations in 1984 introduced Bunnykins to an even wider audience, and led to the first collectors book, published by Richard Dennis. Fans were introduced to the entire range of nurseryware and figures, including the six large-size models from 1939, which are extremely hard to find. Apart from these elusive models, it was relatively easy to form a complete collection of figures in the mid 1980s, as the DB range consisted of just 28 models with only four withdrawals. *Autumn Days, Springtime, The Artist* and *Grandpa's Story*, withdrawn in 1982 and 1983, are now very sought after on the secondary market, but subsequent developments have generated much rarer characters. In 1986, Royal Doulton USA ordered new colourways of *Mr and Mrs Easter Bunnykins* to sell at a programme of artist demonstrations, and these are now extremely difficult to find. Similarly, the two special colourways of *Bedtime Bunnykins*, made for D. H. Holmes and Belks department stores in 1987 and 1988, are now increasing in price as serious collectors try to get hold of them.

Although most Bunnykins characters are modelled with young children in mind, there have been several subjects exclusively for collectors, notably *Collector Bunnykins* which was commissioned by the International Collectors Club in 1987. As it was only offered for a six month period, it is now one of the rarest models in the DB range. *The Royal Doulton Collectors Band*, featuring the first limited-edition Bunnykins figures, was launched at the London Doulton Fair in 1990, and since then there have been several limited pieces for exclusive distribution and special occasions. The overwhelming response to these special commissions was highlighted in 1993 when the *Sergeant Mountie Bunnykins* sold out within hours of its launch at the Canadian Doulton show. Similarly, many of the limited editions commissioned by UK International Ceramics are now fully subscribed.

With this in mind, it is a good idea to buy the new Bunnykins figures as soon as they are issued. Royal Doulton has now allocated 180 DB numbers and, although a few intervening numbers have not been issued, notably *Ballet Bunnykins*, DB 44, committed collectors now have quite a challenge to find them all. Figures are now regularly withdrawn from the range, adding to the excitement of the chase and, like many fellow collectors, you can always dream of finding all the rare 1939 models!

COLLECTING BRAMBLY HEDGE FIGURES

Since their introduction in 1983, the Brambly Hedge mice have overrun households in many parts of the world. They are scurrying about the shelves as Royal Doulton figures and even climbing up the walls on decorative plates. Far from being undesirable, these particular mice are considered indispensable members of the family. Children frequently receive them as gifts from doting grandparents, but adults have also been seduced by the cosy, timeless mouse world which Jill Barklem has created. The mood of rustic nostalgia has all been painstakingly researched. The interiors of the field mice homes are of the sort common in English farmhouses at the end of the 19th century, and the food served is genuine country fare, based on old recipes and tasted in Jill Barklem's kitchen. The Brambly Hedge residents were all expertly drawn with the aid of her two mouse models, a keen understanding of zoology and a knowledge of historical costume.

The same attention to detail went into the Royal Doulton figures designed by Harry Sales. As he explains, "One important feature in the concept was that I chose poses which, when the figures are together, appear to be reacting to one another. I can imagine the fun children and the young at heart will have arranging the figures in conversational situations." Essentially this sums up the collectability of the Brambly Hedge mice, and as there are only 25 figures in the series, they can all be displayed effectively together on one shelf. Royal Doulton retired the entire collection in 1997 but there are plans for more figures in the future. In the meantime, there is one unusual modelling variation to look out for, as *Mr Toadflax's* tail was altered shortly after its introduction.

COLLECTING SNOWMAN FIGURES

Initially, the seasonal appeal of the Snowman tended to limit his collectability, as most purchases were made around Christmas time, and he was more popular in areas which regularly experience snow. Having said this, for some fans the wintry connotations were overshadowed by the inherent quality and humour of the models and there are now keen collectors in sunny

Florida as well as in Australia, where beach barbecues are typical Christmas celebrations.

Between 1985 and 1990, young children regularly received the new Snowman models in their Christmas stockings, and the characters have been widely used as holiday decorations. Like the Brambly Hedge models, they were designed to interact, and the little figure of *James*, gazing up in wonder can be positioned with various Snowman characters, whilst the band works very well as a separate display grouping. There are 19 figures and two musical boxes to collect and, as the range was withdrawn in 1994 they can now be quite difficult to locate. In fact, prices have been snowballing, particularly for the figures that were not in production for long, notably *The Snowman Skiing*.

COLLECTING STORYBOOK CHARACTERS

The Beatrix Potter, Brambly Hedge and Snowman stories have already been discussed in some detail, as there are so many figures to collect in each of the categories. However, the Beswick artists have also sought inspiration in other children's stories, some better known than others.

The American author-illustrator, Joan Walsh Anglund, enjoyed quite a vogue in the 1960s following the publication of *A Friend is Someone Who Likes You* (1958). Three of her drawings of cute children with minimal features were modelled by Albert Hallam for the Beswick range in 1969, but they were withdrawn soon after, making them extremely hard to find today.

The bizarre cast of characters from *Alice's Adventures in Wonderland* has offered a lot more scope for collectors. First published in 1865, this classic tale has entertained generations of young readers and inspired many artistic interpretations. In the early 1900s, Doulton's Lambeth artists modelled some fantastic creatures from the tale, notably the pig-like *Rath* from the "Jabberwocky" poem. The Burslem studio designed an extensive series of nurseryware and, more recently, a collection of character jugs based on the original illustrations by Sir John Tenniel, who firmly fixed the appearance of the Wonderland characters in the public imagination. Harry Sales also consulted the Tenniel illustrations in 1973 when designing Beswick's ALICE IN WONDERLAND™.

Curiously the figures inspired by another great children's classic, *The Wind in the Willows*, did not have the same appeal. Christina Thwaites, a young book illustrator, was commissioned to produce designs for a collection of wall plates and tea wares, and her watercolours of Mr Toad, Ratty, Mole, Badger and others were interpreted by the Beswick modellers. Four figures were launched in 1987 and two more in 1988 as part of a co-ordinated giftware range with the Royal Albert backstamp, but they were withdrawn in 1989. Consequently *Portly* and *Weasel*, the later introductions, were only made for one year, and will no doubt prove particularly hard to find in the future.

With the WIND IN THE WILLOWS™ collection, the Royal Doulton artists have come full circle, reflecting the enthusiasm of their predecessors at Lambeth, notably

Francis Pope who modelled two superb figures of Mr Toad shortly after the book was published. Obviously storybook characters, particularly animals in human guises, have timeless appeal.

COLLECTING CARTOON CHARACTERS

Cartoon characters, whether they be from animated films or comic book strips, are becoming a popular field for collectors. The forthcoming book on the subject, together with introductions, such as *Tom and Jerry*, will surely generate even more interest. Now is the time to start collecting, if you have not already done so.

The characters from David Hand's Animaland are virtually unknown today, but following their film debut in 1948, they were sufficiently well known to inspire Beswick's first series of cartoon figures. Modelled in 1949 and withdrawn in 1955, *Zimmy the Lion* and his seven friends now have a different kind of notoriety, stealing the show when they come up for auction.

In contrast, Mickey Mouse is the best known cartoon character in the world. Within a year of his 1928 screen debut in *Steamboat Willie*, his image was being used to endorse children's products, and by the 1950s there were more than 3,000 different Mickey Mouse items, including plates, dolls, watches and clothes. With all this merchandising activity, it is not surprising that the Beswick studio sought a license for portraying Mickey and his friends in ceramic.

A range of nurseyware was launched in 1954, along with figures of *Mickey* and his girlfriend *Minnie*, *Pluto* his dog and his crazy friends *Goofy* and *Donald Duck*. Characters from some of Walt Disney's feature-length cartoons completed the original WALT DISNEY CHARACTERS™ set of 12 figures. *Peter Pan*, the newest Disney hit in 1953, inspired four characters, *Peter* himself, *Tinkerbell*, *Smee* and *Nana*, whilst the classic *Pinocchio* (1940) provided the puppet hero and his insect conscience *Jiminy Cricket*. Surprisingly only *Thumper* was modelled from another favourite film, *Bambi* (1942), although the fawn appears on the tableware designs. The response to the initial Disney collection encouraged the Beswick factory to launch a second set the following year, featuring *Snow White and the Seven Dwarfs* from Disney's first feature symphony. All the Disney characterisations are superb, making them extremely desirable amongst collectors of Beswick and Disneyana and they are all hard to find, even though they were produced until 1967.

The 1960s saw the rise of a new Disney star, Winnie the Pooh, who became a very popular merchandising character after his cartoon debut in 1966. The Beswick factory was quick off the mark, launching an initial collection of six characters from the film in 1968, followed by two more in 1971. "The Bear of Little Brain" originated in bedtime stories about nursery toys told by AA Milne to his son Christopher Robin in the 1920s, and he was visualised in the resulting books by the illustrator E.H. Shepard. To celebrate the 70th anniversary of the first *Winnie the Pooh* book, Royal Doulton launched a second series of figures in 1996 and these have been a great success. Royal Doulton continue to work closely with the

Walt Disney company today and they have launched two exciting figurine collections featuring Disney *Princesses* and *Villains* exclusively for sale in the Disney stores. The other new Disney collections have been distributed through specialist china shops, notably the *101 Dalmatians* series, which was inspired by the live action film, and the second series of *Snow White and the Seven Dwarfs*, which was prompted by the 60th anniversary of the film. There are plans for a new Disney series featuring Mickey Mouse and his gang during 1998 so don't miss the opportunity to add these to your cartoon collection.

The massive marketing campaigns for Disney characters have made them household names all over the world. British cartoon characters, by comparison, are less well known internationally. The *Daily Express* newspaper was slow to capitalise on the success of Rupert the Bear, who has been the star of their children's comic strip since 1920. Originated by Mary Tourtel, the Rupert stories were enlivened by Alfred Bestall who took over the daily drawings in 1935. Rupert enjoys the most extraordinary adventures with his friends Bill the Badger, Algy Pug and Pong-Ping, always returning safely to his comfortable family home in Nutwood. Rupert Bear annuals sold in millions from the mid 1930s, and his exploits were adapted for TV in the 1970s, but his following is essentially British. No doubt it was for this reason that the five figures in the RUPERT THE BEAR™ collection, designed by Harry Sales in 1980, were relatively short lived.

A similar fate befell the NORMAN THELWELL™ figures, which were in production from 1981 to 1989. Norman Thelwell was a humorous illustrator for *Punch* magazine, who made his reputation with comical observations of young riders and their mounts. *Angels on Horseback*, published in 1957, was the first compilation of his successful cartoons, and many other popular books followed. Thelwell worked closely with Harry Sales to create the most effective figures, both in ceramic and resin, and the results are guaranteed to raise a smile without breaking the bank.

After a gap of nearly 15 years, famous British cartoon characters are back on the drawing board at the Royal Doulton studios once again. *Denis the Menace* and *Desperate Dan*, stars of the long-established children's comics, *The Beano* and *The Dandy*, have been immortalised as character jugs. This is the first time large-size character jugs have been used for portraying cartoons, although there are similarities to the set of six THUNDERBIRDS™ busts modelled by jug designer Bill Harper to celebrate the 30th anniversary of this children's TV show in 1992.

COLLECTING CHARACTER ANIMALS

In the 1880s Doulton's first artist, George Tinworth, was modelling groups of mice engaged in popular human pastimes, and nearly a century later Kitty MacBride did much the same thing with her *Happy Mice*. The appeal of these anthropomorphic creatures is timeless, and collectors have responded with enthusiasm from Victorian times to the present day.

Admittedly, developing a taste for Tinworth's sense of humour will prove very expensive, with models costing several hundreds of pounds each, but the KITTY MACBRIDE™ whimsical mice are still relatively affordable.

Kitty MacBride was a writer and illustrator who began to model little clay figures of mice in 1960. Initially they were sold through a London dealer, but when she could not keep up with the demand she asked the Beswick factory to produce 11 of them commercially, which they did between 1975 and 1983.

The Beswick studio has had a considerable reputation for character animals since the launch of the Beatrix Potter collection in 1948. However, the modellers have not only interpreted illustrations from famous books, from time to time they have envisaged their own comical creatures. Albert Hallam was responsible for a succession of animals with human expressions in the late 1960s. Similar humanising traits can be found in the LITTLE LIKABLES™ collection, which was produced briefly in the mid 1980s. Robert Tabbenor's animals play up the humour of their situation, notably the carefree frog, *Watching the World Go By*, whilst Diane Griffiths takes a more sentimental approach, using human feelings to describe her cartoon-like animals.

The fun has continued in recent years with a collection of footballer cats, produced in 1987 only, and the on-going series of English Country Folk, depicting appropriate animals with human manners and costumes. However, the last laugh is reserved for the Pig Promenade. The absurdity of nine different breeds of pigs playing musical instruments makes this one of the most hilarious series of character animals.

MAKING STORYBOOK CHARACTERS

All the current storybook characters are made at the John Beswick factory in Longton, which became part of the Royal Doulton group in 1969. They have over fifty years' experience in the production of humorous figures and character animals, and essentially the methods have not changed since the earliest days of the Beatrix Potter figures.

First of all the designer has to familiarise himself thoroughly with the character to be portrayed, reading the story and studying the illustration. Having chosen the most suitable pose for interpretation in ceramic, he will produce reference drawings for the modeller. Often he can only see one side of the character in the original illustration, so he has to improvise for his three-dimensional model.

In consultation with the designer, the modeller will create the figure in modelling clay, and if satisfactory, a set of master moulds will be made in plaster of Paris. The number of mould parts will depend on the complexity of the figure, and sometimes the head and arms have to be moulded separately. Two or three prototype figures will be cast from the master mould for colour trials and subsequent approval by the original artist or his agent.

In the case of the Beatrix Potter figures, all the models are scrutinised by the licensing agents, Copyrights, working on behalf of Miss Potter's original publishers, Frederick Warne. Raymond Briggs, who was responsible for the Snowman, is generally quite relaxed about letting experts in other media interpret his drawings. He thought Royal Doulton's models were marvellous and really captured the spirit of the story, although he maintained he would "jolly well say so" if he thought they had got it wrong! Jill Barklem, the creator of Brambly Hedge, likes to get very involved in the licensing of her characters, and design manager Harry Sales spent a lot of time working with her on the finer points of detail. Sometimes slight modifications need to be made to the model or the colour scheme before the figure is approved by all concerned.

The next stage is to produce plaster of Paris working moulds from the master, and supplies are sent to the casting department. An earthenware body is used to cast all the character figures produced at the John Beswick studio, and it is poured into the mould in liquid form, known as slip. The moisture in the slip is absorbed into the plaster of Paris moulds and a "skin" of clay forms the interior.

Once the clay has set to the required thickness, the excess clay is poured out and the mould is carefully dismantled. Any separate mould parts, such as projecting arms, will be joined on at this stage using slip as an adhesive, and the seams will be gently sponged away. The figure is then allowed to dry slowly before it goes for its first firing. The high temperature in the kiln drives out the moisture in the body and the figure shrinks by about 1/12th of its original size, forming a hard "biscuit" body.

Skilled decorators will paint the figure, using special under-glaze ceramic colours. They work from an approved colour sample and great care is taken to match the colours to the original book illustrations. A second firing hardens on the colour before the figure is coated with a solution of liquid glaze. When the figure is fired in the glost kiln, it emerges with a shiny transparent finish which enhances and permanently protects the vibrant colours underneath. After a final inspection, the figures are dispatched to china shops all over the world where they will capture the hearts of collectors young and old.

RESIN FIGURES

Several collectables manufacturers began experimenting with new sculptural materials in the 1980s and developed different types of resin bodies that allow more intricately modelled detail than conventional ceramic processes. Royal Doulton launched its new "bonded ceramic body" in 1984, and two storybook collections were included in its Beswick Studio Sculptures, as the range was known. Seven subjects were chosen from the *Tales of Beatrix Potter* and two from the Thelwell series, but production was short lived, despite the minute detailing of the animals' fur and the tiny pebbles and grasses in their habitat, which would have been impossible to achieve in traditional earthenware. Royal Doulton ceased production of resin at the end of 1985, but designs have been commissioned from resin specialists, notably the *Paddington Bear* and *St. Tiggywinkles* series.

BUYING CURRENT AND DISCONTINUED STORYBOOK CHARACTERS

The Royal Doulton Company owns many well-known china factories, including John Beswick, Royal Albert and Royal Doulton itself, and different trademarks are used for historical reasons or depending on the type of product. The Bunnykins, Brambly Hedge and Snowman collections feature the Royal Doulton backstamp, the Pig Promenade and English Country Folk carry a Beswick backstamp, whilst the Beatrix Potter figures, originally part of the Beswick range, are now marked Royal Albert, although this will revert to Beswick in July 1998. All these varied collections are produced at the John Beswick factory in Longton, Stoke-on-Trent, and models still being made at the factory today are referred to as "current." Most of the current storybook figures can be purchased in specialist china shops or from mail-order companies specialising in collectables. However, some Bunnykins figures have been commissioned for exclusive distribution, by Royal Doulton retailers and can only be obtained from them directly.

Up-to-date information about new introductions to the storybook collections is included in *Gallery* magazine, which is published quarterly by the Royal Doulton International Collectors Club. The Club regularly commissions exclusive collectables for its membership, and Storybook figures have been featured in the past. Members also receive information about withdrawals to the collection in the various branch newsletters.

Once a piece has been withdrawn from production, it is referred to as "discontinued" or "retired," and it enters the secondary market. Many specialist Royal Doulton dealers around the world carry discontinued storybook characters. Some have shops or showrooms, but most sell by mail order and exhibit regularly at antique shows. Some of the more expensive Bunnykins and Beatrix Potter figures are now being sold at auction, notably *Duchess with Flowers*. Some storybook characters do not yet qualify for the minimum lot price but it is still worth watching out for group lots at auctions or estate sales, in case some of the character animals have been included. Perhaps a rare Beatrix Potter or Bunnykins colourway will not be recognised as such!

WHERE TO BUY

Discontinued Doulton and Beswick collectables can be found in Antique shops, Markets, Auctions, Shows and Fairs. Specialist dealers in Royal Doulton and Beswick collectables attend many of the events listed below.

For Auction happenings it is necessary to subscribe to the catalogues provided by those Houses that hold 20th Century or specialist Doulton Auctions.

UNITED KINGDOM

Auction Houses

BBR AUCTIONS
Elsecar Heritage Centre
Nr. Barnsely, South Yorkshire, S74 8HJ
England
(01226) 745156
Attn: Alan Blakeman

BONHAMS
Montpelier Street, Knightsbridge
London, SW7 1HH
England
(0171) 584 9161

CHRISTIE'S SOUTH KENSINGTON
85 Old Brompton Road, London, SW7 3LD
England
(0171) 581 7611
www.christies.com
Attn: Michael Jeffery

DANIEL & HULME
66 Derby Street, Leek, Staffordshire, ST13 5AJ
England
(0153) 838 3339
www.danielhulme.co.uk
Attn: S. J. Hulme

LOUIS TAYLOR
Britannia House
10 Town Road, Hanley, ST1 2QG
England
(01782) 21411
Attn: Clive Hillier

PHILLIPS
101 New Bond Street, London, W1Y 0AS
England
(0171) 629 6602
www.phillips-auctions.com
Attn: Mark Oliver

SOTHEBY'S SUSSEX
Summers Place
Billingshurst, Sussex, RH14 9AF
England
(01403) 783933

THOMPSON RODDICK & LAURIE
60 Whitesands, Dumfries, DG1 2RS
Scotland
(01387) 255366
Attn: Sybelle Medcalf

PETER WILSON
Victoria Gallery, Market Street
Nantwich, Chesire, CW5 5DG, England
(01270) 623878

Antique Fairs

DOULTON AND BESWICK COLLECTORS FAIR
National Motorcycle Museum
Meriden, Birmingham
Usually March and August.
For information on times and dates:
DOULTON AND BESWICK DEALERS ASSOCIATION
(0181) 303 3316

DOULTON AND BESWICK COLLECTORS FAIR
The Queensway Hall Civic Centre, Dunstable, Bedforshire
Usually in October. For information on times and location:
UK FAIRS LTD.
10 Wilford Bridge Spur, Melton, Woodbridge,
Suffolk, 1P12 1RJ
(01394) 386663

DOULTON GROUP COLLECTORS FAIR
Trentham Gardens, Stoke-on-Trent
Usually the last week in May, or the first week in June.
For information on times and dates:
SINCLAIRS
1st Mary's Court, Tickhill, Doncaster, DN11 9QU
(01302) 745287

INTERNATIONAL ANTIQUE & COLLECTORS FAIR
Newark, Nottinghamshire
Usually six fairs annually. For information on times
and dates:
INTERNATIONAL ANTIQUE & COLLECTORS
FAIR LTD.
P.O. Box 100, Newark, Nottinghamshire, NG2 1DJ
(01636) 702326

WEST LONDON WADE BESWICK & DOULTON FAIR
Brunel University, Kingston Lane, Uxbridge,
Middlesex
Usually three fairs a year. For information on times
and location:
B & D FAIRS
P.O. Box 273, Uxbridge, Middlesex, UB9 4LP
(01895) 834694 or 834357

London Markets

ALFIE'S ANTIQUE MARKET
13-25 Church Street, London
Tuesday - Saturday

CAMDEN PASSAGE MARKET
London
Wednesday and Saturday

NEW CALEDONIA MARKET
Bermondsey Square, London
Friday Morning

PORTOBELLO ROAD MARKET
London
Saturday

UNITED STATES

Auction Houses

CHRISTIE'S EAST
219 East 67th Street
New York, NY 10021
(212) 606-0400
www.christies.com
Attn: Timothy Luke

SOTHEBY'S ARCADE AUCTIONS
1334 York Avenue
New York, NY 10021
(212) 606-7000
www.sothebys.com
Attn: Andrew Cheney

Collectable Shows

ATLANTIQUE CITY
New Atlantic City Convention Centre
Atlantic City, NJ
Usually March and October.
For information on times and dates:
BRIMFIELD ASSOCIATES
P.O. Box 1800
Ocean City, NJ 08226
(609) 926-1800
www.atlantiquecity.com

FLORIDA DOULTON CONVENTION & SALE
Sheraton Inn
2440 West Cypress Creek Road
Ft. Lauderdale, FL., 33309
Usually mid-January
For information on times and dates:
PASCOE & COMPANY or CHARLES DOMBECK
101 Almeria Avenue   9552 N.W. 9th Court
Coral Gables, FL   Plantation, FL
33134   33324
(305) 445-3229   (254) 452-9174

O'HARE NATIONAL ANTIQUES SHOW & SALE
Rosemont Convention Centre,
Chicago, IL
Usually April, August and November.
For information on times and dates:
MANOR HOUSE SHOWS INC.
P.O. Box 7320, Fort Lauderdale, FL 33338
(954) 563-6747

ROYAL DOULTON CONVENTION & SALE
John S. Knight Convention Centre
77 E. Mill Street, Akron, OH 44308
Usually August.
For information on times and dates:
COLONIAL HOUSE PRODUCTIONS
182 Front Street, Berea, OH, 44017
(800) 344-9299

CANADA

Auction Houses

MAYNARDS
415 West 2nd Avenue, Vancouver, BC, V5Y 1E3
(604) 876-1311

RITCHIES
288 King Street East, Toronto, ON, M5A 1K4
(416) 364-1864
Attn: Caroline Kaiser

Collectable Shows

CANADIAN ART & COLLECTIBLE SHOW & SALE
Kitchener Memorial Auditorium
Kitchener, ON
Usually early May.
For information on times and location:
George or Jackie Benninger
P.O. Box 130, Durham, ON, N0G 1R0
(519) 369-6950

CANADIAN DOULTON & COLLECTABLE FAIR
Toronto, ON
Usually early September.
For information on times and location:
George or Jackie Benninger
P.O. Box 130, Durham, ON, N0G 1R0
(519) 369-6950

ROYAL DOULTON INTERNATIONAL COLLECTORS CLUB

Founded in 1980 The Royal Doulton International Collectors Club provides an information service on all aspects of the company's products, past and present. A Club magazine, *Gallery*, is published four times per year with news on new products and current events that will assist the collector. Upon joining the club, each new member will receive a free gift and invitations to special events and exclusive offers.

A new visitor centre was opened in the summer of 1996 incorporating a display and design area especially for the Royal Doulton figure collection.

The Visitor Centre is located at:
Nile Street, Burslem, Stoke-on-Trent, ST6 2AJ, England. For opening times and factory tour information please telephone (01782) 292292.

To join the club, please contact your local stockist, or contact the club directly at the address and numbers located below:

ROYAL DOULTON PLC
Minton House, London Road
Stoke-on-Trent, ST4 7QD, England

Telephone:
In the UK: (01782) 292292
In the USA and Canada: 1-800-747-3045 (toll free)
In Austrailia: 011 800-142-624 (toll free)
Fax: (01782) 292127
www.royal-doulton.com
e-mail: icc@royal-doulton.com

DOULTON CHAPTERS

Chapters of RDICC have formed across North America and are worthy of consideration for collectors in these areas.

NEW ENGLAND CHAPTER
Anne Babchyck, President
239 Cedar Street, Dedham, MA 02026
(781) 329-0214
Charles Briggs, Secretary
21 Walpole Street, Norwood, MA 02062
(781) 784-8121

NORTHERN CALIFORNIAN CHAPTER
P.O. Box 3665, Walnut Creek, CA 94598

OHIO CHAPTER
Dick Maschmeier
5556 Whitehaven Ave., North Olmstead, OH, 44070

MID-AMERICA CHAPTER
P.O. Box 483, McHenry, IL 60050

EDMONTON CHAPTER
Mildred's Collectibles
6814 104 Street, Edmonton, AB

FURTHER READING

Storybook Figures

Collecting Cartoon Classics and other Character Figures, by Louise Irvine
Royal Doulton Bunnykins Figures, by Louise Irvine
Bunnykins Collectors Book, by Louise Irvine
Beatrix Potter Figures and Giftware, edited by Louise Irvine
The Beswick Price Guide, by Harvey May

Animals, Figures and Character Jugs

Royal Doulton Figures, by Desmond Eyles, Louise Irvine and Valerie Baynton
The Charlton Standard Catalogue of Beswick Animals, by Diane & John Callow and Marilyn and Peter Sweet
The Charlton Standard Catalogue of Royal Doulton Animals, by Jean Dale
The Charlton Standard Catalogue of Royal Doulton Beswick Figurines, by Jean Dale
The Charlton Standard Catalogue of Royal Doulton Beswick Jugs, by Jean Dale
Collecting Character and Toby Jugs, by Jocelyn Lukins
Collecting Doulton Animals, by Jocelyn Lukins
Doulton Flambé Animals, by Jocelyn Lukins
The Character Jug Collectors Handbook, by Kevin Pearson
The Doulton Figure Collectors Handbook, by Kevin Pearson

General

The Charlton Standard Catalogue of Beswick Pottery, by Diane and John Callow
The Charlton Standard Catalogue of Bunnykins, by Jean Dale
Discovering Royal Doulton, by Michael Doulton
The Doulton Story, by Paul Atterbury and Louise Irvine
Royal Doulton Series Wares, by Louise Irvine (Vols. 1-5)
Limited Edition Loving Cups and Jugs, by Louise Irvine and Richard Dennis
Doulton for the Collector, by Jocelyn Lukins
Doulton Kingsware Flasks, by Jocelyn Lukins
Doulton Burslem Advertising Wares, by Jocelyn Lukins
Doulton Lambeth Advertising Wares, by Jocelyn Lukins
The Doulton Lambeth Wares, by Desmond Eyles
The Doulton Burslem Wares, by Desmond Eyles
Hannah Barlow, by Peter Rose
George Tinworth, by Peter Rose
Sir Henry Doulton Biography, by Edmund Gosse
Phillips Collectors Guide, by Catherine Braithwaite
Royal Doulton, by Jennifer Queree
John Beswick: A World of Imagination. Catalogue reprint (1950-1996)

Magazines and Newsletters

Rabbitting On (Bunnykins Newsletter) Contact Leah Selig: 2 Harper Street, Merrylands 2160, New South Wales, Australia. Tel/Fax: 612 9637 2410 (International), 02 9637 2410 (Australia)

Collect it! Contact subscription department at: P.O. Box 3658, Bracknell, Berkshire RG12 7XZ. Telephone: (1344) 868 280 or e-mail: collectit@dialpipex.com

Collecting Doulton Magazine, published by Francis Joseph, edited by Doug Pinchin

ALICE IN WONDERLAND

BESWICK EARTHENWARE SERIES
ROYAL DOULTON RESIN SERIES

ALICE IN WONDERLAND

EARTHENWARE SERIES 1973-1983

2476
ALICE™
Style One

Designer:	Albert Hallam and Graham Tongue
Height:	4 ¾", 12.1 cm
Colour:	Dark blue dress, white apron with red trim
Issued:	1973 - 1983

Beswick		Price		
Number	U.S. $	Can. $	U.K. £	Aust. $
2476	550.00	700.00	275.00	600.00

2477
WHITE RABBIT™
Style One

Designer:	Graham Tongue
Height:	4 ¾", 12.1 cm
Colour:	White rabbit wearing a brown coat, yellow waistcoat
Issued:	1973 - 1983

Beswick		Price		
Number	U.S. $	Can. $	U.K. £	Aust. $
2477	550.00	650.00	275.00	600.00

2478
MOCK TURTLE™

Designer:	Graham Tongue
Height:	4 ¼", 10.8 cm
Colour:	Browns and grey
Issued:	1973 - 1983

Beswick		Price		
Number	U.S. $	Can. $	U.K. £	Aust. $
2478	400.00	450.00	150.00	200.00

2479
MAD HATTER™
Style One

Designer:	Albert Hallam
Height:	4 ¼", 10.8 cm
Colour:	Burgundy coat, yellow and blue checked trousers, yellow and red bowtie, grey hat
Issued:	1973 - 1983

Beswick		Price		
Number	U.S. $	Can. $	U.K. £	Aust. $
2479	425.00	550.00	225.00	500.00

2480
CHESHIRE CAT™
Style One

Designer:	Albert Hallam and Graham Tongue
Height:	1 ½", 3.8 cm
Colour:	Tabby cat
Issued:	1973 - 1982

Beswick		Price		
Number	U.S. $	Can. $	U.K. £	Aust. $
2480	800.00	1,000.00	475.00	750.00

2485
GRYPHON™

Designer:	Albert Hallam
Height:	3 ¼", 8.3 cm
Colour:	Browns and greens
Issued:	1973 - 1983

Beswick Number	Price U.S. $	Can. $	U.K. £	Aust. $
2485	325.00	400.00	125.00	200.00

2489
KING OF HEARTS™

Designer:	Graham Tongue
Height:	3 ¾", 9.5 cm
Colour:	Burgundy, yellow, white, blue and green
Issued:	1973 - 1983

Beswick Number	Price U.S. $	Can. $	U.K. £	Aust. $
2489	130.00	150.00	60.00	175.00

2490
QUEEN OF HEARTS™
Style One

Designer:	Graham Tongue
Height:	4", 10.1 cm
Colour:	Blue, green, yellow, white and burgundy
Issued:	1973 - 1983

Beswick Number	Price U.S. $	Can. $	U.K. £	Aust. $
2490	130.00	150.00	60.00	175.00

2545
DODO™
Style One

Designer: David Lyttleton
Height: 4", 10.1 cm
Colour: Browns and greens
Issued: 1975 - 1983

Beswick		*Price*			
Number		*U.S. $*	*Can. $*	*U.K. £*	*Aust. $*
2545		375.00	550.00	160.00	325.00

2546
FISH FOOTMAN™

Designer: David Lyttleton
Height: 4 ¾", 14.6 cm
Colour: Blue, gold, white and brown
Issued: 1975 - 1983

Beswick		*Price*			
Number		*U.S. $*	*Can. $*	*U.K. £*	*Aust. $*
2546		450.00	550.00	200.00	500.00

2547
FROG FOOTMAN™

Designer: David Lyttleton
Height: 4 ¼", 10.8 cm
Colour: Maroon jacket with yellow
            trim, blue trousers
Issued: 1975 - 1983

Beswick		*Price*			
Number		*U.S. $*	*Can. $*	*U.K. £*	*Aust. $*
2547		450.00	550.00	250.00	500.00

ALICE IN WONDERLAND

RESIN SERIES 1997-1997

ALICE™
Style Two

Designer:	Adrian Hughes
Height:	4", 10.1 cm
Colour:	Pale blue and white dress, red and white toadstool, green base
Issued:	1997 - 1997

Doulton Number	Price			
	U.S. $	Can. $	U.K. £	Aust. $
—	40.00	50.00	25.00	50.00
Complete Set (6 pcs.)	250.00	300.00	150.00	300.00

CHESHIRE CAT™
Style Two

Designer:	Adrian Hughes
Height:	4", 10.1 cm
Colour:	Orange striped cat, blue butterfly, red ladybird, brown tree stump, green base
Issued:	1997 - 1997

Doulton Number	Price			
	U.S. $	Can. $	U.K. £	Aust. $
—	40.00	50.00	25.00	50.00

DODO™
Style Two

Designer:	Adrian Hughes
Height:	4", 10.1 cm
Colour:	White bird with blue wing tips, yellow head and black beak
Issued:	1997 - 1997

Doulton Number	Price			
	U.S. $	Can. $	U.K. £	Aust. $
—	40.00	50.00	25.00	50.00

MAD HATTER™
Style Two

Designer:	Adrian Hughes
Height:	4", 10.1 cm
Colour:	Brown trousers and top hat, green jacket, blue waistcoat, green base
Issued:	1997 - 1997

Doulton Number		Price		
	U.S. $	Can. $	U.K. £	Aust. $
—	40.00	50.00	25.00	50.00

QUEEN OF HEARTS™
Style Two

Designer:	Adrian Hughes
Height:	4", 10.1 cm
Colour:	Red coat trimmed with white, white dress with red and black design, black and red crown
Issued:	1997 - 1997

Doulton Number		Price		
	U.S. $	Can. $	U.K. £	Aust. $
—	40.00	50.00	25.00	50.00

WHITE RABBIT™
Style Two

Designer:	Adrian Hughes
Height:	4", 10.1 cm
Colour:	White rabbit with brown jacket and green waistcoat, green base
Issued:	1997 - 1997

Doulton Number		Price		
	U.S. $	Can. $	U.K. £	Aust. $
—	40.00	50.00	25.00	50.00

BEATRIX POTTER FIGURES

BEATRIX POTTER BACKSTAMPS

BP-1   BESWICK GOLD CIRCLE
ISSUED 1948 TO 1954

BP-1 was used on 21 figures between 1948 and 1954. There are two varieties of this backstamp, the first a circle and the second a modification of the circle. The modification was necessary due to the small base on two figures - Mrs. Rabbit and the Tailor of Gloucester. The backstamp circle was flattened and the copyright was written in script lettering.

The following is a list of figures that can be found with a BP-1 backstamp:

Benjamin Bunny, first version
Flopsy, Mopsy and Cottontail
Foxy Whiskered Gentleman, first version
Hunca Munca
Jemima Puddle-duck, first version
Johnny Town-mouse
Lady Mouse
Little Pig Robinson, first variation
Miss Moppet, first variation
Mr. Jeremy Fisher, first and second variations
Mrs. Rabbit, first version
Mrs. Tiggy Winkle, first variation
Mrs. Tittlemouse
Peter Rabbit, first version
Ribby
Samuel Whiskers
Squirrel Nutkin, first variation
Tailor of Gloucester, first version
Timmy Tiptoes, first variation
Timmy Willie From Johnny Town-Mouse
Tom Kitten, first version
Tommy Brock, first version, second variation

BP-1 Beswick Gold Circle

BP-2   BESWICK GOLD OVAL
ISSUED 1952 TO 1972

The gold oval was in use for 18 years, between 1955 and 1972, and it was used on 38 figures. Pig-Wig, introduced in 1972, was the last in line for the gold oval backstamp, and in some quarters they still doubt that it officially exists.

The following is a list of figures that can found with a BP-2 backstamp:

Amiable Guinea Pig
Anna Maria
Appley Dappley, first version
Aunt Pettitoes
Benjamin Bunny, first and second versions
Cecily Parsley, first version
Cousin Ribby
Duchess (with flowers)
Flopsy, Mopsy and Cottontail
Foxy Whiskered Gentleman, first version
Goody Tiptoes
Hunca Munca
Jemima Puddle-duck, first version
Johnny Town-mouse
Lady Mouse
Little Pig Robinson, first variation
Miss Moppet, first variation
Mr. Benjamin Bunny, first version
Mr. Jeremy Fisher, first version
Mrs. Flopsy Bunny
Mrs. Rabbit, first version
Mrs. Tiggy Winkle, first and second variations
Mrs. Tittlemouse
Old Mr. Brown
Old Woman Who Lived in a Shoe, The
Peter Rabbit, first version
Pickles
Pigling Bland, first variation
Pig-Wig
Ribby
Samuel Whiskers
Squirrel Nutkin, first variation
Tabitha Twitchit, first variation
Tailor of Gloucester, first version
Timmy Tiptoes, first and second variations
Timmy Willie From Johnny Town-Mouse
Tom Kitten, first version
Tommy Brock, first and second versions

BP-2 Beswick Gold Oval

BP-3   **BESWICK BROWN LINE**
ISSUED 1973 TO 1988

These brown line backstamps (Beswick and England are in a straight line) appear on 92 figures, including the different versions. The brown line backstamp saw three major revisions during the 16 years it was in use.

BP-3a Potters, no date, issued 1973 to 1974
(no copyright date)

BP-3b Potters, date, issued 1974 to 1985
(copyright date)

BP-3c Potter, date, issued 1985 to 1988
(no s on Potter)

BP-4   **BESWICK SIGNATURE**
ISSUED 1988 TO 1989

This era saw the Beswick backstamp converted to the Royal Doulton backstamp. The connection with Beswick was kept by the addition of the John Beswick signature to the backstamp. In use for a year to a year and a half, this is one of the shortest time periods for a backstamp.

Beswick Signature

BP-5   **ROYAL ALBERT GOLD CROWN**
ISSUED 1989

The gold backstamp was reinstituted for 1989 to mark the change from the Doulton/Beswick backstamps to Royal Albert. It was used on only the following six figures:

> Benjamin Bunny, third version
> Flopsy, Mopsy and Cottontail
> Hunca Munca
> Jemima Puddleduck, first version
> Mrs. Rabbit and Bunnies
> Peter Rabbit, first version, second variation

BP-5 Gold Crown

BP-6   **ROYAL ALBERT BROWN CROWN**
ISSUED 1989 TO DATE

This backstamp was issued in two sizes. A small version was used on the standard figures with a larger size for the large size figures. The small size was issued in 1989 and the large size was issued in 1993. A variation of the small size exists without the crown for small base figures.

BP-6a Small brown crown   BP-6b Large brown crown

BP-7   **100th ANNIVERSARY OF PETER RABBIT**
1893 TO 1993

Issued only on the large size Peter Rabbit to commemorate the 100th anniversary of Peter Rabbit.

BP-7 Peter Rabbit Centennary

BP-8　　**100th ANNIVERSARY OF THE
BESWICK STUDIOS 1894-1994**

Issued to commemorate the 100th anniversary of the founding of the Beswick studios. This backstamp was only available on Jemima Puddle-duck.

BP-8 100th Anniversary of Beswick Studios

BP-9　　**50th ANNIVERSARY OF
BEATRIX POTTER AT
BESWICK STUDIOS 1947-1997**

1997 was the 50th anniversary of the production of Beatrix Potter figurines being made at the John Beswick Studios in Longton.

BP-9 50th Anniversary

BP-10　　**BESWICK WARE GOLD
1997**

This gold backstamp was coupled with gold highlights on the following figurines:

>Benjamin Bunny, third version, second variation
>Benjamin Bunny, fourth version, second variation
>Hunca Munca, second variation
>Jemima Puddle-duck, first version, second variation
>Jemima Puddle-duck, second version,
>　　second variation
>Mrs Tiggy-Winkle, first version, third variation
>Mrs Tiggy-Winkle, second version, second variation
>Peter and the Red Pocket Handkerchief,
>　　first version, second variation
>Peter Rabbit, first version, third variation
>Peter Rabbit, second version, second variation
>Tom Kitten, first version, third variation

BP-10 Beswick Gold

BP-11　　**BESWICK
1998 TO DATE**

A new Beswick backstamp is to be introduced in 1998. So far only two pieces have this backstamp:

>Peter Rabbit Gardening
>Tom Kitten in the Rockery

AMIABLE GUINEA PIG™

Modeller: Albert Hallam
Height: 3 ½", 8.9 cm
Colour: Tan jacket, white waistcoat, yellow trousers
Issued: 1967 - 1983

Back Stamp	Beswick Number	Doulton Number	U.S. $	Price Can. $	U.K. £	Aust. $
BP-2	2061	P2061	700.00	800.00	350.00	775.00
BP-3a			375.00	600.00	250.00	550.00
BP-3b			350.00	550.00	225.00	500.00

Note: The colour of the coat varies from tan to brown.

AND THIS PIG HAD NONE™

Modeller: Martyn Alcock
Height: 4", 10.1 cm
Colour: Mauve dress, mottled burgundy and green shawl, brown hat
Issued: 1992 to the present

Back Stamp	Beswick Number	Doulton Number	U.S. $	Price Can. $	U.K. £	Aust. $
BP-6a	3319	P3319	38.00	58.00	16.00	90.00

ANNA MARIA™

Modeller: Albert Hallam
Height: 3", 7.6 cm
Colour: Blue dress and white apron
Issued: 1963 - 1983

Back Stamp	Beswick Number	Doulton Number	U.S. $	Price Can. $	U.K. £	Aust. $
BP-2	1851	P1851	525.00	600.00	250.00	600.00
BP-3a			300.00	375.00	175.00	400.00
BP-3b			250.00	300.00	150.00	350.00

Note: Dress is bright blue in earlier versions and pale blue in later versions.

APPLEY DAPPLY™
First Version (Bottle Out)

Modeller:	Albert Hallam
Height:	3 ¼", 8.3 cm
Colour:	Brown mouse, white apron, blue trim, blue bow, yellow basket, tray of jam tarts
Issued:	1971 - 1975

Back Stamp	Beswick Number	Doulton Number	U.S. $	Price Can. $	U.K. £	Aust. $
BP-2	2333	P2333/1	775.00	925.00	350.00	600.00
BP-3a			400.00	500.00	225.00	300.00
BP-3b			375.00	475.00	200.00	275.00

APPLEY DAPPLY™
Second Version (Bottle In)

Modeller:	Albert Hallam
Height:	3 ¼", 8.3 cm
Colour:	Brown mouse, white apron, blue trim, blue bow, yellow basket, tray of jam tarts
Issued:	1975 to the present

Back Stamp	Beswick Number	Doulton Number	U.S. $	Price Can. $	U.K. £	Aust. $
BP-3b	2333	P2333/2	80.00	90.00	50.00	100.00
BP-3c			110.00	125.00	75.00	125.00
BP-6a			38.00	58.00	16.00	90.00

AUNT PETTITOES™

Modeller:	Albert Hallam
Height:	3 ¾", 9.5 cm
Colour:	Blue dress and white cap with blue polka dots
Issued:	1970 - 1993

Back Stamp	Beswick Number	Doulton Number	U.S. $	Price Can. $	U.K. £	Aust. $
BP-2	2276	P2276	525.00	600.00	200.00	600.00
BP-3a			100.00	135.00	65.00	150.00
BP-3b			85.00	100.00	50.00	100.00
BP-3c			100.00	135.00	65.00	150.00
BP-6a			50.00	60.00	30.00	75.00

Note: The dress is light blue in earlier versions and bright blue in later versions.

BABBITTY BUMBLE™

Modeller:	Warren Platt
Height:	2 ¾", 7.0 cm
Colour:	Black and gold
Issued:	1989 - 1993

Back Stamp	Beswick Number	Doulton Number	U.S. $	Price Can. $	U.K. £	Aust. $
BP-6a	2971	P2971	110.00	175.00	50.00	135.00

BENJAMIN ATE A LETTUCE LEAF™

Modeller:	Martyn Alcock
Height:	4 ¾", 11.9 cm
Colour:	Brown, white and yellow
Issued:	1992 to the present

Back Stamp	Beswick Number	Doulton Number	U.S. $	Price Can. $	U.K. £	Aust. $
BP-6a	3317	P3317	38.00	58.00	16.00	65.00

BENJAMIN BUNNY™
First Version (Ears Out, Shoes Out)

Modeller:	Arthur Gredington
Height:	4", 10.1 cm
Size:	Small
Colour:	Variation No. 1 pale green jacket
	Variation No. 2 brown jacket
Issued:	1948 - 1974

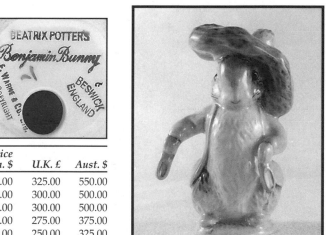

Back Stamp	Beswick Number	Colour Variation	U.S. $	Price Can. $	U.K. £	Aust. $
BP-1	1105/1	Pale green	550.00	625.00	325.00	550.00
BP-2		Pale green	500.00	575.00	300.00	500.00
BP-2		Brown	500.00	575.00	300.00	500.00
BP-3a		Pale green	400.00	425.00	275.00	375.00
BP-3b		Brown	350.00	400.00	250.00	325.00

BENJAMIN BUNNY™
Second Version (Ears Out, Shoes In)

Modeller:	Arthur Gredington
Height:	4", 10.1 cm
Size:	Small
Colour:	Variation No. 1 pale green jacket
	Variation No. 2 brown jacket
Issued:	1972 - c.1980

Back Stamp	Beswick Number	Colour Variation	U.S. $	Price Can. $	U.K. £	Aust. $
BP-2	1105/2	Pale green	500.00	550.00	300.00	500.00
BP-3a		Pale green	375.00	375.00	275.00	350.00
BP-3a		Brown	375.00	375.00	275.00	350.00
BP-3b		Pale green	300.00	300.00	250.00	300.00
BP-3b		Brown	300.00	300.00	250.00	300.00

BENJAMIN BUNNY™
Third Version, First Variation (Ears In, Shoes In)

Modeller:	Arthur Gredington
Height:	4", 10.1 cm
Size:	Small
Colour:	Brown jacket, green beret with orange pompon
Issued:	c.1980 to the present

Back Stamp	Beswick Number	Doulton Number	U.S. $	Price Can. $	U.K. £	Aust. $
BP-3b	1105/3	P1105/3	80.00	90.00	50.00	60.00
BP-3c			90.00	110.00	65.00	100.00
BP-4			100.00	120.00	75.00	100.00
BP-5			140.00	165.00	100.00	175.00
BP-6a			38.00	58.00	16.00	65.00

BENJAMIN BUNNY™
Third Version, Second Variation (Gold Shoes)

Modeller:	Arthur Gredington
Height:	4", 10.1 cm
Size:	Small
Colour:	Brown jacket, green beret with orange pompon, gold shoes
Issued:	1998 - 1998

Back Stamp	Beswick Number	Doulton Number	U.S. $	Price Can. $	U.K. £	Aust. $
BP-10	—	PG1105	60.00	100.00	35.00	125.00

BENJAMIN BUNNY™
Fourth Version, First Variation

Modeller:	Martyn Alcock
Height:	6 ¼", 15.9 cm
Size:	Large
Colour:	Tan jacket, green beret with orange pompon
Issued:	1994 - 1997

Back Stamp	Beswick Number	Doulton Number	U.S. $	Price Can. $	U.K.£	Aust. $
BP-6b	3403	P3403	75.00	105.00	35.00	135.00

BENJAMIN BUNNY™
Fourth Version, Second Variation
(Gold Shoes)

Modeller:	Martyn Alcock
Height:	6 ¼", 15.9 cm
Size:	Large
Colour:	Tan jacket, green beret with orange pompon, gold shoes
Issued:	1997 in a limited edition of 1,947

Back Stamp	Beswick Number	Doulton Number	U.S. $	Price Can. $	U.K. £	Aust. $
BP-10	—	PG3403	—	—	35.00	—

BENJAMIN BUNNY SAT ON A BANK™
First Version (Head Looks Down)

Modeller:	David Lyttleton
Height:	3 ¾", 9.5 cm
Colour:	Brown jacket
Issued:	1983 - 1983

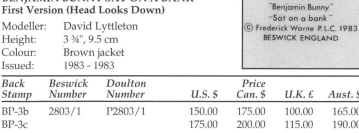

BEATRIX POTTER'S
"Benjamin Bunny"
"Sat on a bank"
© Frederick Warne P.L.C. 1983
BESWICK ENGLAND

Back Stamp	Beswick Number	Doulton Number	U.S. $	Price Can. $	U.K. £	Aust. $
BP-3b	2803/1	P2803/1	150.00	175.00	100.00	165.00
BP-3c			175.00	200.00	115.00	190.00

BENJAMIN BUNNY SAT ON A BANK™
Second Version (Head Looks Up)

Modeller:	David Lyttleton
Height:	3 ¾", 9.5 cm
Colour:	Golden brown jacket
Issued:	1983 - 1997

Back Stamp	Beswick Number	Doulton Number	U.S. $	Price Can. $	U.K. £	Aust. $
BP-3b	2803/2	P2803/2	120.00	150.00	100.00	150.00
BP-3c			150.00	185.00	115.00	175.00
BP-6a			35.00	50.00	15.00	60.00

BENJAMIN WAKES UP™

Modeller:	Amanda Hughes-Lubeck
Height:	2 ¼", 5.7 cm
Colour:	Green, white and orange
Issued:	1991 - 1997

Back Stamp	Beswick Number	Doulton Number	U.S. $	Price Can. $	U.K. £	Aust. $
BP-6a	3234	P3234	40.00	55.00	15.00	60.00

CECILY PARSLEY™
First Version (Blue Dress, Head Down)

Modeller:	Arthur Gredington
Height:	4", 10.1 cm
Colour:	Bright blue dress, white apron, brown pail
Issued:	1965 - 1985

Back Stamp	Beswick Number	Doulton Number	U.S. $	Price Can. $	U.K. £	Aust. $
BP-2	1941/1	P1941/1	300.00	400.00	175.00	350.00
BP-3a			135.00	150.00	75.00	125.00
BP-3b			100.00	110.00	50.00	100.00
BP-3c			115.00	150.00	60.00	125.00

CECILY PARSLEY™
Second Version (Pale Blue Dress, Head Up)

Modeller: Arthur Gredington
Height: 4", 10.1 cm
Colour: Pale blue dress, white apron
Issued: 1985 - 1993

BEATRIX POTTER
"Cecily Parsley"
© Frederick Warne & Co. 1965
Licensed by Copyrights
BESWICK ENGLAND

Back Stamp	Beswick Number	Doulton Number	U.S. $	Price Can. $	U.K. £	Aust. $
BP-3c	1941/2	P1941/2	150.00	150.00	50.00	110.00
BP-6a			65.00	75.00	35.00	65.00

CHIPPY HACKEE™

Modeller: David Lyttleton
Height: 3 ¾", 9.5 cm
Colour: Pale green blanket, white handkerchief, green foot bath
Issued: 1979 - 1993

BEATRIX POTTER'S
Chippy Hackee
F. Warne & Co.Ltd.
© Copyright 1979
BESWICK ENGLAND

Back Stamp	Beswick Number	Doulton Number	U.S. $	Price Can. $	U.K. £	Aust. $
BP-3b	2627	P2627	100.00	125.00	50.00	120.00
BP-3c			125.00	165.00	70.00	150.00
BP-6a			65.00	75.00	35.00	35.00

Note: The colour of the blanket may range from pale green to pale yellow.

CHRISTMAS STOCKING™

Modeller: Martyn Alcock
Height: 3 ¼", 8.3 cm
Colour: Brown mice, red and white striped stocking
Issued: 1991 - 1994

ROYAL ALBERT ®
ENGLAND
The Christmas Stocking
Beatrix Potter
© F. WARNE & CO. 1991
© 1991 ROYAL ALBERT LTD

Back Stamp	Beswick Number	Doulton Number	U.S. $	Price Can. $	U.K. £	Aust. $
BP-6a	3257	P3257	200.00	175.00	60.00	100.00

COTTONTAIL™

Modeller: David Lyttleton
Height: 3 ¾", 9.5 cm
Colour: Blue dress, brown chair
Issued: 1985 - 1996

Back Stamp	Beswick Number	Doulton Number	U.S. $	Price Can. $	U.K.£	Aust. $
BP-3b	2878	P2878	75.00	75.00	50.00	75.00
BP-3c			100.00	110.00	65.00	110.00
BP-4			110.00	125.00	70.00	125.00
BP-6a			40.00	60.00	30.00	80.00

COUSIN RIBBY™

Modeller: Albert Hallam
Height: 3 ½", 8.9 cm
Colour: Pink skirt and hat, green apron, blue shawl, yellow basket
Issued: 1970 - 1993

Back Stamp	Beswick Number	Doulton Number	U.S. $	Price Can. $	U.K. £	Aust. $
BP-2	2284	P2284	500.00	575.00	250.00	500.00
BP-3a			125.00	150.00	75.00	125.00
BP-3b			75.00	80.00	45.00	80.00
BP-3c			115.00	135.00	75.00	125.00
BP-6a			50.00	65.00	40.00	60.00

DIGGORY DIGGORY DELVET™

Modeller: David Lyttleton
Height: 2 ¾", 7.0 cm
Colour: Grey mole
Issued: 1982 - 1997

Back Stamp	Beswick Number	Doulton Number	U.S. $	Price Can. $	U.K. £	Aust. $
BP-3b	2713	P2713	80.00	85.00	50.00	150.00
BP-3c			100.00	135.00	65.00	165.00
BP-6a			50.00	65.00	25.00	75.00

DUCHESS™
Style One (Holding Flowers)

Modeller:	Graham Orwell
Height:	3 ¾", 9.5 cm
Colour:	Black dog, multi-coloured flowers
Issued:	1955 - 1967

Back Stamp	Beswick Number	Doulton Number	U.S. $	Price Can. $	U.K. £	Aust. $
BP-2	1355	P1355	3,500.00	4,500.00	1,650.00	4,000.00

Note: Italized prices are indications only, and the actual selling price may be higher or lower, depending on market conditions.

DUCHESS™
Style Two (Holding a Pie)

Modeller:	Graham Tongue
Height:	4", 10.1 cm
Colour:	Black dog, blue bow, light brown pie
Issued:	1979 - 1982

Back Stamp	Beswick Number	Doulton Number	U.S. $	Price Can. $	U.K. £	Aust. $
BP-3b	2601	P2601	425.00	575.00	250.00	600.00

FIERCE BAD RABBIT™
First Version (Feet Out)

Modeller:	David Lyttleton
Height:	4 ¾", 12.1 cm
Colour:	Dark brown and white rabbit, red-brown carrot, green seat
Issued:	1977 - 1980

Back Stamp	Beswick Number	Doulton Number	U.S. $	Price Can. $	U.K. £	Aust. $
BP-3b	2586/1	P2586/1	275.00	375.00	195.00	325.00

FIERCE BAD RABBIT™
Second Version (Feet In)

Modeller:	David Lyttleton
Height:	4 ¾", 12.1 cm
Colour:	Light brown and white rabbit, red-brown carrot, green seat
Issued:	1980 - 1997

BEATRIX POTTER
"Fierce Bad Rabbit"
© Frederick Warne & Co. 1977
Licensed by Copyrights
BESWICK ENGLAND

Back Stamp	Beswick Number	Doulton Number	U.S. $	Price Can. $	U.K. £	Aust. $
BP-3b	2586/2	P2586/2	110.00	150.00	75.00	125.00
BP-3c			140.00	200.00	95.00	150.00
BP-4			110.00	125.00	55.00	125.00
BP-6a			50.00	65.00	25.00	75.00

FLOPSY, MOPSY AND COTTONTAIL™

Modeller:	Arthur Gredington
Height:	2 ½", 6.4 cm
Colour:	Brown and white rabbits wearing rose-pink cloaks
Issued:	1954 - 1997

BEATRIX POTTER'S
Flopsy, Mopsy
and Cotton Tail
F. WARNE & CO. LTD.
COPYRIGHT
BESWICK ENGLAND

Back Stamp	Beswick Number	Doulton Number	U.S. $	Price Can. $	U.K. £	Aust. $
BP-1	1274	P1274	400.00	450.00	175.00	395.00
BP-2			300.00	275.00	125.00	300.00
BP-3a			125.00	150.00	75.00	125.00
BP-3b			85.00	80.00	55.00	80.00
BP-3c			110.00	125.00	75.00	125.00
BP-4			100.00	150.00	50.00	90.00
BP-5			175.00	200.00	100.00	150.00
BP-6a			40.00	60.00	25.00	60.00

Note: Colour variations of the cloaks exist.

FOXY READING COUNTRY NEWS™

Modeller:	Amanda Hughes-Lubeck
Height:	4 ¼", 10.8 cm
Colour:	Brown and green
Issued:	1990 - 1997

ROYAL ALBERT ®
ENGLAND
Foxy Reading
Beatrix Potter
© F. WARNE & CO. 1990
© 1990 ROYAL ALBERT LTD

Back Stamp	Beswick Number	Doulton Number	U.S. $	Price Can. $	U.K. £	Aust. $
BP-6a	3219	P3219	65.00	85.00	30.00	100.00

FOXY WHISKERED GENTLEMAN™
First Version

Modeller:	Arthur Gredington
Height:	4 ¾", 12.1 cm
Size:	Small
Colour:	Pale green jacket and trousers, pink waistcoat
Issued:	1954 - 1997

Back Stamp	Beswick Number	Doulton Number	U.S. $	Price Can. $	U.K. £	Aust. $
BP-1	1277	P1277	400.00	450.00	225.00	400.00
BP-2			300.00	325.00	150.00	325.00
BP-3a			150.00	175.00	85.00	175.00
BP-3b			120.00	125.00	60.00	115.00
BP-3c			135.00	175.00	85.00	175.00
BP-4			100.00	200.00	75.00	150.00
BP-6a			40.00	60.00	16.00	65.00

Note: Variations occur with the head looking either right or left.

FOXY WHISKERED GENTLEMAN™
Second Version

Modeller:	Arthur Gredington
Height:	6", 15 cm
Size:	Large
Colour:	Pale green jacket and trousers, pink waistcoat
Issued:	1995 - 1997

Back Stamp	Beswick Number	Doulton Number	U.S. $	Price Can. $	U.K. £	Aust. $
BP-6b	3450	P3450	75.00	105.00	30.00	85.00

GENTLEMAN MOUSE MADE A BOW™

Modeller:	Ted Chawner
Height:	3", 7.6 cm
Colour:	Brown, blue and white
Issued:	1990 - 1996

Back Stamp	Beswick Number	Doulton Number	U.S. $	Price Can. $	U.K. £	Aust. $
BP-6a	3200	P3200	50.00	65.00	25.00	85.00

GINGER™

Modeller:	David Lyttleton
Height:	3 ¾", 9.5 cm
Colour:	Green, white and brown
Issued:	1976 - 1982

BEATRIX POTTER'S
"Ginger"
F. Warne & Co.Ltd.
© Copyright 1976
BESWICK ENGLAND

Back Stamp	Beswick Number	Doulton Number	U.S. $	Price Can. $	U.K. £	Aust. $
BP-3b	2559	P2559	900.00	1,100.00	475.00	700.00

Note: The jacket colour varies from light to dark green.

GOODY TIPTOES™

Modeller:	Arthur Gredington
Height:	3 ½", 8.9 cm
Colour:	Grey squirrel wearing pink dress and white apron, brown sack with yellow nuts
Issued:	1961 - 1997

BEATRIX POTTER'S
Goody Tiptoes
F. WARNE & CO. LTD.
COPYRIGHT
BESWICK
ENGLAND

Back Stamp	Beswick Number	Doulton Number	U.S. $	Price Can. $	U.K. £	Aust. $
BP-2	1675	P1675	325.00	375.00	175.00	300.00
BP-3a			110.00	110.00	65.00	110.00
BP-3b			75.00	80.00	40.00	80.00
BP-3c			110.00	110.00	65.00	110.00
BP-6a			50.00	60.00	20.00	75.00

Note: This model has two different bases and the pink dress varies in shade.

GOODY AND TIMMY TIPTOES™

Modeller:	David Lyttleton
Height:	4", 10.1 cm
Colour:	Timmy - rose coat Goody - pink overdress with green and biege underskirt, green umbrella
Issued:	1986 - 1996

BEATRIX POTTER
"Goody & Timmy Tiptoes"
© Frederick Warne & Co. 1986
Licensed by Copyrights
BESWICK ENGLAND

Back Stamp	Beswick Number	Doulton Number	U.S. $	Price Can. $	U.K. £	Aust. $
BP-3c	2957	P2957	300.00	400.00	175.00	300.00
BP-6a			125.00	115.00	50.00	90.00

HUNCA MUNCA™

Modeller:	Arthur Gredington
Height:	2 ¾", 7 cm
Colour:	Blue dress, white apron, pink blanket and straw cradle
Issued:	1951 to the present

Back Stamp	Beswick Number	Doulton Number	U.S. $	Price Can. $	U.K. £	Aust. $
BP-1	1198	P1198	300.00	350.00	125.00	350.00
BP-2			250.00	300.00	100.00	325.00
BP-3a			125.00	150.00	90.00	150.00
BP-3b			95.00	110.00	65.00	110.00
BP-3c			125.00	150.00	90.00	150.00
BP-4			110.00	135.00	75.00	145.00
BP-5			150.00	160.00	100.00	160.00
BP-6a			38.00	58.00	16.00	65.00

HUNCA MUNCA SPILLS THE BEADS™
First Version

Modeller:	Martyn Alcock
Height:	3 ¼", 8.3 cm
Colour:	Brown mouse, blue and white rice jar
Issued:	1992 - 1996

Back Stamp	Beswick Number	Doulton Number	U.S. $	Price Can. $	U.K. £	Aust. $
BP-6a	3288	P3288	60.00	65.00	20.00	85.00

HUNCA MUNCA SWEEPING™
First Variation

Modeller:	David Lyttleton
Height:	3 ½", 8.9 cm
Colour:	Mauve patterned dress with white apron, green broom handle
Issued:	1977 to the present

Back Stamp	Beswick Number	Doulton Number	U.S. $	Price Can. $	U.K. £	Aust. $
BP-3b	2584	P2584	110.00	150.00	65.00	175.00
BP-3c			150.00	175.00	90.00	200.00
BP-4			100.00	200.00	85.00	225.00
BP-6a			38.00	58.00	16.00	65.00

HUNCA MUNCA SWEEPING™
Second Variation (Gold Dustpan)

Modeller:	David Lyttleton
Height:	3 ½", 8.9 cm
Colour:	Mauve patterned dress with white apron, green broom handle, gold dustpan
Issued:	1998 - 1998

Back Stamp	Beswick Number	Doulton Number	U.S. $	Price Can. $	U.K. £	Aust. $
BP-10	—	PG2584	56.00	95.00	25.00	—

JEMIMA PUDDLE-DUCK™
First Version, First Variation

Modeller:	Arthur Gredington
Height:	4 ¾", 12.1 cm
Size:	Small
Colour:	Mauve or pink shawl, light blue bonnet, yellow and beige scarf clip
Issued:	1948 to the present

Back Stamp	Beswick Number	Doulton Number	U.S. $	Price Can. $	U.K. £	Aust. $
BP-1	1092	P1092	275.00	325.00	150.00	350.00
BP-2			225.00	250.00	125.00	300.00
BP-3a			100.00	130.00	90.00	140.00
BP-3b			75.00	90.00	65.00	100.00
BP-3c			100.00	130.00	90.00	140.00
BP-4			95.00	125.00	50.00	125.00
BP-5			140.00	200.00	100.00	185.00
BP-6a			40.00	60.00	16.00	70.00

JEMIMA PUDDLE-DUCK™
First Version, Second Variation
(Gold Scarf Clip)

Modeller:	Arthur Gredington
Height:	4 ¼", 10.75 cm
Size:	Small
Colour:	White duck, mauve or pink shawl, light blue bonnet, gold scarf clip
Issued:	1997 - 1997

Back Stamp	Beswick Number	Doulton Number	U.S. $	Price Can. $	U.K. £	Aust. $
BP-10	—	PG1092	60.00	100.00	35.00	125.00

JEMIMA PUDDLE-DUCK™
Second Version, First Variation

Modeller:	Martyn Alcock
Height:	6", 15 cm
Size:	Large
Colour:	White duck, mauve shawl, light blue bonnet
Issued:	1993 - 1997

Beswick Ware
MADE IN ENGLAND
**BEATRIX POTTER'S
JEMIMA PUDDLE-DUCK**
BESWICK CENTENARY
1894 – 1994
© F.WARNE & CO.1993
© 1993 ROYAL DOULTON

Back Stamp	Beswick Number	Doulton Number	U.S. $	Price Can. $	U.K. £	Aust. $
BP-6b	—	P3373	75.00	105.00	30.00	135.00
BP-8	Beswick Centenary		95.00	125.00	50.00	150.00

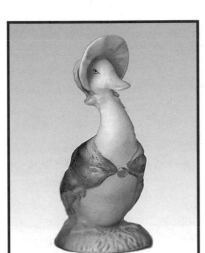

JEMIMA PUDDLE-DUCK™
Second Version, Second Variation
(Gold Scarf Clip)

Modeller:	Martyn Alcock
Height:	6", 15.0 cm
Size:	Large
Colour:	White duck, mauve shawl, light blue bonnet, gold scarf clip
Issued:	1998 in a limited edition of 1,947

Back Stamp	Beswick Number	Doulton Number	U.S. $	Price Can. $	U.K. £	Aust. $
BP-10	—	PG3373	—	—	35.00	—

JEMIMA PUDDLE-DUCK MADE A FEATHER NEST™

Modeller:	David Lyttleton
Height:	2 ¼", 5.7 cm
Colour:	Blue hat, mauve or pink shawl, white duck
Issued:	1983 - 1997

BEATRIX POTTER'S
Jemima Puddleduck
Made a feather nest
© Frederick Warne P LC. 1983
BESWICK
ENGLAND

Back Stamp	Beswick Number	Doulton Number	U.S. $	Price Can. $	U.K. £	Aust. $
BP-3b	2823	P2823	70.00	70.00	40.00	100.00
BP-3c			90.00	85.00	65.00	125.00
BP-4			95.00	110.00	50.00	135.00
BP-6a			40.00	60.00	30.00	65.00

Note: This model was issued with either a mauve or pink shawl.

JEMIMA PUDDLE-DUCK WITH FOXY WHISKERED GENTLEMAN™

Modeller:	Ted Chawner
Height:	4 ¾", 12.1 cm
Colour:	Brown, green, white and blue
Issued:	1990 to the present

ROYAL ALBERT ®
ENGLAND
Jemima Puddleduck with
Foxy Whiskered Gentleman
Beatrix Potter
© F WARNE & CO 1990
© 1990 ROYAL ALBERT LTD

Back Stamp	Beswick Number	Doulton Number	U.S. $	Price Can. $	U.K. £	Aust. $
BP-6a	3193	P3193	61.00	87.00	26.00	110.00

JOHN JOINER™

Modeller:	Graham Tongue
Height:	2 ½", 6.4 cm
Colour:	Brown dog wearing green jacket
Issued:	1990 - 1997

ROYAL ALBERT ®
ENGLAND
John Joiner
Beatrix Potter
© F. WARNE & CO. 1990
© 1990 ROYAL ALBERT LTD

Back Stamp	Beswick Number	Doulton Number	U.S. $	Price Can. $	U.K. £	Aust. $
BP-6a	2965	P2965	40.00	55.00	20.00	100.00

JOHNNY TOWN-MOUSE™

Modeller:	Arthur Gredington
Height:	3 ½", 8.9 cm
Colour:	Pale blue jacket, white and brown waistcoat
Issued:	1954 - 1993

BEATRIX POTTER'S
Johnny Town-Mouse
WARNE & Co. LTD.
COPYRIGHT
BESWICK
ENGLAND

Back Stamp	Beswick Number	Doulton Number	U.S. $	Price Can. $	U.K. £	Aust. $
BP-1	1276	P1276	275.00	350.00	135.00	400.00
BP-2			225.00	250.00	110.00	275.00
BP-3a			100.00	125.00	60.00	150.00
BP-3b			65.00	90.00	45.00	110.00
BP-3c			100.00	125.00	60.00	150.00
BP-6a			50.00	65.00	30.00	65.00

Note: Jacket colouring varies from pale to deep blue.

JOHNNY TOWN-MOUSE WITH BAG™

Modeller:	Ted Chawner
Height:	3 ½", 8.9 cm
Colour:	Light brown coat and hat, yellow-cream waistcoat
Issued:	1988 - 1994

Back Stamp	Beswick Number	Doulton Number	U.S. $	Price Can. $	U.K. £	Aust. $
BP-3c	3094	P3094	400.00	450.00	175.00	425.00
BP-4			400.00	450.00	175.00	425.00
BP-6a			200.00	150.00	45.00	110.00

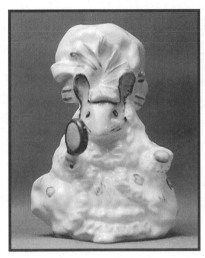

LADY MOUSE™

Modeller:	Arthur Gredington
Height:	4", 10.1 cm
Colour:	White dress with yellow trim and blue polka-dot sleeves, white hat with purple and blue highlights
Issued:	1950 to the present

Back Stamp	Beswick Number	Doulton Number	U.S. $	Price Can. $	U.K. £	Aust. $
BP-1	1183	P1183	325.00	375.00	150.00	400.00
BP-2			275.00	300.00	110.00	350.00
BP-3a			100.00	200.00	80.00	160.00
BP-3b			75.00	150.00	55.00	125.00
BP-3c			100.00	200.00	80.00	160.00
BP-6a			38.00	58.00	16.00	65.00

LADY MOUSE MADE A CURTSEY™

Modeller:	Amanda Hughes-Lubeck
Height:	3 ¼", 8.3 cm
Colour:	Purple-pink and white
Issued:	1990 - 1997

Back Stamp	Beswick Number	Doulton Number	U.S. $	Price Can. $	U.K. £	Aust. $
BP-6a	3220	P3220	40.00	62.00	20.00	85.00

LITTLE BLACK RABBIT™

Modeller:	David Lyttleton
Height:	4 ½", 11.4 cm
Colour:	Black rabbit wearing green waistcoat
Issued:	1977 - 1997

BEATRIX POTTER'S
"Little Black Rabbit"
F. Warne & Co.Ltd.
© Copyright 1977
BESWICK ENGLAND

Back Stamp	Beswick Number	Doulton Number	U.S. $	Price Can. $	U.K. £	Aust. $
BP-3b	2585	P2585	75.00	90.00	55.00	110.00
BP-3c			100.00	125.00	75.00	125.00
BP-4			150.00	175.00	100.00	175.00
BP-6a			40.00	60.00	25.00	90.00

Note: The jacket colouring varies from light to dark green.

LITTLE PIG ROBINSON™
First Variation (Blue Stripes)

Modeller:	Arthur Gredington
Height:	4", 10.2 cm
Colour:	White and blue striped dress, brown basket with yellow cauliflowers
Issued:	1948 - 1974

Back Stamp	Beswick Number	Doulton Number	U.S. $	Price Can. $	U.K. £	Aust. $
BP-1	1104/1	P1104/1	475.00	650.00	250.00	600.00
BP-2			400.00	550.00	225.00	500.00
BP-3a			400.00	525.00	200.00	500.00

LITTLE PIG ROBINSON™
Second Variation (Blue Checked)

Modeller:	Arthur Gredington
Height:	3 ½", 8.9 cm
Colour:	Blue dress, brown basket with cream cauliflowers
Issued:	c.1974 to the present

BEATRIX POTTER'S
"Little Pig Robinson"

F. Warne & Co.Ltd.
© Copyright 1948
BESWICK
ENGLAND

Back Stamp	Beswick Number	Doulton Number	U.S. $	Price Can. $	U.K. £	Aust. $
BP-3b	1104/2	P1104/2	75.00	125.00	45.00	100.00
BP-3c			110.00	150.00	75.00	135.00
BP-6a			38.00	60.00	16.00	65.00

LITTLE PIG ROBINSON SPYING™

Modeller: Ted Chawner
Height: 3 ½", 8.9 cm
Colour: Blue and white striped dress, rose-pink chair
Issued: 1987 - 1993

Back Stamp	Beswick Number	Doulton Number	U.S. $	Price Can. $	U.K. £	Aust. $
BP-3c	3031	P3031	300.00	425.00	175.00	350.00
BP-6a			115.00	130.00	40.00	90.00

MISS DORMOUSE™

Modeller: Martyn Alcock
Height: 4", 10.1 cm
Colour: Blue, white and pink
Issued: 1991 - 1995

Back Stamp	Beswick Number	Doulton Number	U.S. $	Price Can. $	U.K. £	Aust. $
BP-6a	3251	P3251	60.00	100.00	45.00	100.00

MISS MOPPET™
First Variation (Mottled Brown Cat)

Modeller: Arthur Gredington
Height: 3", 7.6 cm
Colour: Dark brown cat, blue checkered kerchief
Issued: 1954 - c.1978

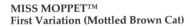

Back Stamp	Beswick Number	Doulton Number	U.S. $	Price Can. $	U.K. £	Aust. $
BP-1	1275/1	P1275/1	250.00	325.00	150.00	350.00
BP-2			225.00	275.00	100.00	300.00
BP-3a			200.00	250.00	80.00	275.00
BP-3b			200.00	250.00	80.00	275.00

MISS MOPPET™
Second Variation (Brown Striped Cat)

Modeller:	Arthur Gredington
Height:	3", 7.6 cm
Colour:	Light brown cat, blue checkered kerchief
Issued:	1978 to the present

BEATRIX POTTER'S
"Miss. Moppet"
F. Warne & Co.Ltd.
© Copyright 1954
BESWICK ENGLAND

Back Stamp	Beswick Number	Doulton Number	U.S. $	Price Can. $	U.K. £	Aust. $
BP-3b	1275/2	P1275/2	60.00	90.00	45.00	90.00
BP-3c			75.00	110.00	65.00	120.00
BP-6a			38.00	58.00	16.00	65.00

MITTENS AND MOPPET™

Modeller:	Ted Chawner
Height:	3 ¾", 9.5 cm
Colour:	Blue, brown and grey
Issued:	1990 - 1994

ROYAL ALBERT ®
ENGLAND
Mittens and Moppet
Beatrix Potter
© F. WARNE & CO. 1989
© 1989 ROYAL ALBERT LTD

Back Stamp	Beswick Number	Doulton Number	U.S. $	Price Can. $	U.K. £	Aust. $
BP-6a	3197	P3197	175.00	150.00	45.00	110.00

MOTHER LADYBIRD™

Modeller:	Warren Platt
Height:	2 ½", 6 .4 cm
Colour:	Red and black
Issued:	1989 - 1996

ROYAL ALBERT ®
ENGLAND
Mother Ladybird
Beatrix Potter
© F. WARNE & CO. 1989
© 1989 ROYAL ALBERT LTD

Back Stamp	Beswick Number	Doulton Number	U.S. $	Price Can. $	U.K. £	Aust. $
BP-6a	2966	P2966	55.00	75.00	35.00	75.00

MR. ALDERMAN PTOLEMY™

Modeller: Graham Tongue
Height: 3 ½", 8.9 cm
Colour: Brown, grey and green
Issued: 1973 - 1997

Back Stamp	Beswick Number	Doulton Number	U.S. $	Price Can. $	U.K. £	Aust. $
BP-3a	2424	P2424	225.00	275.00	125.00	250.00
BP-3b			200.00	225.00	95.00	225.00
BP-3c			225.00	275.00	125.00	250.00
BP-6a			40.00	60.00	20.00	80.00

MR. BENJAMIN BUNNY™
First Version (Pipe Out)

Modeller: Arthur Gredington
Height: 4 ¼", 10.8 cm
Colour: Dark maroon jacket, yellow waistcoat
Issued: 1965 - 1974

Back Stamp	Beswick Number	Doulton Number	U.S. $	Price Can. $	U.K. £	Aust. $
BP-2	1940/1	P1940/1	650.00	825.00	300.00	750.00
BP-3a			550.00	650.00	275.00	625.00

MR. BENJAMIN BUNNY™
Second Version (Pipe In)

Modeller: Arthur Gredington
Height: 4 ¼", 10.8 cm
Colour: Variation No. 1 dark maroon jacket
Variation No. 2 lilac jacket
Issued: 1. c.1970 - c.1974
2. 1975 to the present

Back Stamp	Beswick Number	Colour Variation	U.S. $	Price Can. $	U.K. £	Aust. $
BP-3a	1940/2	Dark maroon	500.00	650.00	275.00	600.00
BP-3a		Lilac	95.00	125.00	65.00	135.00
BP-3b		Dark maroon	500.00	650.00	275.00	600.00
BP-3b		Lilac	75.00	85.00	40.00	90.00
BP-3c		Lilac	95.00	125.00	65.00	135.00
BP-4		Lilac	100.00	150.00	50.00	150.00
BP-6a		Lilac	38.00	58.00	16.00	65.00

MR. BENJAMIN BUNNY AND PETER RABBIT™

Modeller:	Alan Maslankowski
Height:	4", 10.1 cm
Colour:	Benjamin Bunny - lilac jacket, yellow waistcoat Peter Rabbit - blue jacket
Issued:	1975 - 1995

BEATRIX POTTER'S
"Mr. Benjamin Bunny
& Peter Rabbit"
F. Warne & Co.Ltd.
© Copyright 1975
BESWICK ENGLAND

Back Stamp	Beswick Number	Doulton Number	U.S. $	Price Can. $	U.K. £	Aust. $
BP-3b	2509	P2509	175.00	225.00	85.00	250.00
BP-3c			200.00	250.00	110.00	275.00
BP-6a			70.00	115.00	40.00	90.00

MR. DRAKE PUDDLE-DUCK™

Modeller:	David Lyttleton
Height:	4", 10.1 cm
Colour:	White duck, blue waistcoat and trousers
Issued:	1979 to the present

BEATRIX POTTER
"Mr. Drake Puddle-Duck"
© Frederick Warne & Co. 1979
Licensed by Copyrights
BESWICK ENGLAND

Back Stamp	Beswick Number	Doulton Number	U.S. $	Price Can. $	U.K. £	Aust. $
BP-3b	2628	P2628	75.00	100.00	45.00	100.00
BP-3c			90.00	125.00	70.00	135.00
BP-4			85.00	150.00	75.00	125.00
BP-6a			38.00	58.00	16.00	65.00

MR JACKSON™
First Variation (Green Toad)

Modeller:	Albert Hallam
Height:	2 ¾", 7.0 cm
Colour:	Green toad wearing mauve jacket
Issued:	1974 - c.1974

BEATRIX POTTER'S
"Mr Jackson"
F. Warne & Co.Ltd.
Copyright
BESWICK ENGLAND

Back Stamp	Beswick Number	Doulton Number	U.S. $	Price Can. $	U.K. £	Aust. $
BP-3a	2453/1	P2453/1	600.00	700.00	275.00	600.00

MR JACKSON™
Second Variation (Brown Toad)

Modeller: Albert Hallam
Height: 2 ¾", 7.0 cm
Colour: Brown toad wearing
mauve jacket
Issued: 1975 - 1997

BEATRIX POTTER'S
"Mr Jackson"
F. Warne & Co.Ltd.
© Copyright 1974
BESWICK ENGLAND

Back Stamp	Beswick Number	Doulton Number	U.S. $	Price Can. $	U.K. £	Aust. $
BP-3b	2453/2	P2453/2	100.00	110.00	65.00	125.00
BP-3c			115.00	150.00	90.00	160.00
BP-6a			40.00	60.00	25.00	70.00

MR. JEREMY FISHER™
First Version, First Variation (Spotted Legs)

Modeller: Arthur Gredington
Height: 3", 7.6 cm
Size: Small
Colour: Lilac coat, green frog
with small brown spots
on head and legs
Issued: 1950 - c.1974

BEATRIX POTTER'S
"Mr Jeremy Fisher"
F. Warne & Co. Ltd
COPYRIGHT
BESWICK
ENGLAND

Back Stamp	Beswick Number	Doulton Number	U.S. $	Price Can. $	U.K. £	Aust. $
BP-1	1157/1	P1157/1	400.00	500.00	225.00	525.00
BP-2			350.00	375.00	175.00	375.00
BP-3a			225.00	275.00	95.00	275.00
BP-3b			175.00	225.00	90.00	225.00

MR. JEREMY FISHER™
First Version, Second Variation (Striped Legs)

Modeller: Arthur Gredington
Height: 3", 7.6 cm
Size: Small
Colour: Lilac coat, green frog with
large spots on head and
stripes on legs
Issued: c.1950 to the present

BEATRIX POTTER'S
"Mr Jeremy Fisher"
Copyright
BESWICK • ENGLAND

Back Stamp	Beswick Number	Doulton Number	U.S. $	Price Can. $	U.K. £	Aust. $
BP-1	1157/2	P1157/2	375.00	500.00	225.00	500.00
BP-3b			80.00	110.00	50.00	110.00
BP-3c			100.00	125.00	75.00	125.00
BP-6a			38.00	58.00	16.00	70.00

Note: BP-3c backstamp name exists with and without "Mr."

MR. JEREMY FISHER™
Second Version

Modeller:	Martyn Alcock
Height:	5", 12.7 cm
Size:	Large
Colour:	Lilac coat, green frog with stripes on legs
Issued:	1994 - 1997

Back Stamp	Beswick Number	Doulton Number	U.S. $	Price Can. $	U.K. £	Aust. $
BP-6b	3372	P3372	90.00	105.00	30.00	135.00

MR. JEREMY FISHER DIGGING™

Modeller:	Ted Chawner
Height:	3 ¾", 9.5 cm
Colour:	Mauve coat, pink waistcoat, white cravat, green frog with brown highlights
Issued:	1988 - 1994

BEATRIX POTTER
"Mr. Jeremy Fisher Digging"
© F. Warne & Co. 1988
Licensed by Copyrights
John Beswick
Studio of Royal Doulton
England

Back Stamp	Beswick Number	Doulton Number	U.S. $	Price Can. $	U.K. £	Aust. $
BP-4	3090	P3090	350.00	475.00	175.00	450.00
BP-6a			125.00	150.00	45.00	125.00

Note: Jeremy Fisher's skin may have dark or light spots.

MR. McGREGOR™

Modeller:	Martyn Alcock
Height:	5 ¼", 13.5 cm
Colour:	Brown hat and trousers, tan vest and pale blue shirt
Issued:	1995 to the present

ROYAL ALBERT ®
ENGLAND
Mr McGregor
Beatrix Potter
© F. WARNE & CO. 1995
© 1995 ROYAL ALBERT LTD

Back Stamp	Beswick Number	Doulton Number	U.S. $	Price Can. $	U.K. £	Aust. $
BP-6a	3506	P3506	48.00	70.00	19.00	90.00

MR. TOD™

Modeller:	Ted Chawner
Height:	4 ¾", 12.1 cm
Colour:	Green suit, red waistcoat, dark brown walking stick
Issued:	1988 - 1993

Back Stamp	Beswick Number	Doulton Number	U.S. $	Price Can. $	U.K. £	Aust. $
BP-4	3091/1	P3091/1	375.00	500.00	225.00	425.00
BP-6a			150.00	175.00	45.00	150.00

Note: Variations occur with the head facing right or left and the base in either green or brown.

MRS FLOPSY BUNNY™

Modeller:	Arthur Gredington
Height:	4", 10.1 cm
Colour:	Blue dress, pink bag
Issued:	1965 to the present

Back Stamp	Beswick Number	Doulton Number	U.S. $	Price Can. $	U.K. £	Aust. $
BP-2	1942	P1942	250.00	275.00	125.00	275.00
BP-3a			160.00	200.00	75.00	175.00
BP-3b			65.00	90.00	45.00	100.00
BP-3c			95.00	130.00	60.00	130.00
BP-4			95.00	150.00	55.00	160.00
BP-6a			38.00	58.00	16.00	70.00

Note: Dress is bright blue on earlier models and pale blue on later models.

MRS RABBIT™
First Version (Umbrella Out)

Modeller:	Arthur Gredington
Height:	4 ¼", 10.8 cm
Size:	Small
Colour:	Variation No. 1 pink and yellow striped dress; Variation No. 2 lilac and pale green striped dress
Issued:	1951 - c.1974

Back Stamp	Beswick Number	Variation	U.S. $	Price Can. $	U.K.£	Aust. $
BP-1	1200/1	Var. 1	575.00	750.00	300.00	600.00
BP-2		Var. 1	525.00	675.00	250.00	550.00
BP-2		Var. 2	525.00	675.00	250.00	550.00
BP-3a		Var. 2	350.00	375.00	175.00	400.00

Note: The base is too small to carry the circular Beswick England backstamp. It is flattened and the copyright date is carried in script.

MRS RABBIT™
Second Version (Umbrella Moulded to Dress)

Modeller:	Arthur Gredington
Height:	4 ¼", 10.8 cm
Size:	Small
Colour:	Lilac and yellow striped dress, red collar and cap, light straw coloured basket
Issued:	c.1975 to the present

Back Stamp	Beswick Number	Doulton Number	U.S. $	Price Can. $	U.K. £	Aust. $
BP-3b	1200/2	P1200/2	75.00	80.00	50.00	115.00
BP-3c			95.00	110.00	75.00	125.00
BP-4			95.00	200.00	70.00	150.00
BP-6a			38.00	58.00	16.00	70.00

MRS RABBIT™
Third Version

Modeller:	Martyn Alcock
Height:	6 ¼", 15.9 cm
Size:	Large
Colour:	White, pink, yellow and green
Issued:	1994 - 1997

Back Stamp	Beswick Number	Doulton Number	U.S. $	Price Can. $	U.K. £	Aust. $
BP-6b	3398	P3398	75.00	105.00	35.00	135.00

MRS. RABBIT AND BUNNIES™

Modeller:	David Lyttleton
Height:	3 ¾", 9.5 cm
Colour:	Blue dress with white apron, dark blue chair
Issued:	1976 - 1997

Back Stamp	Beswick Number	Doulton Number	U.S. $	Price Can. $	U.K. £	Aust. $
BP-3b	2543	P2543	90.00	135.00	50.00	140.00
BP-3c			110.00	160.00	75.00	170.00
BP-4			110.00	175.00	65.00	175.00
BP-5			135.00	175.00	100.00	185.00
BP-6a			40.00	60.00	15.00	70.00

MRS RABBIT AND THE FOUR BUNNIES™

Modeller: Shane Ridge
Height: 4 ½", 11.9 cm
Colour: Mrs Rabbit - light blue dress, brown basket;
Bunnies - brown, rose tunic;
Peter: light blue coat, yellow buttons
Issued: 1997 in a limited edition of 1,997

Beswick Ware
MADE IN ENGLAND
MRS. RABBIT AND THE FOUR BUNNIES
1947-1997
© F. WARNE & CO. 1996
© 1996 ROYAL DOULTON
LIMITED EDITION OF 1,997
THIS IS № 54

Back Stamp	Beswick Number	Doulton Number	U.S. $	Price Can. $	U.K. £	Aust. $
BP-9	3672	P3672	2,000.00	2,750.00	850.00	2,750.00

Note: Italized prices are indications only, and the actual selling price may be higher or lower, depending on market conditions.

MRS RABBIT AND PETER™

Modeller: Warren Platt
Height: 3 ½", 8.9 cm
Colour: Mrs Rabbit - light blue dress
Peter - light blue coat
Issued: 1997 to the present

Back Stamp	Beswick Number	Doulton Number	U.S. $	Price Can. $	U.K. £	Aust. $
BP-6a	3646	P3646	72.00	105.00	28.00	90.00

MRS RABBIT COOKING™

Modeller: Martyn Alcock
Height: 4", 10.1 cm
Colour: Blue dress, white apron
Issued: 1992 to the present

Back Stamp	Beswick Number	Doulton Number	U.S. $	Price Can. $	U.K. £	Aust. $
BP-6a	3278	P3278	38.00	58.00	16.00	75.00

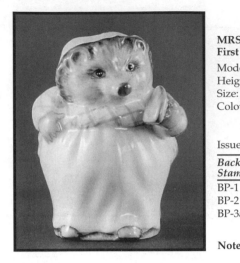

MRS TIGGY-WINKLE™
First Version, First Variation (Diagonal Stripes)

Modeller:	Arthur Gredington
Height:	3 ¼", 8.3 cm
Size:	Small
Colour:	Red-brown and white dress, green and blue striped skirt, white apron
Issued:	1948 - 1974

Back Stamp	Beswick Number	Doulton Number	U.S. $	Price Can.$	U.K. £	Aust. $
BP-1	1107/1	P1107/1	300.00	400.00	150.00	450.00
BP-2			275.00	350.00	125.00	400.00
BP-3a			150.00	200.00	75.00	175.00

Note: This figurine is also recognisable by the heavily patterned bustle.

MRS TIGGY-WINKLE™
First Version, Second Variation (Plaid)

Modeller:	Arthur Gredington
Height:	3 ¼", 8.3 cm
Size:	Small
Colour:	Red-brown and white dress, green and blue striped skirt, white apron
Issued:	1972 to the present

Back Stamp	Beswick Number	Doulton Number	U.S. $	Price Can. $	U.K. £	Aust. $
BP-2	1107/2	P1107/2	275.00	325.00	100.00	350.00
BP-3a			125.00	125.00	75.00	125.00
BP-3b			85.00	90.00	45.00	125.00
BP-3c			110.00	125.00	70.00	150.00
BP-4			110.00	175.00	60.00	150.00
BP-6a			38.00	58.00	16.00	70.00

MRS TIGGY-WINKLE™
First Version, Third Variation (Platinum Iron)

Modeller:	Arthur Gredington
Height:	3 ¼", 8.3 cm
Size:	Small
Colour:	Red-brown and white dress, green and blue striped skirt, white apron, platinum iron
Issued:	1998 - 1998

Back Stamp	Beswick Number	Doulton Number	U.S. $	Price Can. $	U.K. £	Aust. $
BP-10	—	PG1107	56.00	95.00	25.00	90.00

MRS. TIGGY-WINKLE™
Second Version, First Variation

Modeller:	Amanda Hughes-Lubeck
Height:	4 ½", 11.9 cm
Size:	Large
Colour:	Brown, white and brown striped skirt, white apron
Issued:	1996 - 1997

Back Stamp	Beswick Number	Doulton Number	U.S. $	Price Can. $	U.K. £	Aust. $
BP-6b	3437	P3437	75.00	110.00	35.00	125.00

MRS. TIGGY-WINKLE™
Second Version, Second Variation
(Platinum Iron)

Modeller:	Amanda Hughes-Lubeck
Height:	4 ½", 11.9 cm
Size:	Large
Colour:	Brown, white and brown striped skirt, white apron, platinum iron
Issued:	1998 in a limited edition of 1,947

Back Stamp	Beswick Number	Doulton Number	U.S. $	Price Can. $	U.K. £	Aust. $
BP-10	—	PG3437	—	—	35.00	—

BEATRIX POTTER'S
"Mrs. Tiggy Winkle"
'Takes Tea'
© Frederick Warne P.L.C. 1985
BESWICK ENGLAND

MRS. TIGGY WINKLE TAKES TEA™

Modeller:	David Lyttleton
Height:	3 ¼", 8.3 cm
Colour:	Pink and white dress, white and brown mob cap
Issued:	1985 to the present

Back Stamp	Beswick Number	Doulton Number	U.S. $	Price Can. $	U.K. £	Aust. $
BP-3b	2877	P2877	125.00	125.00	100.00	125.00
BP-3c			150.00	125.00	115.00	150.00
BP-4			175.00	250.00	125.00	250.00
BP-6a			38.00	58.00	16.00	70.00

MRS TITTLEMOUSE™

Modeller:	Arthur Gredington
Height:	3 ½", 8.9 cm
Colour:	White and red striped blouse, blue and white striped skirt
Issued:	1948 - 1993

Back Stamp	Beswick Number	Doulton Number	U.S. $	Price Can. $	U.K. £	Aust. $
BP-1	1103	P1103	300.00	450.00	150.00	450.00
BP-2			250.00	350.00	125.00	350.00
BP-3a			100.00	125.00	80.00	135.00
BP-3b			65.00	90.00	60.00	110.00
BP-3c			100.00	125.00	80.00	135.00
BP-6a			55.00	70.00	35.00	70.00

NO MORE TWIST™

Modeller:	Martyn Alcock
Height:	3 ½", 9.2 cm
Colour:	Brown and white mouse
Issued:	1992 - 1997

Back Stamp	Beswick Number	Doulton Number	U.S. $	Price Can. $	U.K. £	Aust. $
BP-6a	3325	P3325	40.00	60.00	25.00	95.00

OLD MR. BOUNCER™

Modeller:	David Lyttleton
Height:	3", 7.6 cm
Colour:	Brown jacket and trousers, blue scarf
Issued:	1986 - 1995

Back Stamp	Beswick Number	Doulton Number	U.S. $	Price Can. $	U.K.£	Aust. $
BP-3c	2956	P2956	100.00	175.00	65.00	130.00
BP-6a			50.00	75.00	30.00	75.00

OLD MR BROWN™

Modeller:	Albert Hallam
Height:	3 ¼", 8.3 cm
Colour:	Brown owl and red squirrel
Issued:	1963 to the present

Back Stamp	Beswick Number	Doulton Number	U.S. $	Price Can. $	U.K. £	Aust. $
BP-2	1796	P1796	225.00	350.00	150.00	275.00
BP-3a			95.00	150.00	70.00	115.00
BP-3b			65.00	90.00	45.00	95.00
BP-3c			90.00	115.00	70.00	115.00
BP-6a			38.00	58.00	16.00	70.00

Note: The colour of the squirrel may vary from orange to brown.

OLD MR PRICKLEPIN™

Modeller:	David Lyttleton
Height:	2 ½", 6.4 cm
Colour:	Brown
Issued:	1983 - 1989

BEATRIX POTTER'S
"Old Mr Pricklepin"
© Frederick Warne P.L.C. 1983
BESWICK ENGLAND

Back Stamp	Beswick Number	Doulton Number	U.S. $	Price Can. $	U.K. £	Aust. $
BP-3b	2767	P2767	110.00	110.00	60.00	110.00
BP-3c			125.00	135.00	75.00	125.00
BP-6a			135.00	150.00	100.00	175.00

PETER AND THE RED POCKET HANDKERCHIEF™
First Version, First Variation

Modeller:	Martyn Alcock
Height:	4 ¾", 12.3 cm
Size:	Small
Colour:	Brown blanket, light blue coat
Issued:	1991 to the present

ROYAL ALBERT ®
ENGLAND
Peter and the
Red Pocket Handkerchief
Beatrix Potter
© F. WARNE & CO. 1990
© 1990 ROYAL ALBERT LTD

Back Stamp	Beswick Number	Doulton Number	U.S. $	Price Can. $	U.K. £	Aust. $
BP-6a	3242	P3242	48.00	79.00	17.00	79.00

PETER AND THE RED POCKET HANDKERCHIEF™
First Version, Second Variation (Gold Buttons)

Modeller:	Martyn Alcock
Height:	4 ¾", 12.3 cm
Size:	Small
Colour:	Red-brown blanket, light blue coat
Issued:	1997 to the present

Back Stamp	Beswick Number	Doulton Number	U.S. $	Price Can. $	U.K. £	Aust. $
BP-10	—	PG3242	—	—	29.99	—

Note: Exclusive to Peter Rabbit and Friends, U.K.

PETER AND THE RED POCKET HANDKERCHIEF™
Second Version

Modeller:	Amanda Hughes-Lubeck
Height:	7 ¼", 18.4 cm
Size:	Large
Colour:	Red-brown blanket, light blue coat
Issued:	1996 - 1997

Back Stamp	Beswick Number	Doulton Number	U.S. $	Price Can. $	U.K. £	Aust. $
BP-6b	3592	P3592	75.00	125.00	40.00	125.00

PETER ATE A RADISH™

Modeller:	Warren Platt
Height:	4", 10.1 cm
Colour:	Blue jacket, brown and white rabbit, red radishes
Issued:	1995 to the present

Back Stamp	Beswick Number	Doulton Number	U.S. $	Price Can. $	U.K. £	Aust. $
BP-6a	3533	P3533	48.00	75.00	18.00	92.00

PETER IN BED™

Modeller:	Martyn Alcock
Height:	2 ¾", 7.0 cm
Colour:	Blue, white, pink and green
Issued:	1995 to the present

Back Stamp	Beswick Number	Doulton Number	U.S. $	Price Can. $	U.K. £	Aust. $
BP-6a	3473	P3473	48.00	80.00	20.00	89.00

PETER IN THE GOOSEBERRY NET™

Modeller:	David Lyttleton
Height:	2", 4.6 cm
Colour:	Brown and white rabbit wearing blue jacket, green netting
Issued:	1989 - 1995

ROYAL ALBERT ®
ENGLAND
Peter in the Gooseberry Net
Beatrix Potter
© F. WARNE & CO. 1989
© 1989 ROYAL ALBERT LTD

Back Stamp	Beswick Number	Doulton Number	U.S. $	Price Can. $	U.K. £	Aust. $
BP-6a	3157	P3157	75.00	100.00	25.00	90.00

PETER RABBIT™
First Version, First Variation (Deep Blue Jacket)

Modeller:	Arthur Gredington
Height:	4 ½", 11.4 cm
Size:	Small
Colour:	Brown and white rabbit wearing dark blue jacket
Issued:	1948 - c.1980

BEATRIX POTTER'S
Peter Rabbit
BESWICK
ENGLAND
COPYRIGHT
F. WARNE & CO. Ltd.

Back Stamp	Beswick Number	Doulton Number	U.S. $	Price Can. $	U.K. £	Aust. $
BP-1	1098/1	P1098/1	250.00	350.00	150.00	375.00
BP-2			225.00	250.00	125.00	300.00
BP-3a			150.00	175.00	95.00	200.00
BP-3b			125.00	150.00	75.00	165.00

Note: Peter Rabbit was issued with two different bases.

PETER RABBIT™
First Version, Second Variation
(Light Blue Jacket)

Modeller:	Arthur Gredington
Height:	4 ½", 11.4 cm
Size:	Small
Colour:	Brown and white rabbit wearing light blue jacket
Issued:	c.1980 to the present

BEATRIX POTTER
"Peter Rabbit"
© F. Warne & Co. 1948
Licensed by Copyrights
John Beswick
Studio of Royal Doulton
England

Back Stamp	Beswick Number	Doulton Number	U.S. $	Price Can. $	U.K. £	Aust. $
BP-3b	1098/2	P1098/2	70.00	80.00	50.00	125.00
BP-3c			90.00	110.00	70.00	135.00
BP-4			90.00	150.00	55.00	145.00
BP-5			125.00	175.00	100.00	165.00
BP-6a			38.00	58.00	16.00	70.00

PETER RABBIT™
First Version, Third Variation
(Light Blue Jacket, Gold Buttons)

Modeller:	Arthur Gredington
Height:	4 ½", 11.9 cm
Size:	Small
Colour:	Brown and white rabbit wearing light blue jacket with gold buttons
Issued:	1997 - 1997

Beswick Ware
MADE IN ENGLAND
Peter Rabbit
Beatrix Potter
© F. WARNE & CO. 1997
© 1997 ROYAL DOULTON

Back Stamp	Beswick Number	Doulton Number	U.S. $	Price Can. $	U.K. £	Aust. $
BP-10	—	PG1098	50.00	95.00	25.00	100.00

PETER RABBIT™
Second Version, First Variation

Modeller:	Martyn Alcock
Height:	6 ¾", 17.1 cm
Size:	Large
Colour:	Brown rabbit wearing a light blue jacket
Issued:	1993 - 1997

BEATRIX POTTER'S
Peter Rabbit ™
© F. WARNE & CO.1992
© 1992 ROYAL DOULTON
PETER RABBIT
1893 100 1993
F. WARNE & Co
BESWICK
ENGLAND

Back Stamp	Beswick Number	Doulton Number	U.S. $	Price Can. $	U.K. £	Aust. $
BP-6b	3356	P3356	75.00	125.00	30.00	135.00
BP-7	100th Anniversary		100.00	135.00	50.00	150.00

PETER RABBIT™
Second Version, Second Variation
(Gold Buttons)

Modeller:	Martyn Alcock
Height:	6 ¾", 17.1 cm
Size:	Large
Colour:	Brown rabbit wearing light blue jacket with gold buttons
Issued:	1997 in a limited edtion of 1,947

Back Stamp	Beswick Number	Doulton Number	U.S. $	Price Can. $	U.K. £	Aust. $
BP-10	—	PG3356	—	—	35.00	—

PETER RABBIT GARDENING™

Modeller:	Warren Platt
Height:	5", 12.7 cm
Colour:	Blue jacket, brown shovel, basket of carrots
Issued:	1998 to the present

Back Stamp	Beswick Number	Doulton Number	U.S. $	Price Can. $	U.K. £	Aust. $
BP 11	3739	P3739	47.50	85.00	20.00	100.00

PETER WITH DAFFODILS™

Modeller:	Warren Platt
Height:	4 ¾", 12.1 cm
Colour:	Light blue coat, yellow daffodils
Issued:	1996 to the present

Back Stamp	Beswick Number	Doulton Number	U.S. $	Price Can. $	U.K. £	Aust. $
BP-6a	3597	P3597	48.00	84.00	19.00	100.00

ROYAL ALBERT ®
ENGLAND
Peter with Daffodils
Beatrix Potter
© F. WARNE & CA 1996
© 1996 ROYAL ALBERT LTD

PETER WITH POSTBAG

Modeller:	Amanda Hughes-Lubeck
Height:	4 ¾", 12.1 cm
Colour:	Light brown rabbit and postbag, lilac jacket trimmed in red
Issued:	1996 to the present

Back Stamp	Beswick Number	Doulton Number	U.S. $	Price Can. $	U.K. £	Aust. $
BP-6a	3591	P3591	48.00	84.00	19.00	100.00

PICKLES™

Modeller:	Albert Hallam
Height:	4 ½", 11.4 cm
Colour:	Black face dog with brown jacket and white apron, pink book
Issued:	1971 - 1982

Back Stamp	Beswick Number	Doulton Number	U.S. $	Price Can. $	U.K. £	Aust. $
BP-2	2334	P2334	850.00	1,150.00	475.00	850.00
BP-3a			500.00	650.00	300.00	675.00
BP-3b			475.00	600.00	275.00	600.00

PIGLING BLAND™
First Variation (Deep Maroon Jacket)

Modeller:	Graham Orwell
Height:	4 ¼", 10.8 cm
Colour:	Purple jacket, blue waistcoat, yellow trousers
Issued:	1955 - 1974

Back Stamp	Beswick Number	Doulton Number	U.S. $	Price Can. $	U.K. £	Aust. $
BP-2	1365/1	P1365/1	550.00	650.00	250.00	800.00
BP-3a			300.00	400.00	215.00	400.00
BP-3b			275.00	375.00	195.00	375.00

JEMIMA PUDDLE-DUCK™

Large Size   Wall Plaque   Gold Backstamp   Character Jug

DISPLAY STAND

Pig-Wig™   Simpkin™   Duchess™   Ginger™   Amiable Guinea Pig™

TIMMY TIPTOES™
First Version   Second Version

SQUIRREL NUTKIN™
First Version   Second Version

TOM KITTEN™
First Version   Second Version

PETER RABBIT™
First Version   Second Version

APPLEY DAPPLY™

First Version   Second Version   First Version   **MRS. TIGGY WINKLE™**

Second Version on a Tree Lamp Base

TOMMY BROCK™   **MR. BENJAMIN BUNNY™**

Spade Out   Spade In   First Version   Second Version

MISS MOPPET™
First Version   Second Version

TABITHA TWITCHIT™
First Version   Second Version

LITTLE PIG ROBINSON™
First Version   Second Version

PIGLING BLAND™
First Version   Second Version

FIERCE BAD RABBIT™
First Version   Second Version

BENJAMIN BUNNY SAT ON A BANK™
First Version   Second Version

MR. JEREMY FISHER™
First Version   Second Version

MR. JACKSON™
First Version   Second Version

BENJAMIN BUNNY™

First Version   Second Version   Third Version

MRS. RABBIT™

First Version   Second Version

CECILEY PARSLEY™

First Version   Second Version

TOM KITTEN™

Character Jug   **Large Size**   **First Version**   **Second Version**

PETER RABBIT™

Large Size   **First Version**   **Second Version**   **Character Jug**

TOMMY BROCK™

First Version **Second Version** **Third Version** **Fourth Version**

DUCHESS™

Style Two **Style One**

PIGLING BLAND™
Second Variation (Lilac Jacket)

Modeller:	Graham Orwell
Height:	4 ¼", 10.8 cm
Colour:	Lilac jacket, blue waistcoat, yellow trousers
Issued:	c.1975 to the present

Back Stamp	Beswick Number	Doulton Number	U.S. $	Price Can. $	U.K. £	Aust. $
BP-3b	1365/2	P1365/2	70.00	110.00	50.00	300.00
BP-3c			95.00	135.00	70.00	300.00
BP-6a			38.00	58.00	16.00	90.00

PIGLING EATS HIS PORRIDGE™

Modeller:	Martyn Alcock
Height:	4", 10.1 cm
Colour:	Brown coat, blue waistcoat and yellow trousers
Issued:	1991 - 1994

Back Stamp	Beswick Number	Doulton Number	U.S. $	Price Can. $	U.K. £	Aust. $
BP-6a	3252	P3252	125.00	195.00	35.00	90.00

PIG-WIG™

Modeller:	Albert Hallam
Height:	4", 10.1 cm
Colour:	Variation 1 (BP-2) grey pig, pale blue dress
	Variation 2 (BP-3) black pig, deep blue dress
Issued:	1972 - 1982

Back Stamp	Beswick Number	Doulton Number	U.S. $	Price Can. $	U.K. £	Aust. $
BP-2	2381	P2381	Extremely rare. Only two known.			
BP-3a			650.00	950.00	425.00	925.00
BP-3b			625.00	875.00	400.00	900.00

POORLY PETER RABBIT™

Modeller:	David Lyttleton
Height:	3 ¾", 9.5 cm
Colour:	Brown-red and white blanket
Issued:	1976 - 1997

Back Stamp	Beswick Number	Doulton Number	U.S. $	Price Can. $	U.K. £	Aust. $
BP-3b	2560	P2560	80.00	95.00	50.00	100.00
BP-3c			90.00	115.00	70.00	125.00
BP-4			85.00	150.00	65.00	130.00
BP-6a			40.00	60.00	20.00	65.00

Note: Later models have a lighter brown blanket.

REBECCAH PUDDLE-DUCK™

Modeller:	David Lyttleton
Height:	3 ¼", 8.3 cm
Colour:	White goose, pale blue coat and hat
Issued:	1981 to the present

Back Stamp	Beswick Number	Doulton Number	U.S. $	Price Can. $	U.K. £	Aust. $
BP-3b	2647	P2647	70.00	90.00	45.00	100.00
BP-3c			90.00	120.00	65.00	125.00
BP-4			95.00	130.00	55.00	125.00
BP-6a			38.00	58.00	16.00	80.00

RIBBY™

Modeller:	Arthur Gredington
Height:	3 ¼", 8.3 cm
Colour:	White dress with blue rings, white apron, pink and white striped shawl
Issued:	1951 to the present

Back Stamp	Beswick Number	Doulton Number	U.S. $	Price Can. $	U.K. £	Aust. $
BP-1	1199	P1199	325.00	425.00	200.00	400.00
BP-2			250.00	325.00	150.00	300.00
BP-3a			100.00	135.00	70.00	125.00
BP-3b			70.00	80.00	50.00	95.00
BP-3c			95.00	110.00	70.00	125.00
BP-6a			38.00	58.00	16.00	65.00

Note: The name shown on BP-6a is Mrs Ribby.

RIBBY AND THE PATTY PAN™

Modeller:	Martyn Alcock
Height:	3 ½", 8.9 cm
Colour:	Blue dress, white apron
Issued:	1992 to the present

Back Stamp	Beswick Number	Doulton Number	U.S. $	Price Can. $	U.K. £	Aust. $
BP-6a	3280	P3280	38.00	58.00	16.00	70.00

SALLY HENNY PENNY™

Modeller:	Albert Hallam
Height:	4", 10.1 cm
Colour:	Brown and gold chicken, black hat and cloak, two yellow chicks
Issued:	1974 - 1993

Back Stamp	Beswick Number	Doulton Number	U.S. $	Price Can. $	U.K. £	Aust. $
BP-3a	2452	P2452	95.00	125.00	70.00	150.00
BP-3b			70.00	80.00	50.00	110.00
BP-3c			90.00	100.00	70.00	125.00
BP-6a			65.00	60.00	35.00	85.00

SAMUEL WHISKERS™

Modeller:	Arthur Gredington
Height:	3 ¼", 8.3 cm
Colour:	Light green coat, yellow waistcoat and trousers
Issued:	1948 - 1995

Back Stamp	Beswick Number	Doulton Number	U.S. $	Price Can. $	U.K. £	Aust. $
BP-1	1106	P1106	325.00	475.00	150.00	475.00
BP-2			300.00	375.00	130.00	350.00
BP-3a			100.00	150.00	70.00	135.00
BP-3b			65.00	80.00	45.00	80.00
BP-3c			100.00	100.00	70.00	110.00
BP-4			100.00	150.00	55.00	150.00
BP-6a			60.00	60.00	30.00	60.00

SIMPKIN™

Modeller:	Alan Maslankowski
Height:	4", 10.1 cm
Colour:	Green coat
Issued:	1975 - 1983

Back Stamp	Beswick Number	Doulton Number	U.S. $	Price Can. $	U.K. £	Aust. $
BP-3b	2508	P2508	800.00	1,200.00	475.00	800.00

SIR ISAAC NEWTON™

Modeller:	Graham Tongue
Height:	3 ¾", 9.5 cm
Colour:	Pale green jacket, yellow waistcoat with tan markings
Issued:	1973 - 1984

Back Stamp	Beswick Number	Doulton Number	U.S. $	Price Can. $	U.K. £	Aust. $
BP-3a	2425	P2425	525.00	725.00	300.00	650.00
BP-3b			475.00	675.00	250.00	625.00

Note: The colour and size of Sir Isaac Newton may vary.

SQUIRREL NUTKIN™
First Variation (Red-brown Squirrel)

Modeller:	Arthur Gredington
Height:	3 ¾", 9.5 cm
Colour:	Red-brown squirrel holding green-brown nut
Issued:	1948 - c.1980

Back Stamp	Beswick Number	Doulton Number	U.S. $	Price Can. $	U.K. £	Aust. $
BP-1	1102/1	P1102/1	250.00	325.00	150.00	375.00
BP-2			225.00	275.00	125.00	300.00
BP-3a			150.00	200.00	115.00	225.00
BP-3b			125.00	175.00	95.00	250.00

SQUIRREL NUTKIN™
Second Variation (Golden Brown Squirrel)

Modeller:	Arthur Gredington
Height:	3 ¾", 9.5 cm
Colour:	Golden brown squirrel holding green nut
Issued:	c.1980 to the present

Back Stamp	Beswick Number	Doulton Number	U.S. $	Price Can. $	U.K. £	Aust. $
BP-3b	1102/2	P1102/2	65.00	90.00	50.00	100.00
BP-3c			95.00	115.00	70.00	125.00
BP-6a			38.00	58.00	16.00	75.00

SUSAN™

Modeller:	David Lyttleton
Height:	4", 10.1 cm
Colour:	Blue dress, green, pink and black shawl and hat
Issued:	1983 - 1989

Back Stamp	Beswick Number	Doulton Number	U.S. $	Price Can. $	U.K. £	Aust. $
BP-3b	2716	P2716	300.00	300.00	100.00	300.00
BP-3c			325.00	250.00	125.00	325.00
BP-6a			310.00	350.00	150.00	300.00

Note: The colour and size of Susan may vary.

TABITHA TWITCHIT™
First Variation (Blue Striped Top)

Modeller:	Arthur Gredington
Height:	3 ½", 8.9 cm
Colour:	Blue and white striped dress, white apron
Issued:	1961 - 1974

Back Stamp	Beswick Number	Doulton Number	U.S. $	Price Can. $	U.K. £	Aust. $
BP-2	1676/1	P1676/1	375.00	450.00	175.00	400.00
BP-3a			230.00	275.00	150.00	350.00
BP-3b			200.00	250.00	125.00	275.00

TABITHA TWITCHETT™
Second Variation (White Top)

Modeller:	Arthur Gredington
Height:	3 ½", 8.9 cm
Colour:	Blue and white striped dress, white apron
Issued:	c.1975 - 1995

Back Stamp	Beswick Number	Doulton Number	U.S. $	Price Can. $	U.K. £	Aust. $
BP-3b	1676/2	P1676/2	75.00	90.00	50.00	175.00
BP-3c			95.00	115.00	70.00	200.00
BP-6a			50.00	60.00	30.00	75.00

Note: BP-3b and forward has Twitchit spelled "Twitchett."

TABITHA TWITCHIT AND MISS MOPPET™

Modeller:	David Lyttleton
Height:	3 ½", 8.9 cm
Colour:	Lilac dress, white apron, yellow sponge and hassock
Issued:	1976 - 1993

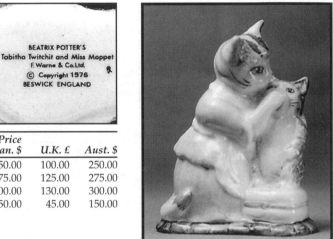

Back Stamp	Beswick Number	Doulton Number	U.S. $	Price Can. $	U.K. £	Aust. $
BP-3b	2544	P2544	235.00	250.00	100.00	250.00
BP-3c			240.00	275.00	125.00	275.00
BP-4			275.00	300.00	130.00	300.00
BP-6a			110.00	150.00	45.00	150.00

TAILOR OF GLOUCESTER™
First Version

Modeller:	Arthur Gredington
Height:	3 ½", 8.9 cm
Size:	Small
Colour:	Brown mouse, yellow bobbin of red thread
Issued:	1949 to the present

Back Stamp	Beswick Number	Doulton Number	U.S. $	Price Can. $	U.K. £	Aust. $
BP-1	1108	P1108	300.00	450.00	200.00	475.00
BP-2			250.00	350.00	125.00	375.00
BP-3a			85.00	110.00	70.00	125.00
BP-3b			65.00	85.00	50.00	100.00
BP-3c			85.00	110.00	70.00	125.00
BP-4			85.00	150.00	50.00	135.00
BP-6a			38.00	60.00	16.00	65.00

TAILOR OF GLOUCESTER™
Second Version

Modeller:	Arthur Gredington
Height:	6", 15.0 cm
Size:	Large
Colour:	Brown mouse, yellow bobbin of red thread
Issued:	1995 - 1997

Back Stamp	Beswick Number	Doulton Number	U.S. $	Price Can. $	U.K. £	Aust. $
BP-6b	3449	P3449	75.00	105.00	30.00	135.00

THE OLD WOMAN WHO LIVED IN A SHOE™

Modeller:	Colin Melbourne
Size:	2 ¾" x 3 ¾", 7.0 cm x 9.5 cm
Colour:	Blue shoe
Issued:	1959 - 1997

Back Stamp	Beswick Number	Doulton Number	U.S. $	Price Can. $	U.K. £	Aust. $
BP-2	1545	P1545	225.00	275.00	100.00	325.00
BP-3a			95.00	110.00	65.00	120.00
BP-3b			65.00	80.00	45.00	90.00
BP-3c			95.00	100.00	65.00	120.00
BP-6a			45.00	60.00	20.00	95.00

THE OLD WOMAN WHO LIVED IN A SHOE KNITTING™

Modeller:	David Lyttleton
Height:	3", 7.5 cm
Colour:	Purple dress, white apron, pale blue shawl and mob cap, yellow chair
Issued:	1983 - 1997

Back Stamp	Beswick Number	Doulton Number	U.S. $	Price Can. $	U.K.£	Aust. $
BP-3b	2804	P2804	225.00	350.00	150.00	300.00
BP-3c			275.00	375.00	175.00	325.00
BP-6a			40.00	60.00	16.00	75.00

THOMASINA TITTLEMOUSE™

Modeller:	David Lyttleton
Height:	3 ¼", 8.3 cm
Colour:	Brown and pink highlights
Issued:	1981 - 1989

BEATRIX POTTER'S
"Thomasina Tittlemouse"
F. Warne & Co Ltd.
© Copyright 1981
BESWICK ENGLAND

Correct

BEATRIX POTTER
"Tomasina Tittlemouse"
© Frederick Warne & Co. 1981
Licensed by Copyrights
BESWICK ENGLAND

Error

Backstamp Variations

Back Stamp	Beswick Number	Doulton Number	U.S. $	Price Can. $	U.K. £	Aust. $
BP-3b	2668	P2668	135.00	200.00	60.00	215.00
BP-3c	Error		165.00	225.00	80.00	240.00
BP-6a			125.00	75.00	40.00	75.00

TIMMY TIPTOES™
First Variation
(Red Jacket)

Modeller:	Arthur Gredington
Height:	3 ¾", 9.5 cm
Colour:	Variation No. 1- brown-grey squirrel, red jacket
	Variation No. 2 - grey squirrel, red jacket
Issued:	1948 - c.1980

BEATRIX POTTER'S
Timmy Tiptoes
WARNE & CO. LTD.
COPYRIGHT
BESWICK ENGLAND

Back Stamp	Beswick Number	Doulton Number	U.S. $	Price Can. $	U.K. £	Aust. $
BP-1	1101/1	P1101/1	290.00	400.00	175.00	375.00
BP-2	Brown-grey squirrel		240.00	350.00	135.00	325.00
BP-2	Grey squirrel		240.00	350.00	135.00	325.00
BP-3a	Brown-grey squirrel		165.00	175.00	85.00	225.00
BP-3b	Grey squirrel		175.00	175.00	85.00	225.00

TIMMY TIPTOES™
Second Variation
(Light Pink Jacket, Grey Squirrel)

Modeller:	Arthur Gredington
Height:	3 ½", 8.9 cm
Colour:	Grey squirrel wearing pink jacket
Issued:	c.1970 - 1997

ROYAL ALBERT ®
ENGLAND
Timmy Tiptoes
Beatrix Potter
© F. WARNE & CO. 1948
© 1989 ROYAL ALBERT LTD

Back Stamp	Beswick Number	Doulton Number	U.S. $	Price Can. $	U.K. £	Aust. $
BP-2	1101/2	P1101/2	240.00	350.00	135.00	325.00
BP-3b			75.00	85.00	45.00	125.00
BP-3c			100.00	110.00	65.00	150.00
BP-6a			40.00	60.00	20.00	75.00

TIMMY WILLIE FROM JOHNNY TOWN-MOUSE™

Modeller:	Arthur Gredington
Height:	2 ½", 6.4 cm
Colour:	Brown and white mouse, green base
Issued:	1949 - 1993

Back Stamp	Beswick Number	Doulton Number	U.S. $	Price Can. $	U.K. £	Aust. $
BP-1	1109	P1109	250.00	350.00	150.00	375.00
BP-2			225.00	300.00	125.00	325.00
BP-3a			95.00	115.00	70.00	125.00
BP-3b			70.00	90.00	50.00	100.00
BP-3c			95.00	115.00	70.00	125.00
BP-4			95.00	125.00	65.00	135.00
BP-6a			50.00	60.00	30.00	65.00

TIMMY WILLIE SLEEPING™

Modeller:	Graham Tongue
Size:	1 ¼" x 3 ¾", 3.2 cm x 9.5 cm
Colour:	Green, white and brown
Issued:	1986 - 1996

Back Stamp	Beswick Number	Doulton Number	U.S. $	Price Can. $	U.K. £	Aust. $
BP-3c	2996	P2996	250.00	300.00	125.00	300.00
BP-6a			50.00	75.00	35.00	75.00

TOM KITTTEN™
First Version, First Variation (Deep Blue Outfit)

Modeller:	Arthur Gredington
Height:	3 ½", 8.9 cm
Size:	Small
Colour:	Tabby kitten wearing blue trousers and jacket, dark green base
Issued:	1948 - c.1980

Back Stamp	Beswick Number	Doulton Number	U.S. $	Price Can. $	U.K. £	Aust. $
BP-1	1100/1	P1100/1	275.00	400.00	125.00	375.00
BP-2			225.00	250.00	115.00	275.00
BP-3a			125.00	110.00	70.00	100.00
BP-3b			100.00	90.00	50.00	90.00

TOM KITTEN™
First Version, Second Variation
(Light Blue Outfit)

Modeller:	Arthur Gredington	
Height:	3 ½", 8.9 cm	
Size:	Small	
Colour:	Tabby kitten wearing light blue trousers and jacket, light green base	
Issued:	c.1980 to the present	

Back Stamp	Beswick Number	Doulton Number	U.S. $	Price Can. $	U.K. £	Aust. $
BP-3b	1100/2	P1100/2	75.00	80.00	50.00	90.00
BP-3c			90.00	100.00	70.00	110.00
BP-4			90.00	150.00	65.00	130.00
BP-6a			38.00	58.00	16.00	65.00

Note: Tom Kitten was issued with two different style bases.

TOM KITTEN™
First Version, Third Variation
(Gold Buttons)

Modeller:	Arthur Gredington
Height:	3 ½", 8.9 cm
Size:	Small
Colour:	Tabby kitten wearing light blue trousers and jacket with gold buttons
Issued:	1997 - 1997

Back Stamp	Beswick Number	Doulton Number	U.S. $	Price Can. $	U.K. £	Aust. $
BP-10	—	PG1100	60.00	100.00	35.00	125.00

TOM KITTEN™
Second Version

Modeller:	Martyn Alcock	
Height:	5 ¼", 13.3 cm	
Size:	Large	
Colour:	Tabby kitten wearing light blue trousers and jacket, light green base	
Issued:	1994 - 1997	

Back Stamp	Beswick Number	Doulton Number	U.S. $	Price Can. $	U.K. £	Aust. $
BP-7	3405	P3405	75.00	105.00	35.00	135.00

TOM KITTEN AND BUTTERFLY™

Modeller:	Ted Chawner
Height:	3 ½", 8.9 cm
Colour:	Blue outfit, yellow hat
Issued:	1987 - 1994

Back Stamp	Beswick Number	Doulton Number	U.S. $	Price Can. $	U.K. £	Aust. $
BP-3c	3030	P3030	400.00	425.00	200.00	300.00
BP-6a			150.00	125.00	45.00	95.00

TOM KITTEN IN THE ROCKERY™

Modeller:	Warren Platt
Height:	3 ½", 8.9 cm
Colour:	Pale blue jacket and trousers, yellow hat
Issued:	1998 to the present

Back Stamp	Beswick Number	Doulton Number	U.S. $	Price Can. $	U.K. £	Aust. $
BP-11	3719	P3719	36.00	55.00	16.00	65.00

TOM THUMB™

Modeller:	Warren Platt
Height:	3 ¼", 8.3 cm
Colour:	Rose-pink and yellow chimney
Issued:	1987 - 1997

Back Stamp	Beswick Number	Doulton Number	U.S. $	Price Can. $	U.K. £	Aust. $
BP-3c	2989	P2989	175.00	250.00	100.00	200.00
BP-6a			40.00	60.00	20.00	75.00

TOMMY BROCK™
First Version, First Variation
(Handle Out, Small Eye Patch)

Modeller:	Graham Orwell
Height:	3 ½", 8.9 cm
Colour:	Blue jacket, pink waistcoat, yellow-green trousers
Issued:	1955 - 1974

Back Stamp	Beswick Number	Doulton Number	U.S. $	Price Can. $	U.K. £	Aust. $
BP-2	1348/1	P1348/1	600.00	900.00	275.00	675.00
BP-3a			550.00	700.00	250.00	575.00

TOMMY BROCK™
First Version, Second Variation
(Handle Out, Large Eye Patch)

Modeller:	Graham Orwell
Height:	3 ½", 8.9 cm
Colour:	Blue jacket, pink waistcoat, yellow trousers
Issued:	c.1970 - c.1974

Back Stamp	Beswick Number	Doulton Number	U.S. $	Price Can. $	U.K. £	Aust. $
BP-1	1348/2	P1348/2	600.00	750.00	300.00	725.00
BP-2			575.00	700.00	275.00	675.00
BP-3a			500.00	550.00	250.00	575.00

TOMMY BROCK™
Second Version, First Variation
(Handle In, Small Eye Patch)

Modeller:	Graham Orwell
Height:	3 ½", 8.9 cm
Colour:	Blue-grey jacket, pink waistcoat, yellow trousers
Issued:	c.1974 - 1976

Back Stamp	Beswick Number	Doulton Number	U.S. $	Price Can. $	U.K. £	Aust. $
BP-3a	1348/3	P1348/3	175.00	275.00	75.00	250.00
BP-3b			150.00	275.00	75.00	250.00

TOMMY BROCK™
**Second Version, Second Variation
(Handle In, Large Eye Patch)**

Modeller:	Graham Orwell
Height:	3 ½", 8.9 cm
Colour:	Blue-grey jacket, red waistcoat, yellow trousers
Issued:	c.1975 to the present

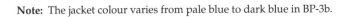

Back Stamp	Beswick Number	Doulton Number	U.S. $	Price Can. $	U.K. £	Aust. $
BP-3b	1348/4	P1348/4	80.00	90.00	50.00	135.00
BP-3c			100.00	110.00	70.00	160.00
BP-4			100.00	150.00	60.00	140.00
BP-6a			38.00	60.00	16.00	75.00

Note: The jacket colour varies from pale blue to dark blue in BP-3b.

Sir Isaac Newton, Amiable Guinea Pig, Simpkin, Ginger, Pig-wig, Pickles

BEATRIX POTTER MISCELLANEOUS

CHARACTER JUGS AND PLAQUES

JEMIMA PUDDLE-DUCK CHARACTER JUG™

Modeller:	Ted Chawner
Height:	4", 10.1 cm
Colour:	Blue, pink and white
Issued:	1989 - 1992

BEATRIX POTTER
`Jemima Puddle-Duck`
© F. Warne & Co. 1988
Licensed by Copyrights

John Beswick

Studio of Royal Doulton
England

Back Stamp	Beswick Number	Doulton Number	U.S. $	Price Can. $	U.K. £	Aust. $
BP-4	3088	P3088	250.00	275.00	75.00	150.00
BP-6a			150.00	175.00	85.00	150.00

MR. JEREMY FISHER CHARACTER JUG™

Modeller:	Graham Tongue
Height:	3", 7.6 cm
Colour:	Mauve
Issued:	1987 - 1992

John Beswick
ENGLAND
BEATRIX POTTER
"Jeremy Fisher"
© 1987 Frederick Warne & Co.
Licensed by Copyrights

Back Stamp	Beswick Number	Doulton Number	U.S. $	Price Can. $	U.K. £	Aust. $
BP-4	2960	P2960	225.00	225.00	70.00	150.00
BP-6a			165.00	175.00	80.00	150.00

MRS. TIGGY-WINKLE CHARACTER JUG™

Modeller:	Ted Chawner
Height:	3", 7.6 cm
Colour:	White dress with blue stripes
Issued:	1988 - 1992

Back Stamp	Beswick Number	Doulton Number	U.S. $	Price Can. $	U.K. £	Aust.$
BP-4	3102	P3102	250.00	225.00	75.00	200.00
BP-6a			175.00	175.00	85.00	150.00

OLD MR. BROWN
CHARACTER JUG™

Modeller:	Graham Tongue
Height:	3", 7.6 cm
Colour:	Brown and cream
Issued:	1987 - 1992

Back Stamp	Beswick Number	Doulton Number	U.S. $	Price Can. $	U.K.	Aust. $
BP-4	2959	P2959	250.00	225.00	70.00	220.00
BP-6a			175.00	175.00	80.00	165.00

PETER RABBIT
CHARACTER JUG™

Modeller:	Graham Tongue
Height:	3", 7.6 cm
Colour:	Brown, blue and white
Issued:	1987 - 1992

Back Stamp	Beswick Number	Doulton Number	U.S. $	Price Can. $	U.K. £	Aust. $
BP-4	3006	P3006	225.00	250.00	70.00	250.00
BP-6a			175.00	190.00	80.00	200.00

TOM KITTEN
CHARACTER JUG™

Modeller:	Ted Chawner
Height:	3", 7.6 cm
Colour:	Brown, blue and white
Issued:	1989 - 1992

Back Stamp	Beswick Number	Doulton Number	U.S. $	Price Can. $	U.K. £	Aust. $
BP-4	3103	P3103	275.00	235.00	75.00	150.00
BP-6a			200.00	190.00	85.00	175.00

JEMIMA PUDDLE-DUCK PLAQUE™

Modeller:	Albert Hallam
Height:	6", 15.2 cm
Colour:	White duck, mauve shawl, pale blue bonnet
Issued:	1967 - 1969

Back Stamp	Beswick Number	Doulton Number	U.S. $	Price Can. $	U.K. £	Aust. $
BP-2	2082	P2082		Extremely rare		

JEMIMA PUDDLE-DUCK WITH FOXY WHISKERED GENTLEMAN PLAQUE™

Modeller:	Harry Sales and David Lyttleton
Size:	7 ½" x 7 ½", 19.1 cm x 19.1 cm
Colour:	Brown, green, white and blue
Issued:	1977 - 1982

Back Stamp	Beswick Number	Doulton Number	U.S. $	Price Can. $	U.K. £	Aust. $
BP-3	2594	P2594	225.00	275.00	110.00	350.00

MRS. TITTLEMOUSE PLAQUE™

Modeller:	Harry Sales
Height:	7 ½" x 7 ½", 19.1 cm x 19.1 cm
Colour:	Blue, pink and green
Issued:	1982 - 1984

Back Stamp	Beswick Number	Doulton Number	U.S. $	Price Can. $	U.K. £	Aust. $
BP-3	2685	P2685	300.00	350.00	150.00	350.00

PETER RABBIT PLAQUE™
First Version

Modeller:	Graham Tongue
Height:	6", 15.2 cm
Colour:	Brown rabbit wearing a blue coat
Issued:	1967 - 1969

Back Stamp	Beswick Number	Doulton Number	U.S. $	Price Can. $	U.K. £	Aust. $
BP-2	2083	P2083		Extremely rare		

Photograph not available at press time

PETER RABBIT PLAQUE™
Second Version

Modeller:	Harry Sales and David Lyttleton
Size:	7 ½" x 7 ½", 19.1 cm x 19.1 cm
Colour:	Blue, green, brown and orange
Issued:	1979 - 1983

Back Stamp	Beswick Number	Doulton Number	U.S. $	Price Can. $	U.K. £	Aust. $
BP-3	2650	P2650	225.00	275.00	100.00	375.00

TOM KITTEN PLAQUE™

Modeller:	Graham Tongue
Height:	6", 15.2 cm
Colour:	Unknown
Issued:	1967 - 1969

Back Stamp	Beswick Number	Doulton Number	U.S. $	Price Can. $	U.K.	Aust. $
BP-2	2085	P2085		Extremely rare		

Photograph not available at press time

DISPLAY STAND

Modeller: Andrew Brindley
Size: 12 ½" x 12 ½",
31.7 cm x 31.7 cm
Colour: Brown, light brown
Issued: 1970 - 1997

Back Stamp	Beswick Number	Doulton Number	U.S. $	Price Can. $	U.K. £	Aust. $
Beswick	2295	P2295	150.00	125.00	75.00	125.00
Doulton			75.00	65.00	25.00	75.00

TREE LAMP BASE™

Modeller: Albert Hallam and
James Hayward
Height: 7", 17.8 cm
Colour: Brown and green
Issued: 1958 - 1982

Back Stamp	Beswick Number	Doulton Number	U.S. $	Price Can. $	U.K. £	Aust. $
BP-2	1531	P1531	450.00	425.00	200.00	400.00
BP-3			375.00	350.00	150.00	325.00

Note: The price of this lamp will vary in accordance with the figure found on the base.

BEATRIX POTTER

RESIN STUDIO SCULPTURES

SS1
TIMMY WILLIE™

Designer:	Harry Sales
Modeller:	Graham Tongue
Height:	4 ¼", 10.8 cm
Colour:	Green and brown
Issued:	1985 - 1985

Beswick	Price			
Number	U.S. $	Can. $	U.K. £	Aust. $
SS1	150.00	200.00	85.00	225.00

SS2
FLOPSY BUNNIES™

Designer:	Harry Sales
Modeller:	Graham Tongue
Height:	5", 12.7 cm
Colour:	Browns and green
Issued:	1985 - 1985

Beswick	Price			
Number	U.S. $	Can. $	U.K. £	Aust. $
SS2	150.00	200.00	95.00	225.00

SS3
MR. JEREMY FISHER™

Designer:	Harry Sales
Modeller:	David Lyttleton
Height:	4", 10.1 cm
Colour:	Beige, green and cream
Issued:	1985 - 1985

Beswick	Price			
Number	U.S. $	Can. $	U.K. £	Aust. $
SS3	150.00	250.00	100.00	275.00

SS4
PETER RABBIT™

Designer:	Harry Sales
Modeller:	Graham Tongue
Height:	7", 17.8 cm
Colour:	Browns, blue and green
Issued:	1985 - 1985

Beswick Number	U.S. $	Price Can. $	U.K. £	Aust. $
SS4	150.00	250.00	100.00	275.00

SS11
MRS. TIGGY WINKLE™

Designer:	Harry Sales
Modeller:	Graham Tongue
Height:	5", 12.7 cm
Colour:	Browns, green, white and blue
Issued:	1985 - 1985

Beswick Number	U.S. $	Price Can. $	U.K. £	Aust. $
SS11	150.00	250.00	100.00	275.00

SS26
YOCK YOCK™
(In The Tub)

Designer:	Harry Sales
Modeller:	David Lyttleton
Height:	1 7/8", 5.0 cm
Colour:	Pink and brown
Issued:	1986 - 1986

Beswick Number	U.S. $	Price Can. $	U.K. £	Aust. $
SS26	375.00	475.00	250.00	450.00

SS27
PETER RABBIT™
(In The Watering Can)

Designer:	Harry Sales
Modeller:	David Lyttleton
Height:	3 ¼", 8.3 cm
Colour:	Browns and blue
Issued:	1986 - 1986

Beswick Number		Price		
	U.S. $	Can. $	U.K. £	Aust. $
SS27	475.00	500.00	350.00	450.00

BEDTIME CHORUS

1801
PIANIST™

Designer: Albert Hallam
Height: 3", 7.6 cm
Colour: Pale blue and yellow
Issued: 1962 - 1969

| Beswick | Price | | | |
Number	U.S. $	Can. $	U.K. £	Aust. $
1801	165.00	200.00	100.00	120.00

1802
PIANO™

Designer: Albert Hallam
Height: 3", 7.6 cm
Colour: Brown and white
Issued: 1962 - 1969

| Beswick | Price | | | |
Number	U.S. $	Can. $	U.K. £	Aust. $
1802	140.00	175.00	50.00	100.00

1803
CAT - SINGING™

Designer: Albert Hallam
Height: 1 ¼", 3.2 cm
Colour: Ginger stripe
Issued: 1962 - 1971

| Beswick | Price | | | |
Number	U.S. $	Can. $	U.K. £	Aust. $
1803	125.00	175.00	55.00	100.00

1804
BOY WITHOUT SPECTACLES™

Designer:	Albert Hallam
Height:	3 ½", 8.9 cm
Colour:	Yellow, white and blue
Issued:	1962 - 1969

Beswick		Price		
Number	U.S. $	Can. $	U.K. £	Aust. $
1804	275.00	350.00	125.00	120.00

1805
BOY WITH SPECTACLES™

Designer:	Albert Hallam
Height:	3", 7.6 cm
Colour:	Green, white and blue
Issued:	1962 - 1969

Beswick		Price		
Number	U.S. $	Can. $	U.K. £	Aust. $
1805	325.00	400.00	160.00	120.00

1824
DOG - SINGING™

Designer:	Albert Hallam
Height:	1 ½", 3.8 cm
Colour:	Tan
Issued:	1962 - 1971

Beswick		Price		
Number	U.S. $	Can. $	U.K. £	Aust. $
1824	100.00	175.00	55.00	120.00

1825
BOY WITH GUITAR™

Designer:	Albert Hallam
Height:	3", 7.6 cm
Colour:	Blue-grey, brown and blue
Issued:	1962 - 1969

Beswick		Price		
Number	U.S. $	Can. $	U.K. £	Aust. $
1825	275.00	375.00	125.00	120.00

1826
GIRL WITH HARP™

Designer:	Albert Hallam
Height:	3 ½", 8.9 cm
Colour:	Purple, red and brown
Issued:	1962 - 1969

Beswick		Price		
Number	U.S. $	Can. $	U.K. £	Aust. $
1826	275.00	375.00	125.00	120.00

BESWICK BEARS

BESWICK RESIN BEARS
BESWICK EARTHENWARE BEARS

BESWICK BEARS

RESIN BEARS 1993-1993

BB001
WILLIAM™

Designer:	Unknown
Height:	2 ¼", 5.7 cm
Colour:	Brown bear, blue apron, white and rose book
Issued:	1993 - 1993

Beswick	Price			
Number	U.S. $	Can. $	U.K. £	Aust. $
BB001	100.00	150.00	50.00	100.00

BB002
BILLY™

Designer:	Unknown
Height:	4", 10.1 cm
Colour:	Brown bear, green waistcoat, blue hat, yellow, red and blue ball
Issued:	1993 - 1993

BILLY
kicked his ball up high
and it landed "SPLAT"
in the apple pie.
Beswick Bears
BB002

Beswick	Price			
Number	U.S. $	Can. $	U.K. £	Aust. $
BB002	75.00	110.00	40.00	100.00

BB003
HARRY™

Designer:	Unknown
Height:	3 ¼", 8.3 cm
Colour:	Brown bear, blue waistcoat, brown hat, white plates
Issued:	1993 - 1993

HARRY
slipped – he'd made a mistake.
He dropped the plates,
but saved his cake.
Beswick Bears
BB003

Beswick	Price			
Number	U.S. $	Can. $	U.K. £	Aust. $
BB003	75.00	110.00	40.00	100.00

BB004
BOBBY™

Designer:	Unknown
Height:	4", 10.1 cm
Colour:	Brown bear, blue waistcoat, brown hat, yellow ball, black and red bat
Issued:	1993 - 1993

Beswick		*Price*		
Number	*U.S. $*	*Can. $*	*U.K. £*	*Aust. $*
BB004	75.00	110.00	40.00	100.00

BB005
JAMES™

Designer:	Unknown
Height:	3 ¾", 9.5 cm
Colour:	Brown bear, yellow waistcoat, blue hat, blue parcel with pink ribbon
Issued:	1993 - 1993

Beswick		*Price*		
Number	*U.S. $*	*Can. $*	*U.K. £*	*Aust. $*
BB005	75.00	110.00	40.00	100.00

BB006
SUSIE™

Designer:	Unknown
Height:	3 ½", 8.9 cm
Colour:	Brown bear, blue dress, brown recorder
Issued:	1993 - 1993

Beswick		*Price*		
Number	*U.S. $*	*Can. $*	*U.K. £*	*Aust. $*
BB006	75.00	110.00	40.00	100.00

BB007
ANGELA™

Designer: Unknown
Height: 3 ¼", 8.3 cm
Colour: Brown bear, yellow dress,
white flowers
Issued: 1993 - 1993

ANGELA
kneels to pick some flowers
Happily dreaming for
hours and hours.
Beswick Bears
BB007

Beswick Number	Price			
	U.S. $	Can. $	U.K. £	Aust. $
BB007	75.00	110.00	40.00	100.00

BB008
CHARLOTTE™

Designer: Unknown
Height: 4", 10.1 cm
Colour: Brown bear, pink dress,
blue and yellow parasol
Issued: 1993 - 1993

CHARLOTTE
tries to keep in the shade.
Twirling her parasol,
a pretty young maid.
Beswick Bears
BB008

Beswick Number	Price			
	U.S. $	Can. $	U.K. £	Aust. $
BB008	75.00	110.00	40.00	100.00

BB009
SAM™

Designer: Unknown
Height: 3 ½", 8.9 cm
Colour: Brown bear, rose waistcoat,
yellow banjo
Issued: 1993 - 1993

SAM
plays his banjo all day long.
Amusing friends
with a tune and a song.
Beswick Bears
BB009

Beswick Number	Price			
	U.S. $	Can. $	U.K. £	Aust. $
BB009	75.00	110.00	40.00	100.00

BB010
LIZZY™

Designer: Unknown
Height: 2 ¼", 5.7 cm
Colour: Brown bear, pink dress,
 paint box
Issued: 1993 - 1993

Beswick Number	Price			
	U.S. $	Can. $	U.K. £	Aust. $
BB010	75.00	110.00	40.00	100.00

BB011
EMILY™

Designer: Unknown
Height: 3 ½", 8.9 cm
Colour: Brown bear, pale blue dress,
 brown picnic hamper
Issued: 1993 - 1993

Beswick Number	Price			
	U.S. $	Can. $	U.K. £	Aust. $
BB011	75.00	110.00	40.00	100.00

BB012
SARAH™

Designer: Unknown
Height: 3 ¼", 8.3 cm
Colour: Brown bear, green dress,
 white cup and saucer
Issued: 1993 - 1993

Beswick Number	Price			
	U.S. $	Can. $	U.K. £	Aust. $
BB012	75.00	110.00	40.00	100.00

BESWICK BEARS

EARTHENWARE SERIES 1997 to the present

ARCHIE

Designer:	Unknown
Height:	4 ½", 11.9 cm
Colour:	Brown bear with light blue waistcoat and red and white spotted handkerchief
Issued:	1997 to the present
Series:	The Beswick Bears Collection by Compton and Woodhouse

Beswick Number	Price			
	U.S. $	Can. $	U.K. £	Aust. $
—	—	—	39.95	—

BENJAMIN

Designer:	Unknown
Height:	4 ½", 11.9 cm
Colour:	Brown bear wearing a bright yellow scarf
Issued:	1996 to the present
Series:	The Beswick Bears Collection by Compton and Woodhouse

Beswick Number	Price			
	U.S. $	Can. $	U.K. £	Aust. $
—	—	—	39.95	—

BERTIE

Designer:	Unknown
Height:	4 ½", 11.9 cm
Colour:	Dark brown bear, light brown straw hat with red and purple band, yellow cane
Issued:	1997 to the present
Series:	The Beswick Bears Collection by Compton and Woodhouse

Beswick Number	Price			
	U.S. $	Can. $	U.K. £	Aust. $
—	—	—	39.95	—

BRAMBLY HEDGE

DBH1
POPPY EYEBRIGHT™

Designer:	Harry Sales
Modeller:	David Lyttleton
Height:	3 ¼", 8.3 cm
Colour:	Grey-white and pink dress, white apron trimmed with blue flowers
Issued:	1983 - 1997

Back Stamp	Price			
	U.S. $	Can. $	U.K. £	Aust. $
BH-1	50.00	65.00	25.00	75.00

DBH2
MR APPLE™

Designer:	Harry Sales
Modeller:	David Lyttleton
Height:	3 ¼", 8.3 cm
Colour:	Black trousers, white and blue striped shirt, white apron
Issued:	1983 - 1997

Back Stamp	Price			
	U.S. $	Can. $	U.K. £	Aust. $
BH-1	50.00	65.00	25.00	70.00

DBH3
MRS. APPLE™

Designer:	Harry Sales
Modeller:	David Lyttleton
Height:	3 ¼", 8.3 cm
Colour:	White and blue striped dress, white apron
Issued:	1983 - 1997

Back Stamp	Price			
	U.S. $	Can. $	U.K. £	Aust. $
BH-1	50.00	65.00	25.00	70.00

DBH4
LORD WOODMOUSE™

Designer:	Harry Sales
Modeller:	David Lyttleton
Height:	3 ¼", 8.3 cm
Colour:	Green trousers, brown coat and burgundy waistcoat
Issued:	1983 - 1997

Back Stamp	U.S. $	Price Can. $	U.K. £	Aust. $
BH-1	50.00	65.00	25.00	75.00

DBH5
LADY WOODMOUSE™

Designer:	Harry Sales
Modeller:	David Lyttleton
Height:	3 ¼", 8.3 cm
Colour:	Red and white striped dress, white apron
Issued:	1983 - 1997

Back Stamp	U.S. $	Price Can. $	U.K. £	Aust. $
BH-1	50.00	65.00	25.00	75.00

DBH6
DUSTY DOGWOOD™

Designer:	Harry Sales
Modeller:	David Lyttleton
Height:	3 ¼", 8.3 cm
Colour:	Dark grey suit, red waistcoat
Issued:	1984 - 1995

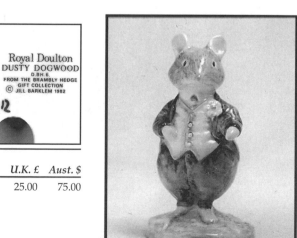

Royal Doulton
DUSTY DOGWOOD
D.BH.6
FROM THE BRAMBLY HEDGE
GIFT COLLECTION
© JILL BARKLEM 1982

Back Stamp	U.S. $	Price Can. $	U.K. £	Aust. $
BH-1	50.00	65.00	25.00	75.00

DBH7
WILFRED TOADFLAX™

Designer:	Harry Sales
Modeller:	David Lyttleton
Height:	3 ¼", 8.3 cm
Colour:	Grey trousers, red and white striped shirt
Issued:	1983 - 1997

Royal Doulton
WILFRED TOADFLAX
DBH 7
FROM THE BRAMBLY HEDGE
GIFT COLLECTION
© JILL BARKLEM 1982

Back Stamp	Price			
	U.S. $	Can. $	U.K. £	Aust. $
BH-1	50.00	65.00	25.00	75.00

DBH8
PRIMROSE WOODMOUSE™

Designer:	Harry Sales
Modeller:	David Lyttleton
Height:	3 ¼", 8.3 cm
Colour:	Yellow dress with white apron
Issued:	1983 - 1997

Royal Doulton
PRIMROSE WOODMOUSE
DBH 8
FROM THE BRAMBLY HEDGE
GIFT COLLECTION
© JILL BARKLEM 1982

Back Stamp	Price			
	U.S. $	Can. $	U.K. £	Aust. $
BH-1	50.00	65.00	25.00	70.00

DBH9
OLD MRS EYEBRIGHT™

Designer:	Harry Sales
Modeller:	David Lyttleton
Height:	3 ¼", 8.3 cm
Colour:	Mauve skirt, white and pink striped shawl, white apron
Issued:	1984 - 1995

Royal Doulton
OLD MRS EYEBRIGHT
DBH 9
FROM THE BRAMBLY HEDGE
GIFT COLLECTION
© JILL BARKLEM 1983

Back Stamp	Price			
	U.S. $	Can. $	U.K. £	Aust. $
BH-1	60.00	75.00	30.00	70.00

DBH10
MR. TOADFLAX™

Designer:	Harry Sales
Modeller:	David Lyttleton
Height:	3 ¼", 8.3 cm
Colour:	Blue and white striped shirt, pink trousers
Issued:	1984 - 1997

Back Stamp	Price			
	U.S. $	Can. $	U.K. £	Aust. $
BH-1	50.00	65.00	25.00	70.00

DBH11
MRS. TOADFLAX™

Designer:	Harry Sales
Modeller:	David Lyttleton
Height:	3 ¼", 8.3 cm
Colour:	Green and white striped dress, white apron
Issued:	1985 - 1995

Back Stamp	Price			
	U.S. $	Can. $	U.K. £	Aust. $
BH-1	60.00	75.00	30.00	75.00

DBH12
CATKIN™

Designer:	Harry Sales
Modeller:	David Lyttleton
Height:	3 ¼", 8.3 cm
Colour:	Yellow dress and white apron
Issued:	1985 - 1994

Back Stamp	Price			
	U.S. $	Can. $	U.K. £	Aust. $
BH-1	100.00	125.00	60.00	100.00

DBH13
OLD VOLE™

Designer:	Harry Sales
Modeller:	David Lyttleton
Height:	3 ¼", 8.3 cm
Colour:	Green jacket, blue trousers, yellow waistcoat
Issued:	1985 - 1992

Back Stamp	Price			
	U.S. $	Can. $	U.K. £	Aust. $
BH-1	175.00	250.00	110.00	135.00

DBH14
BASIL™

Designer:	Harry Sales
Modeller:	David Lyttleton
Height:	3 ¼", 8.3 cm
Colour:	Brown waistcoat, green and white striped trousers
Issued:	1985 - 1992

Back Stamp	Price			
	U.S. $	Can. $	U.K. £	Aust. $
BH-1	175.00	250.00	110.00	135.00

DBH15
MRS. CRUSTYBREAD™

Designer:	Graham Tongue
Modeller:	Ted Chawner
Height:	3 ¼", 8.3 cm
Colour:	Yellow dress, white apron and cap
Issued:	1987 - 1994

Back Stamp	Price			
	U.S. $	Can. $	U.K. £	Aust. $
BH-1	100.00	125.00	60.00	120.00

DBH16
CLOVER™

Designer:	Graham Tongue
Modeller:	Graham Tongue
Height:	3 ¼", 8.3 cm
Colour:	Burgundy dress, white apron
Issued:	1987 - 1997

Back Stamp	Price			
	U.S. $	Can. $	U.K. £	Aust. $
BH-1	50.00	65.00	25.00	70.00

DBH17
TEASEL™

Designer:	Graham Tongue
Modeller:	Ted Chawner
Height:	3 ¼", 8.3 cm
Colour:	Blue-grey dungarees, blue and white striped shirt
Issued:	1987 - 1992

Back Stamp	Price			
	U.S. $	Can. $	U.K. £	Aust. $
BH-1	175.00	250.00	110.00	175.00

DBH18
STORE STUMP MONEY BOX™

Designer:	Martyn Alcock
Height:	3 ¼", 8.3 cm
Colour:	Browns
Issued:	1987 - 1989

Back Stamp	Price			
	U.S. $	Can. $	U.K. £	Aust. $
BH-1	200.00	200.00	100.00	100.00

DBH19
LILY WEAVER™

Designer:	Graham Tongue
Modeller:	Ted Chawner
Height:	3 ¼", 8.3 cm
Colour:	White dress with green and mauve, white cap
Issued:	1988 - 1993

Royal Doulton®
LILY WEAVER
D B H 19
FROM THE BRAMBLY HEDGE
GIFT COLLECTION
1988 JILL BARKLEM

Back Stamp	Price			
	U.S. $	Can. $	U.K. £	Aust. $
BH-1	175.00	225.00	100.00	120.00

DBH20
FLAX WEAVER™

Designer:	Graham Tongue
Modeller:	Ted Chawner
Height:	3 ¼", 8.3 cm
Colour:	Grey trousers, grey and white striped shirt
Issued:	1988 - 1993

Royal Doulton®
FLAX WEAVER
D B H 20
FROM THE BRAMBLY HEDGE
GIFT COLLECTION
© 1988 JILL BARKLEM

Back Stamp	Price			
	U.S. $	Can. $	U.K. £	Aust. $
BH-1	150.00	175.00	75.00	120.00

DBH21
CONKER™

Designer:	Graham Tongue
Modeller:	Ted Chawner
Height:	3 ¼", 8.3 cm
Colour:	Green jacket, yellow waistcoat, green striped trousers
Issued:	1988 - 1994

Royal Doulton®
CONKER
D B H 21
FROM THE BRAMBLY HEDGE
GIFT COLLECTION
1988 JILL BARKLEM

Back Stamp	Price			
	U.S. $	Can. $	U.K. £	Aust. $
BH-1	175.00	225.00	110.00	120.00

DBH22
PRIMROSE ENTERTAINS™

Designer:	Graham Tongue
Modeller:	Alan Maslankowski
Height:	3 ¼", 8.3 cm
Colour:	Green and yellow dress
Issued:	1990 - 1995

Back Stamp	Price			
	U.S. $	Can. $	U.K. £	Aust. $
BH-1	125.00	175.00	40.00	135.00

DBH23
WILFRED ENTERTAINS™

Designer:	Graham Tongue
Modeller:	Alan Maslankowski
Height:	3 ¼", 8.3 cm
Colour:	Burgundy and yellow outfit, black hat
Issued:	1990 - 1995

Back Stamp	Price			
	U.S. $	Can. $	U.K. £	Aust $
BH-1	125.00	175.00	40.00	135.00

DBH24
MR. SALTAPPLE™

Designer:	Graham Tongue
Modeller:	Warren Platt
Height:	3 ¼", 8.3 cm
Colour:	Blue and white striped outfit, beige base
Issued:	1993 - 1997

Back Stamp	Price			
	U.S. $	Can. $	U.K. £	Aust. $
BH-1	50.00	65.00	25.00	85.00

DBH25
MRS. SALTAPPLE™

Designer:	Graham Tongue
Modeller:	Warren Platt
Height:	3 ¼", 8.3 cm
Colour:	Rose and cream dress, beige hat and base
Issued:	1993 - 1997

Royal Doulton®
MRS.SALTAPPLE
D B H 25
FROM THE BRAMBLY HEDGE
GIFT COLLECTION
© JILL BARKLEM 1992

Back Stamp	Price			
	U.S. $	Can. $	U.K. £	Aust. $
BH-1	50.00	65.00	25.00	85.00

DBH26
DUSTY AND BABY™

Designer:	Graham Tongue
Modeller:	Martyn Alcock
Height:	3 ¾", 9.5 cm
Colour:	Dusty - blue striped shirt with beige dungarees
	Baby - white gown
Issued:	1995 - 1997

Back Stamp	Price			
	U.S. $	Can. $	U.K. £	Aust. $
BH-1	50.00	65.00	25.00	75.00

BUNNYKINS

DOULTON EARTHENWARE BUNNYKINS
DOULTON RESIN BUNNYKINS

BUNNYKINS BACKSTAMPS

BK-1. DOULTON & CO. LIMITED, 1972 - 1976

These backstamps were used on all figurines introduced between 1972 and 1976.

BK-2. ROYAL DOULTON TABLEWARE LTD, 1976 - 1984

The name Doulton & Co. Limited was changed to Royal Doulton Tableware Ltd., and this backstamp was used on all new figurines introduced between 1976 and 1984. It was also used on all models that had been in production previously, updating the older backstamp (BK-1). In these instances the copyright year on the stamps was kept the same as that of the original backstamp (BK-1).

BK-3. GOLDEN JUBILEE CELEBRATION, 1984

All models manufactured during 1984 carried the words Golden Jubilee Celebration 1984", which were added to the 1976-1984 backstamp (BK-2).

BK-4. ROYAL DOULTON (U.K.), 1985 - 1986

The backstamp of 1976-1984 was modified to Royal Doulton (U.K.). All items introduced between 1985 and 1986 carry this backstamp.

BK-5. ROYAL DOULTON, 1987 TO DATE

BK-SPECIALS. SPECIAL COMMISSION BACKSTAMPS

Many figurines are issued for special events, anniversaries, promotions, etc. All these carry a special stamp.

The backstamp of 1985 - 1986 was again modified by removing the (U.K.). All new figurines introduced since 1987 carry this backstamp.

D6003

D6004

D6002

D6025

D6001

D6024

BUNNYKINS

EARTHENWARE Circa 1939 - to the present

BILLY BUNNYKINS™
D6001

Designer:	Charles Noke
Height:	4 ½", 11.4 cm
Colour:	Red trousers, blue jacket, white bowtie with blue spots
Issued:	1939-c.1940

FARMER BUNNYKINS™
D6003

Designer:	Charles Noke
Height:	7 ½", 19 cm
Colour:	Green, blue, brown, red and white
Issued:	1939-c.1940

FREDDIE BUNNYKINS™
D6024

Designer:	Charles Noke
Height:	3 ¾", 9.5 cm
Colour:	Green trousers, red jacket and yellow bowtie
Issued:	1939-c.1940

MARY BUNNYKINS™
D6002

Designer:	Charles Noke
Height:	6 ½", 16.5 cm
Colour:	Blue and red, white apron
Issued:	1939-c.1940

MOTHER BUNNYKINS™
D6004

Designer:	Charles Noke
Height:	7", 17.5 cm
Colour:	Blue, red, white and brown
Issued:	1939-c.1940

REGGIE BUNNYKINS™
D6025

Designer:	Charles Noke
Height:	3 ¾", 9.5 cm
Colour:	Blue outfit, red bowtie
Issued:	1939-c.1940

Name	Back Stamp	Doulton Number	Price U.S. $	Can. $	U.K. £	Aust. $
Billy Bunnykins	BK-	D6001	3,500.00	3,750.00	2,000.00	3,500.00
Farmer Bunnykins	BK-	D6003	3,750.00	4,000.00	2,000.00	3,500.00
Freddie Bunnykins	BK-	D6024	5,000.00	5,500.00	2,250.00	3,500.00
Mary Bunnykins	BK-	D6002	4,000.00	4,500.00	2,000.00	3,500.00
Mother Bunnykins	BK-	D6004	3,750.00	4,000.00	2,000.00	3,500.00
Reggie Bunnykins	BK-	D6025	4,500.00	4,750.00	2,250.00	3,500.00

D6615A
BUNNYBANK™
First Variation

Designer:	Unknown
Modeller:	Unknown
Height:	8 ½", 21.6 cm
Colour:	Grey rabbit, green coat and hat, maroon drum
Issued:	1967 - 1977

Back Stamp	Price			
	U.S. $	Can. $	U.K. £	Aust. $
BK-	500.00	600.00	250.00	525.00

D6615B
BUNNYBANK™
Second Variation

Designer:	Unknown
Modeller:	Unknown
Height:	9 ¼", 23.5 cm
Colour:	Brown rabbit, green coat and hat, maroon drum
Issued:	1979 - 1991

Back Stamp	Price			
	U.S. $	Can. $	U.K. £	Aust. $
BK-	350.00	475.00	200.00	525.00

Bunnybank
D.6615
© DOULTON & CO.LIMITED 1967

DB1
FAMILY PHOTOGRAPH BUNNYKINS™
First Variation

Designer:	Walter Hayward
Modeller:	Albert Hallam
Height:	4 ½", 11.4 cm
Colour:	Blue, white, burgundy and grey
Issued:	1972 - 1988
Varieties:	DB67; also called Father, Mother and Victoria Bunnykins, DB68

Back Stamp	Price			
	U.S. $	Can. $	U.K. £	Aust. $
BK-1	175.00	200.00	80.00	235.00
BK-2	175.00	200.00	80.00	235.00
BK-3	200.00	250.00	135.00	260.00

DB2
BUNTIE BUNNYKINS HELPING MOTHER™

Designer:	Walter Hayward
Modeller:	Albert Hallam
Height:	3 ½", 8.9 cm
Colour:	Rose-pink and yellow
Issued:	1972 - 1993

Back Stamp	Price			
	U.S. $	Can. $	U.K. £	Aust. $
BK-1	90.00	115.00	45.00	95.00
BK-2	90.00	115.00	45.00	95.00
BK-3	125.00	275.00	85.00	125.00

DB3
BILLIE BUNNYKINS COOLING OFF™

Designer:	Walter Hayward
Modeller:	Albert Hallam
Height:	3 ¾", 9.5 cm
Colour:	Burgundy, yellow and green-grey
Issued:	1972 - 1987

Back Stamp	Price			
	U.S. $	Can. $	U.K. £	Aust. $
BK-1	275.00	350.00	150.00	300.00
BK-2	275.00	350.00	150.00	300.00
BK-3	300.00	375.00	175.00	325.00

DB4
BILLIE AND BUNTIE BUNNYKINS SLEIGH RIDE™
First Variation

Designer:	Walter Hayward
Modeller:	Albert Hallam
Height:	3 ¼", 8.3 cm
Colour:	Blue, maroon and yellow
Issued:	1972 - 1997
Varieties:	DB81

Back Stamp	Price			
	U.S. $	Can. $	U.K. £	Aust. $
BK-1	45.00	60.00	45.00	75.00
BK-2	45.00	60.00	30.00	75.00
BK-3	125.00	175.00	85.00	110.00

DB5
MR. BUNNYKINS AUTUMN DAYS™

Designer:	Walter Hayward
Modeller:	Albert Hallam
Height:	4", 10.1 cm
Colour:	Maroon, yellow and blue
Issued:	1972 - 1982

Back Stamp	Price			
	U.S. $	Can. $	U.K. £	Aust. $
BK-1	500.00	600.00	300.00	725.00
BK-2	500.00	600.00	300.00	725.00
BK-3	550.00	700.00	350.00	775.00

DB6
MRS. BUNNYKINS CLEAN SWEEP™

Designer:	Walter Hayward
Modeller:	Albert Hallam
Height:	4", 10.1 cm
Colour:	Blue and white
Issued:	1972 - 1991

Back Stamp	Price			
	U.S. $	Can. $	U.K. £	Aust. $
BK-1	115.00	150.00	65.00	125.00
BK-2	115.00	150.00	65.00	125.00
BK-3	125.00	175.00	95.00	150.00

DB7
DAISIE BUNNYKINS SPRING TIME™

Designer:	Walter Hayward
Modeller:	Albert Hallam
Height:	3 ½", 8.9 cm
Colour:	Blue, white and yellow
Issued:	1972 - 1983

DAISIE BUNNYKINS
"Spring Time"
DB7
COPR. 1972
DOULTON & CO. LIMITED
Rd. No. 986231
Rd. No. 12906
R.S.A. Rd. No. 186/72

Back Stamp	Price			
	U.S. $	Can. $	U.K. £	Aust. $
BK-1	525.00	750.00	300.00	750.00
BK-2	525.00	750.00	300.00	750.00
BK-3	575.00	800.00	325.00	800.00

DB8
DOLLIE BUNNYKINS PLAYTIME™
First Variation

Designer:	Walter Hayward
Modeller:	Albert Hallam
Height:	4", 10.1 cm
Colour:	White dress with pink design, blue dress
Issued:	1972 - 1993
Varieties:	DB80

DOLLIE BUNNYKINS
"Playtime"
DB8
COPR. 1972
DOULTON & CO. LIMITED
Rd. No. 956229
Rd. No. 12906
R.S.A. Rd. No. 187/72

Back Stamp	Price			
	U.S. $	Can. $	U.K. £	Aust. $
BK-1	85.00	110.00	40.00	80.00
BK-2	85.00	110.00	40.00	80.00
BK-3	125.00	150.00	75.00	115.00

DB9
STORYTIME BUNNYKINS™
First Variation

Designer:	Walter Hayward
Modeller:	Albert Hallam
Height:	3", 7.6 cm
Colour:	White dress with blue design, pink dress
Issued:	1972 - 1997
Varieties:	DB59; also called Partners in Collecting, DB151

Back Stamp	Price			
	U.S. $	Can. $	U.K. £	Aust. $
BK-1	45.00	55.00	45.00	70.00
BK-2	45.00	55.00	30.00	70.00
BK-3	100.00	150.00	85.00	100.00

DB10
BUSY NEEDLES BUNNYKINS™

Designer:	Walter Hayward
Modeller:	Albert Hallam
Height:	3 ¼", 8.3 cm
Colour:	White, green and maroon
Issued:	1973 - 1988
Varieties:	DB70

Back Stamp	Price			
	U.S. $	Can. $	U.K. £	Aust. $
BK-1	125.00	165.00	70.00	175.00
BK-2	125.00	165.00	70.00	175.00
BK-3	150.00	225.00	125.00	235.00

DB11
RISE AND SHINE BUNNYKINS™

Designer:	Walter Hayward
Modeller:	Albert Hallam
Height:	3 ¾", 9.5 cm
Colour:	Maroon, yellow and blue
Issued:	1973 - 1988

Back Stamp	Price			
	U.S. $	Can. $	U.K. £	Aust. $
BK-1	175.00	195.00	85.00	225.00
BK-2	175.00	195.00	85.00	225.00
BK-3	225.00	250.00	125.00	250.00

DB12
TALLY HO! BUNNYKINS™
First Variation

Designer:	Walter Hayward
Modeller:	Albert Hallam
Height:	3 ¾", 9.5 cm
Colour:	Burgundy, yellow, blue, white and green
Issued:	1973 - 1988
Varieties:	DB78; also called William Bunnykins, DB69

Back Stamp	Price			
	U.S. $	Can. $	U.K. £	Aust. $
BK-1	125.00	200.00	70.00	225.00
BK-2	125.00	200.00	70.00	225.00
BK-3	175.00	250.00	125.00	250.00

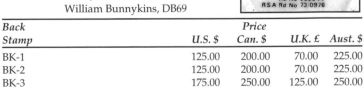

DB13
THE ARTIST BUNNYKINS™

Designer: Walter Hayward
Modeller: Alan Maslankowski
Height: 3 ¾", 9.5 cm
Colour: Burgundy, yellow and blue
Issued: 1974 - 1982

Back Stamp	Price			
	U.S. $	Can. $	U.K. £	Aust. $
BK-1	525.00	700.00	350.00	700.00
BK-2	525.00	700.00	350.00	700.00

DB14
GRANDPA'S STORY BUNNYKINS™

Designer: Walter Hayward
Modeller: Alan Maslankowski
Height: 4", 10.1 cm
Colour: Burgundy, grey, yellow, blue and green
Issued: 1974 - 1983

Back Stamp	Price			
	U.S. $	Can. $	U.K. £	Aust. $
BK-1	500.00	675.00	350.00	775.00
BK-2	500.00	675.00	350.00	775.00

DB15
SLEEPYTIME BUNNYKINS™

Designer: Walter Hayward
Modeller: Alan Maslankowski
Height: 1 ¾", 4.7 cm
Colour: Brown, white, yellow, blue and red
Issued: 1974 - 1993

Back Stamp	Price			
	U.S. $	Can. $	U.K. £	Aust. $
BK-1	100.00	125.00	35.00	80.00
BK-2	100.00	125.00	35.00	80.00
BK-3	140.00	165.00	85.00	110.00

DB16
MR. BUNNYBEAT STRUMMING™

Designer: Harry Sales
Modeller: David Lyttleton
Height: 4 ½", 11.4 cm
Colour: Pink and yellow coat, blue and white striped trousers, white with blue polka-dot neck bow
Issued: 1982 - 1988
Varieties: Also called Rock and Roll Bunnykins, DB 124

Back Stamp	Price			
	U.S. $	Can. $	U.K. £	Aust. $
BK-2	225.00	300.00	150.00	225.00
BK-3	275.00	375.00	200.00	250.00

DB17
SANTA BUNNYKINS HAPPY CHRISTMAS™

Designer: Harry Sales
Modeller: David Lyttleton
Height: 4 ½", 10.8 cm
Colour: Red, white and brown
Issued: 1981 - 1996

Back Stamp	Price			
	U.S. $	Can. $	U.K. £	Aust. $
BK-2	45.00	65.00	35.00	75.00
BK-3	125.00	150.00	85.00	135.00

DB18
MR BUNNYKINS AT THE EASTER PARADE™
First Variation

Designer: Harry Sales
Modeller: David Lyttleton
Height: 5", 12.7 cm
Colour: Red, yellow and brown
Issued: 1982 - 1993
Varieties: DB 51

Back Stamp	Price			
	U.S. $	Can. $	U.K. £	Aust. $
BK-2	110.00	125.00	45.00	95.00
BK-3	150.00	175.00	100.00	125.00

DB19
MRS BUNNYKINS
AT THE EASTER PARADE™
First Variation

Designer:	Harry Sales
Modeller:	David Lyttleton
Height:	4 ½", 11.4 cm
Colour:	Pale blue and maroon
Issued:	1982 - 1996
Varieties:	DB52

Back Stamp	Price			
	U.S. $	Can. $	U.K. £	Aust. $
BK-2	110.00	150.00	25.00	95.00
BK-3	150.00	200.00	85.00	125.00

DB20
ASTRO BUNNYKINS ROCKET MAN™

Designer:	Harry Sales
Modeller:	David Lyttleton
Height:	4 ¼", 10.8 cm
Colour:	White, red, blue and yellow
Issued:	1983 - 1988

Back Stamp	Price			
	U.S. $	Can. $	U.K. £	Aust. $
BK-2	200.00	225.00	85.00	175.00
BK-3	250.00	275.00	125.00	200.00

DB21
HAPPY BIRTHDAY BUNNYKINS™

Designer:	Harry Sales
Modeller:	Graham Tongue
Height:	3 ¾", 9.5 cm
Colour:	Red and blue
Issued:	1983 - 1997

Back Stamp	Price			
	U.S. $	Can. $	U.K. £	Aust. $
BK-2	45.00	65.00	20.00	75.00
BK-3	100.00	150.00	85.00	150.00

DB22
JOGGING BUNNYKINS™

Designer:	Harry Sales
Modeller:	David Lyttleton
Height:	2 ½", 6.4 cm
Colour:	Yellow, blue and white
Issued:	1983 - 1989

Back	Price			
Stamp	U.S. $	Can. $	U.K. £	Aust. $
BK-2	135.00	150.00	75.00	150.00
BK-3	175.00	175.00	110.00	175.00

DB23
SOUSAPHONE BUNNYKINS™
First Variation

Designer:	Harry Sales
Modeller:	David Lyttleton
Height:	3 ½", 8.9 cm
Colour:	Red, blue and yellow
Issued:	1984 - 1990
Varieties:	DB86, DB105
Series:	Bunnykins Oompah Band

Back	Price			
Stamp	U.S. $	Can. $	U.K. £	Aust. $
BK-3	175.00	225.00	100.00	200.00
BK-4	150.00	175.00	65.00	175.00
Set DB23 - 27 (5 pcs.)	875.00	1,000.00	500.00	1,100.00

DB24
TRUMPETER BUNNYKINS™
First Variation

Designer:	Harry Sales
Modeller:	David Lyttleton
Height:	3 ½", 8.9 cm
Colour:	Red, blue and yellow
Issued:	1984 - 1990
Varieties:	DB87, DB106
Series:	Bunnykins Oompah Band

Back	Price			
Stamp	U.S. $	Can. $	U.K. £	Aust. $
BK-3	175.00	225.00	100.00	200.00
BK-4	150.00	175.00	75.00	175.00

DB25
CYMBALS BUNNYKINS™
First Variation

Designer:	Harry Sales
Modeller:	David Lyttleton
Height:	3 ½", 8.9 cm
Colour:	Red, blue and yellow
Issued:	1984 - 1990
Varieties:	DB 88, DB 107
Series:	Bunnykins Oompah Band

| Back Stamp | Price | | | |
	U.S. $	Can. $	U.K. £	Aust. $
BK-3	175.00	225.00	100.00	200.00
BK-4	150.00	175.00	75.00	175.00

DB26A
DRUMMER BUNNYKINS™
First Variation, 50th Anniversary Edition

Designer:	Harry Sales
Modeller:	David Lyttleton
Height:	3 ½", 9.2 cm
Colour:	Blue, yellow, red and cream
Issued:	1984 - 1984
Series:	Bunnykins Oompah Band

| Back Stamp | Price | | | |
	U.S. $	Can. $	U.K. £	Aust. $
BK-3	150.00	200.00	150.00	260.00

DB26B
DRUMMER BUNNYKINS™
Second Variation, Bunnykins Oompah Band Edition

Designer:	Harry Sales
Modeller:	David Lyttleton
Height:	3 ¾", 9.5 cm
Colour:	Blue, yellow, red and cream
Issued:	1984 - 1990
Varieties:	DB 89, DB 108
Series:	Bunnykins Oompah Band

| Back Stamp | Price | | | |
	U.S. $	Can. $	U.K £	Aust. $
BK-4	125.00	175.00	85.00	200.00

DB27
DRUM-MAJOR BUNNYKINS™
First Variation

Designer:	Harry Sales
Modeller:	David Lyttleton
Height:	3 ½", 8.9 cm
Colour:	Red, blue and yellow
Issued:	1984 - 1990
Varieties:	DB 90, DB 109
Series:	Bunnykins Oompah Band

Back Stamp	Price U.S. $	Can. $	U.K. £	Aust. $
BK-3	175.00	225.00	100.00	200.00
BK-4	150.00	175.00	65.00	175.00

DB28A
OLYMPIC BUNNYKINS™
First Variation

Designer:	Harry Sales
Modeller:	David Lyttleton
Height:	3 ¾", 9.4 cm
Colour:	White and blue
Issued:	1984 - 1988

Back Stamp	Price U.S. $	Can. $	U.K. £	Aust. $
BK-3	250.00	300.00	125.00	350.00
BK-4	225.00	275.00	95.00	300.00

DB28B
OLYMPIC BUNNYKINS™
Second Variation

Designer:	Harry Sales
Modeller:	David Lyttleton
Height:	3 ½", 8.9 cm
Colour:	Gold and green
Issued:	1984 - 1984

Back Stamp	Price U.S. $	Can. $	U.K. £	Aust. $
BK-Special	500.00	425.00	175.00	350.00

DB29A
TOUCHDOWN BUNNYKINS™
First Variation

Designer:	Harry Sales
Modeller:	David Lyttleton
Height:	3 ¼", 8.3 cm
Colour:	Blue and white
Issued:	1985 - 1988
Varieties:	DB 29B, 96, 97, 98, 99, 100

"TOUCHDOWN BUNNYKINS"
DB29
© ROYAL DOULTON
TABLEWARE LTD 1984
GOLDEN JUBILEE
CELEBRATION 1984

Back Stamp	Price			
	U.S. $	Can. $	U.K. £	Aust. $
BK-4	175.00	225.00	75.00	250.00
BK-5	175.00	225.00	75.00	250.00

DB29B
TOUCHDOWN BUNNYKINS™
Second Variation (Boston College)

Designer:	Harry Sales
Modeller:	David Lyttleton
Height:	3 ¼", 8.3 cm
Colour:	Maroon and gold
Issued:	1985 in a limited edition of 50
Varieties:	DB29B, 96, 97, 98, 99, 100

Back Stamp	Price			
	U.S. $	Can. $	U.K. £	Aust. $
BK-4	2,750.00	3,000.00	1,500.00	2,000.00

DB30
KNOCKOUT BUNNYKINS™

Designer:	Harry Sales
Modeller:	David Lyttleton
Height:	4", 10.1 cm
Colour:	Yellow, green and white
Issued:	1985 - 1988

"KNOCKOUT BUNNYKINS"
DB 30
© ROYAL DOULTON
TABLEWARE LTD 1984

Back Stamp	Price			
	U.S. $	Can. $	U.K. £	Aust. $
BK-4	325.00	275.00	110.00	275.00
BK-5	325.00	275.00	110.00	275.00

DB31
DOWNHILL BUNNYKINS™

Designer:	Harry Sales
Modeller:	Graham Tongue
Height:	2 ½", 6.4 cm
Colour:	Yellow, green, maroon and grey
Issued:	1985 - 1988

DOWNHILL BUNNYKINS™
DB 31
© ROYAL DOULTON
TABLEWARE LTD 1984

Back Stamp	U.S. $	Price Can. $	U.K. £	Aust. $
BK-3	350.00	400.00	175.00	300.00
BK-4	300.00	350.00	150.00	275.00
BK-5	300.00	350.00	150.00	275.00

DB32
BOGEY BUNNYKINS™

Designer:	Harry Sales
Modeller:	David Lyttleton
Height:	4", 10.1 cm
Colour:	Green, brown and yellow
Issued:	1985 - 1992

"BOGEY BUNNYKINS"
DB 32
© ROYAL DOULTON
TABLEWARE LTD 1984

Back Stamp	U.S. $	Price Can. $	U.K. £	Aust. $
BK-3	275.00	275.00	100.00	150.00
BK-4	225.00	225.00	80.00	125.00
BK-5	225.00	225.00	80.00	125.00

DB33A
TALLY HO!™
Music Box
First Variation, "Tally-Ho!" Figurine

Designer:	Walter Hayward
Modeller:	Albert Hallam
Height:	7", 17.8 cm
Colour:	Red coat, yellow jumper
Issued:	1984 - 1993
Tune:	Rock A Bye Baby

Back Stamp	U.S. $	Price Can. $	U.K. £	Aust. $
BK-4	325.00	275.00	125.00	400.00
BK-5	325.00	275.00	125.00	400.00

DB33B
TALLY HO!™
Music Box
Second Variation, "William Bunnykins" Figurine

Designer:	Walter Hayward
Modeller:	Albert Hallam
Height:	7", 17.8 cm
Colour:	Brown trousers, red coat and maroon tie
Issued:	1988 - 1991
Tune:	Rock A Bye Baby

Back		Price		
Stamp	U.S. $	Can. $	U.K. £	Aust. $
BK-4	325.00	300.00	100.00	400.00
BK-5	325.00	300.00	100.00	400.00

DB34
SANTA BUNNYKINS™
Music Box

Designer:	Harry Sales
Modeller:	David Lyttleton
Height:	7 ¼", 18.4 cm
Colour:	Red, white and brown
Issued:	1984 - 1991
Tune:	White Christmas

Back		Price		
Stamp	U.S. $	Can. $	U.K. £	Aust. $
BK-4	300.00	300.00	100.00	350.00
BK-5	300.00	300.00	100.00	350.00

DB35
ASTRO BUNNYKINS ROCKET MAN™
Music Box

Designer:	Harry Sales
Modeller:	David Lyttleton
Height:	7", 17.8 cm
Colour:	White, red and blue
Issued:	1984 - 1989
Tune:	Fly Me To The Moon

Back		Price		
Stamp	U.S. $	Can. $	U.K. £	Aust. $
BK-4	450.00	475.00	125.00	450.00
BK-5	450.00	475.00	125.00	450.00

DB36
HAPPY BIRTHDAY BUNNYKINS™
Music Box

Designer: Harry Sales
Modeller: Graham Tongue
Height: 7", 17.8 cm
Colour: Red and white
Issued: 1984 - 1993
Tune: Happy Birthday To You

Back Stamp	Price			
	U.S. $	Can. $	U.K. £	Aust. $
BK-4	350.00	300.00	85.00	300.00
BK-5	350.00	300.00	85.00	300.00

DB37
JOGGING BUNNYKINS™
Music Box

Designer: Harry Sales
Modeller: David Lyttleton
Height: 5 ½", 14.0 cm
Colour: Yellow and blue
Issued: 1987 - 1989
Tune: King of the Road

Back Stamp	Price			
	U.S. $	Can. $	U.K. £	Aust. $
BK-5	500.00	500.00	135.00	500.00

DB38
MR. BUNNYBEAT STRUMMING™
Music Box

Designer: Harry Sales
Modeller: David Lyttleton
Height: 7 ½", 19.1 cm
Colour: Pink, white and yellow
Issued: 1987 - 1989
Tune: Hey Jude

Back Stamp	Price			
	U.S. $	Can. $	U.K. £	Aust. $
BK-5	550.00	500.00	175.00	500.00

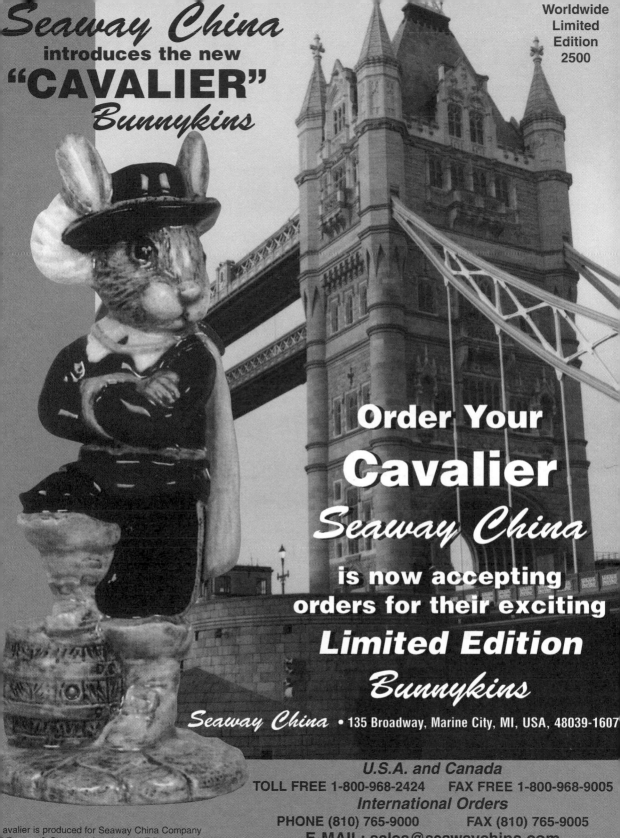

Royal Doulton News

Store Specializes in Discontinued

Characters Look For New Home

Marine City, MI: With an entire store full of Royal Doulton, people often look to *Seaway China* in Marine City, MI to find that special discontinued Beatrix Potter, Bunnykins, Brambly Hedge, or Snowman. Hundreds of Royal Doulton collectors count on *Seaway* to locate their special needs. In addition to their own 32 page color catalog, *Seaway* can mail or fax special lists of Royal Doulton Collectibles. *Seaway China* are specialists in discontinued figures and character jugs.

For more information call **1-800-968-2424**.

Shown above are a collection of Bunnykins at Seaway China. Call Seaway China at 1-800-968-2424 for more information about Bunnykins.

DB39
MRS. BUNNYKINS
AT THE EASTER PARADE™
Music Box

Designer:	Harry Sales
Modeller:	David Lyttleton
Height:	7", 17.8 cm
Colour:	Blue, yellow and maroon
Issued:	1987 - 1991
Tune:	Easter Parade

Back Stamp	Price			
	U.S. $	Can. $	U.K. £	Aust. $
BK-5	400.00	500.00	95.00	500.00

DB40
AEROBIC BUNNYKINS™

Designer:	Harry Sales
Modeller:	David Lyttleton
Height:	2 ¾", 7.0 cm
Colour:	Yellow and pale blue
Issued:	1985 - 1988

"AEROBIC BUNNYKINS"
DB 40
© ROYAL DOULTON (U.K.) 1984

Back Stamp	Price			
	U.S. $	Can. $	U.K. £	Aust. $
BK-4	275.00	325.00	100.00	300.00
BK-5	275.00	325.00	100.00	300.00

"FREEFALL BUNNYKINS"
DB 41
© ROYAL DOULTON (U.K.) 1984

DB41
FREEFALL BUNNYKINS™

Designer:	Harry Sales
Modeller:	David Lyttleton
Height:	2 ¼", 5.7 cm
Colour:	Grey, yellow and white
Issued:	1986 - 1989

Back Stamp	Price			
	U.S. $	Can. $	U.K. £	Aust. $
BK-4	350.00	400.00	175.00	300.00
BK-5	350.00	400.00	175.00	300.00

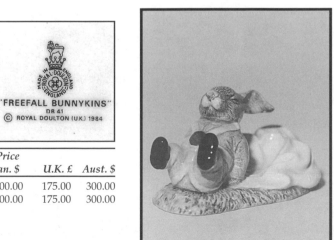

DB42
ACE BUNNYKINS™

Designer:	Harry Sales		
Modeller:	David Lyttleton		
Height:	3 ¾", 9.5 cm		
Colour:	White and blue		
Issued:	1986 - 1989		

Back		*Price*			
Stamp		*U.S. $*	*Can. $*	*U.K. £*	*Aust. $*
BK-4		275.00	350.00	125.00	250.00
BK-5		275.00	350.00	125.00	250.00

DB43
HOME RUN BUNNYKINS™
(1 on Back of Jersey)

Designer:	Harry Sales
Modeller:	David Lyttleton
Height:	4", 10.1 cm
Colour:	Blue, yellow and white
Issued:	1986 - 1993

Back		*Price*			
Stamp		*U.S. $*	*Can. $*	*U.K. £*	*Aust. $*
BK-4		115.00	130.00	45.00	95.00
BK-5		115.00	130.00	45.00	95.00

DB44: Assigned to Ballet Bunnykins but not issued.

DB45
KING JOHN™
First Variation

Designer:	Harry Sales		
Modeller:	David Lyttleton		
Height:	4", 10.1 cm		
Colour:	Red, yellow and blue		
Issued:	1986 - 1990		
Varieties:	DB91		
Series:	Bunnykins Royal Family		

Back		*Price*			
Stamp		*U.S. $*	*Can. $*	*U.K. £*	*Aust. $*
BK-4		125.00	175.00	75.00	225.00
BK-5		125.00	175.00	75.00	225.00
Set DB45 - 49 (5 pcs.)		650.00	900.00	350.00	1,100.00

DB46
QUEEN SOPHIE™
First Variation

Designer:	Harry Sales
Modeller:	David Lyttleton
Height:	4 ½", 11.4 cm
Colour:	Blue and red
Issued:	1986 - 1990
Varieties:	DB92
Series:	Bunnykins Royal Family

Back Stamp	Price U.S. $	Can. $	U.K. £	Aust. $
BK-4	125.00	175.00	75.00	225.00
BK-5	125.00	175.00	75.00	225.00

DB47
PRINCESS BEATRICE™
First Variation

Designer:	Harry Sales
Modeller:	David Lyttleton
Height:	3 ½", 8.9 cm
Colour:	Pale green
Issued:	1986 - 1990
Varieties:	DB93
Series:	Bunnykins Royal Family

Back Stamp	Price U.S. $	Can. $	U.K. £	Aust. $
BK-4	125.00	175.00	60.00	225.00
BK-5	125.00	175.00	60.00	225.00

DB48
PRINCE FREDERICK™
First Variation

Designer:	Harry Sales
Modeller:	David Lyttleton
Height:	3 ½", 8.9 cm
Colour:	Green, white and red
Issued:	1986 - 1990
Varieties:	DB94
Series:	Bunnykins Royal Family

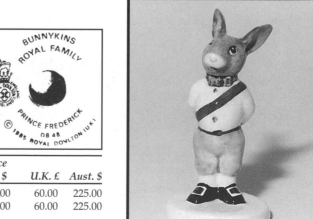

Back Stamp	Price U.S. $	Can. $	U.K. £	Aust. $
BK-4	125.00	175.00	60.00	225.00
BK-5	125.00	175.00	60.00	225.00

DB49
HARRY THE HERALD™
First Variation

Designer:	Harry Sales
Modeller:	David Lyttleton
Height:	3 ½", 8.9 cm
Colour:	Maroon, white and tan
Issued:	1986 - 1990
Varieties:	DB95, DB115
Series:	Bunnykins Royal Family

Back		Price			
Stamp		U.S. $	Can. $	U.K. £	Aust. $
BK-4		150.00	200.00	85.00	235.00
BK-5		150.00	200.00	85.00	235.00

DB50
UNCLE SAM BUNNYKINS™
First Variation

Designer:	Harry Sales
Modeller:	David Lyttleton
Height:	4 ½", 11 cm
Colour:	Blue, red and white
Issued:	1986 to the present
Varieties:	DB175

Back		Price			
Stamp		U.S. $	Can. $	U.K. £	Aust. $
BK-4		45.00	65.00	35.00	75.00
BK-5		45.00	65.00	35.00	75.00

DB51
MR. BUNNYKINS AT THE EASTER PARADE™
Second Variation

Designer:	Harry Sales
Modeller:	David Lyttleton
Height:	5", 12.7 cm
Colour:	Blue tie and hat band, maroon coat, light grey trousers, pink ribbon on package
Issued:	1986 - 1986
Varieties:	DB18

Back		Price			
Stamp		U.S. $	Can. $	U.K. £	Aust. $
BK-4		950.00	950.00	350.00	1,500.00

DB52
MRS. BUNNYKINS AT THE
EASTER PARADE™
Second Variation

Designer: Harry Sales
Modeller: David Lyttleton
Height: 4 ½", 11.4 cm
Colour: Maroon dress, white collar, blue bow on bonnet,
              multi-coloured bows on packages
Issued: 1986 - 1986
Varieties: DB19

Back Stamp	U.S. $	Can. $	Price U.K. £	Aust. $
BK-4	1,000.00	1,000.00	400.00	1,500.00

DB53
CAROL SINGER™
Music Box

Designer: Harry Sales
Modeller: David Lyttleton
Height: 7", 17.8 cm
Colour: Red, yellow and green
Issued: 1986 - 1989
Tune: Silent Night

Back Stamp	U.S. $	Can. $	Price U.K. £	Aust. $
BK-4	500.00	500.00	175.00	500.00
BK-5	500.00	500.00	175.00	500.00

DB54
COLLECTOR BUNNYKINS™

Designer: Harry Sales
Modeller: David Lyttleton
Height: 4 ¼", 10.8 cm
Colour: Brown, blue and grey
Issued: 1987 - 1987
Series: R.D.I.C.C.

INTERNATIONAL COLLECTORS CLUB
ROYAL DOULTON
COLLECTOR BUNNYKINS
DB54
EXCLUSIVELY FOR
COLLECTORS CLUB
© 1986 ROYAL DOULTON
MODELLED BY
D. Lyttleton

Back Stamp	U.S. $	Can. $	Price U.K. £	Aust. $
BK-Special	900.00	1,000.00	525.00	950.00

DB55
BEDTIME BUNNYKINS™
First Variation

Designer:	Graham Tongue
Modeller:	David Lyttleton
Height:	3 ¼", 8.3 cm
Colour:	Blue and white striped pyjamas, brown teddy bear
Issued:	1987 to the present
Varieties:	DB63, 79, 103

Back Stamp	Price			
	U.S. $	Can. $	U.K. £	Aust. $
BK-5	45.00	63.00	16.00	60.00

DB56
BE PREPARED BUNNYKINS™

Designer:	Graham Tongue
Modeller:	David Lyttleton
Height:	4", 10.1 cm
Colour:	Dark green and grey
Issued:	1987 - 1996

Back Stamp	Price			
	U.S. $	Can. $	U.K. £	Aust. $
BK-5	80.00	100.00	25.00	70.00

DB57
SCHOOL DAYS BUNNYKINS™

Designer:	Graham Tongue
Modeller:	David Lyttleton
Height:	3 ½", 8.9 cm
Colour:	Dark green, white and yellow
Issued:	1987 - 1994

Back Stamp	Price			
	U.S. $	Can. $	U.K. £	Aust. $
BK-5	100.00	100.00	35.00	80.00

DB58
AUSTRALIAN BUNNYKINS™

Designer:	Harry Sales
Modeller:	Warren Platt
Height:	4", 10.1 cm
Colour:	Gold and green
Issued:	1988 - 1988

Back Stamp	Price U.S. $	Can. $	U.K. £	Aust. $
BK-Special	1,000.00	1,000.00	675.00	450.00

DB59
STORYTIME BUNNYKINS™
Second Variation

Designer:	Walter Hayward
Modeller:	Albert Hallam
Height:	3", 7.6 cm
Colour:	Left - green polka dots on white dress, yellow shoes
	Right - yellow dress, green shoes
Issued:	1987 - 1987
Varieties:	DB9; also called Partners in Collecting, DB151

Back Stamp	Price U.S. $	Can. $	U.K. £	Aust. $
BK-5	550.00	600.00	200.00	450.00

Note: Produced for distribution at special events in the U.S.A.

DB60
SCHOOLMASTER BUNNYKINS™

Designer:	Graham Tongue
Modeller:	Warren Platt
Height:	4", 10 cm
Colour:	Black, white, green and white
Issued:	1987 - 1996

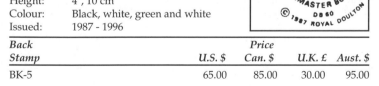

Back Stamp	Price U.S. $	Can. $	U.K. £	Aust. $
BK-5	65.00	85.00	30.00	95.00

DB61
BROWNIE BUNNYKINS™

Designer: Graham Tongue
Modeller: Warren Platt
Height: 4", 10 cm
Colour: Brown uniform, yellow neck-tie
Issued: 1987 - 1993

| Back Stamp | Price | | | |
	U.S. $	Can. $	U.K. £	Aust. $
BK-5	90.00	125.00	50.00	100.00

DB62
SANTA BUNNYKINS HAPPY CHRISTMAS™
Christmas Tree Ornament

Designer: Harry Sales
Modeller: David Lyttleton
Height: Unknown
Colour: Red and white
Issued: 1987 in a limited edition of 1,551

| Back Stamp | Price | | | |
	U.S. $	Can. $	U.K. £	Aust. $
BK-Special	2,500.00	3,000.00	1,250.00	2,500.00

DB63
BEDTIME BUNNYKINS™
Second Variation

Designer: Graham Tongue
Modeller: David Lyttleton
Height: 3 ¼", 8.3 cm
Colour: Red and white striped
             pyjamas, white teddy bear
Issued: 1987 - 1987
Varieties: DB55, 79, 103

| Back Stamp | Price | | | |
	U.S. $	Can. $	U.K. £	Aust. $
BK-Special	500.00	450.00	175.00	300.00

DB64
POLICEMAN BUNNYKINS™

Designer:	Graham Tongue
Modeller:	Martyn Alcock
Height:	4 ¼", 10.8 cm
Colour:	Dark blue uniform
Issued:	1988 to the present

Back Stamp	Price			
	U.S. $	Can. $	U.K. £	Aust. $
BK-5	45.00	52.00	16.00	70.00

DB65
LOLLIPOPMAN BUNNYKINS™

Designer:	Graham Tongue
Modeller:	Martyn Alcock
Height:	3 ¾", 9.5 cm
Colour:	White and yellow
Issued:	1988 - 1991

Back Stamp	Price			
	U.S. $	Can. $	U.K. £	Aust. $
BK-5	150.00	180.00	85.00	225.00

DB66
SCHOOLBOY BUNNYKINS™

Designer:	Graham Tongue
Modeller:	Martyn Alcock
Height:	4", 10.1 cm
Colour:	Blue, white and grey
Issued:	1988 - 1991

Back Stamp	Price			
	U.S. $	Can. $	U.K. £	Aust. $
BK-5	160.00	225.00	100.00	300.00

DB67
FAMILY PHOTOGRAPH BUNNYKINS™
Second Variation

Designer:	Walter Hayward
Modeller:	Albert Hallam
Height:	4 ½", 11.4 cm
Colour:	Pink, black and white
Issued:	1988 - 1988
Varieties:	DB1; also called Father, Mother and Victoria Bunnykins, DB68

BUNNYKINS®
"Family Photograph"
DB67
© 1972 ROYAL DOULTON
NEW COLOURWAY 1988
SPECIAL EVENTS – U.S.A. 1988

Back Stamp	Price			
	U.S. $	Can. $	U.K. £	Aust. $
BK-Special	275.00	350.00	150.00	300.00

DB68
FATHER, MOTHER AND VICTORIA BUNNYKINS™

Designer:	Based on design Family Photograph by Walter Hayward
Modeller:	Martyn Alcock
Height:	4 ½", 11.4 cm
Colour:	Blue, grey, maroon and yellow
Issued:	1988 - 1996
Varieties:	Also called Family Photograph, DB1, 67

FATHER, MOTHER
& VICTORIA BUNNYKINS
DB 68
© 1988 ROYAL DOULTON

Back Stamp	Price			
	U.S. $	Can. $	U.K. £	Aust. $
BK-5	75.00	100.00	30.00	90.00

DB69
WILLIAM BUNNYKINS™

Designer:	Based on a design by Walter Hayward
Modeller:	Martyn Alcock
Height:	4", 10.1 cm
Colour:	Red and white
Issued:	1988 - 1993
Varieties:	Also called Tally Ho! Bunnykins, DB 12, 78

WILLIAM BUNNYKINS
DB 69
© 1988 ROYAL DOULTON

Back Stamp	Price			
	U.S. $	Can. $	U.K. £	Aust. $
BK-5	150.00	125.00	40.00	110.00

DB70
SUSAN BUNNYKINS™

Designer:	Based on a design by Walter Hayward
Modeller:	Martyn Alcock
Height:	3 ¼", 8.3 cm
Colour:	White, blue and yellow
Issued:	1988 - 1993

Back Stamp	Price U.S. $	Can. $	U.K. £	Aust. $
BK-5	100.00	130.00	40.00	110.00

DB71
POLLY BUNNYKINS™

Designer:	Graham Tongue
Modeller:	Martyn Alcock
Height:	3 ½", 8.7 cm
Colour:	Pink
Issued:	1988 - 1993

Back Stamp	Price U.S. $	Can. $	U.K. £	Aust. $
BK-5	100.00	130.00	40.00	110.00

DB72
TOM BUNNYKINS™

Designer:	Graham Tongue
Modeller:	Martyn Alcock
Height:	3", 7.6 cm
Colour:	Browns, white and blue
Issued:	1988 - 1993

Back Stamp	Price U.S. $	Can. $	U.K. £	Aust. $
BK-5	100.00	130.00	40.00	110.00

DB73
HARRY BUNNYKINS™

Designer:	Graham Tongue
Modeller:	Martyn Alcock
Height:	3", 7.9 cm
Colour:	Blue, brown, white and yellow
Issued:	1988 - 1993

Back Stamp	Price			
	U.S. $	Can. $	U.K. £	Aust. $
BK-5	100.00	125.00	40.00	110.00

DB74A
NURSE BUNNYKINS™
First Variation (Red Cross)

Designer:	Graham Tongue
Modeller:	Martyn Alcock
Height:	4 ¼", 10.8 cm
Colour:	Dark and light blue and white, red cross
Issued:	1989 - 1994
Varieties:	DB 74B

Back Stamp	Price			
	U.S. $	Can. $	U.K. £	Aust. $
BK-5	300.00	300.00	100.00	300.00

DB74B
NURSE BUNNYKINS™
Second Variation (Green Cross)

Designer:	Graham Tongue
Modeller:	Martyn Alcock
Height:	4 ¼", 10.8 cm
Colour:	Dark and light blue and white, green cross
Issued:	1994 to the present
Varieties:	DB 74A

Back Stamp	Price			
	U.S. $	Can. $	U.K. £	Aust. $
BK-5	45.00	55.00	16.00	80.00

DB75
FIREMAN BUNNYKINS™

Designer:	Graham Tongue
Modeller:	Martyn Alcock
Height:	4 ¼", 10.8 cm
Colour:	Dark blue and yellow
Issued:	1989 to the present

Back Stamp	Price U.S. $	Can. $	U.K. £	Aust. $
BK-5	45.00	63.00	18.00	70.00

DB76
POSTMAN BUNNYKINS™

Designer:	Graham Tongue
Modeller:	Martyn Alcock
Height:	4 ½", 11.4 cm
Colour:	Dark blue and red
Issued:	1989 - 1993

Back Stamp	Price U.S. $	Can. $	U.K. £	Aust. $
BK-5	125.00	150.00	50.00	125.00

DB77
PAPERBOY BUNNYKINS™

Designer:	Graham Tongue
Modeller:	Martyn Alcock
Height:	4", 10.4 cm
Colour:	Green, yellow, red and white
Issued:	1989 - 1993

Back Stamp	Price U.S. $	Can. $	U.K. £	Aust. $
BK-5	125.00	150.00	50.00	125.00

DB78
TALLY HO! BUNNYKINS™
Second Variation

Designer:	Based on a design by Walter Hayward
Modeller:	Albert Hallam
Height:	4", 10.1 cm
Colour:	Light blue coat and white rocking horse, yellow sweater
Issued:	1988 - 1988
Varieties:	DB12; also called William Bunnykins, DB69

BUNNYKINS ®
"Tally Ho!"
DB 78
© 1974 ROYAL DOULTON
SPECIAL COMMISSION
COLOURWAY

Back Stamp	Price			
	U.S. $	Can. $	U.K. £	Aust. $
BK-Special	300.00	350.00	125.00	320.00

DB79
BEDTIME BUNNYKINS™
Third Variation

Designer:	Graham Tongue
Modeller:	David Lyttleton
Height:	3 ¼", 8.3 cm
Colour:	Light blue and white
Issued:	1988 - 1988
Varieties:	DB55, 63, 103

BEDTIME BUNNYKINS
© 1986 ROYAL DOULTON
100/1988 - 1988
SPECIAL COMMISSION COLOURWAY

Back Stamp	Price			
	U.S. $	Can. $	U.K. £	Aust. $
BK-Special	950.00	1,100.00	650.00	650.00

DB80
DOLLIE BUNNYKINS PLAYTIME™
Second Variation

Designer:	Based on a design by Walter Hayward
Modeller:	Albert Hallam
Height:	4", 10.1 cm
Colour:	White and yellow
Issued:	1988 in a limited edition of 250
Varieties:	DB8

DOLLIE BUNNYKINS
"Playtime"
DB 80
© 1972 ROYAL DOULTON
SPECIAL COLOURWAY COMMISSION
FOR D H HOLMES

Back Stamp	Company	Price			
		U.S. $	Can. $	U.K. £	Aust. $
BK-Special	Higbee	300.00	350.00	85.00	250.00
BK-Special	Holmes	300.00	350.00	85.00	250.00
BK-Special	Hornes	300.00	350.00	85.00	250.00
BK-Special	Strawbridge	300.00	350.00	85.00	250.00

DB81
BILLIE AND BUNTIE BUNNYKINS
SLEIGH RIDE™
Second Variation

Designer:	Based on a design by Walter Hayward
Modeller:	Albert Hallam
Height:	3 ½", 8.9 cm
Colour:	Green, yellow and red
Issued:	1989 - 1989
Varieties:	DB4

Back Stamp	Price U.S. $	Can. $	U.K. £	Aust. $
BK-Special	250.00	300.00	175.00	325.00

DB82
ICE CREAM BUNNYKINS™

Designer:	Graham Tongue
Modeller:	Warren Platt
Height:	4 ½", 11.4 cm
Colour:	White, blue and green
Issued:	1990 - 1993

Back Stamp	Price U.S. $	Can. $	U.K. £	Aust. $
BK-5	150.00	175.00	65.00	150.00

DB83
SUSAN BUNNYKINS AS
QUEEN OF THE MAY™

Designer:	Graham Tongue
Modeller:	Martyn Alcock
Height:	4", 10.2 cm
Colour:	White polka-dot dress, blue and brown chair
Issued:	1990 - 1991

Back Stamp	Price U.S. $	Can. $	U.K. £	Aust. $
BK-5	175.00	225.00	75.00	200.00

DB84
FISHERMAN BUNNYKINS™
Style One

Designer:	Graham Tongue
Modeller:	Warren Platt
Height:	4 ¼", 10.8 cm
Colour:	Maroon, yellow and grey
Issued:	1990 - 1993

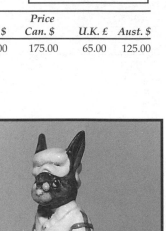

Back Stamp	Price			
	U.S. $	Can. $	U.K. £	Aust. $
BK-5	150.00	175.00	65.00	125.00

DB85
COOK BUNNYKINS™

Designer:	Graham Tongue
Modeller:	Warren Platt
Height:	4 ¼", 10.8 cm
Colour:	White and green
Issued:	1990 - 1994

Back Stamp	Price			
	U.S. $	Can. $	U.K. £	Aust. $
BK-5	100.00	125.00	45.00	135.00

DB86
SOUSAPHONE BUNNYKINS™
From the Oompah Band - Second Variation

Designer:	Harry Sales
Modeller:	David Lyttleton
Height:	3 ½", 8.9 cm
Colour:	Blue uniform and yellow sousaphone
Issued:	1990 in a limited edition of 250
Series:	Royal Doulton Collectors Band
Varieties:	DB23, 105

Back Stamp	Price			
	U.S. $	Can. $	U.K. £	Aust. $
BK-5	500.00	600.00	250.00	500.00
DB86 to 90 (5 pcs.)	2,500.00	3,000.00	1,250.00	2,500.00

DB87
TRUMPETER BUNNYKINS™
From the Oompah Band - Second Variation

Designer:	Harry Sales
Modeller:	David Lyttleton
Height:	3 ¾", 9.5 cm
Colour:	Blue uniform and yellow trumpet
Issued:	1990 in a limited edition of 250
Series:	Royal Doulton Collectors Band
Varieties:	DB24, 106

"TRUMPETER BUNNYKINS"
FROM THE OOMPAH BAND
DB 87
© 1990 ROYAL DOULTON

Back Stamp	Price			
	U.S. $	Can. $	U.K. £	Aust. $
BK-5	500.00	600.00	250.00	500.00

DB88
CYMBALS BUNNYKINS™
From the Oompah Band - Second Variation

Designer:	Harry Sales
Modeller:	David Lyttleton
Height:	3 ½", 8.9 cm
Colour:	Blue uniform and yellow cymbals
Issued:	1990 in a limited edition of 250
Series:	Royal Doulton Collectors Band
Varieties:	DB25, 107

"CYMBAL BUNNYKINS"
FROM THE OOMPAH BAND
DB 88
© 1990 ROYAL DOULTON

Back Stamp	Price			
	U.S. $	Can. $	U.K. £	Aust. $
BK-5	500.00	600.00	250.00	500.00

DB89
DRUMMER BUNNYKINS™
Third Variation

Designer:	Harry Sales
Modeller:	David Lyttleton
Height:	3 ¾", 9.5 cm
Colour:	Blue trousers and sleeves, yellow vest, cream and red drum
Issued:	1990 in a limited edition of 250
Series:	Royal Doulton Collectors Band
Varieties:	DB26, 26A, 26B, 108

"DRUMMER BUNNYKINS"
FROM THE OOMPAH BAND
DB 89
SPECIAL COLOURWAY EDITION OF 250 SETS
EXCLUSIVE FOR UK FAIRS LTD.
© 1990 ROYAL DOULTON

Back Stamp	Price			
	U.S. $	Can. $	U.K. £	Aust. $
BK-Special	500.00	600.00	250.00	500.00

DB90
DRUM-MAJOR BUNNYKINS™
Second Variation

Designer:	Harry Sales
Modeller:	David Lyttleton
Height:	3 ¾", 9.5 cm
Colour:	Blue and yellow uniform
Issued:	1990 in a limited edition of 250
Series:	Royal Doulton Collectors Band
Varieties:	DB27, 109

Back Stamp	Price			
	U.S. $	Can. $	U.K. £	Aust. $
BK-5	500.00	600.00	250.00	500.00

DB91
KING JOHN™
Second Variation

Designer:	Harry Sales
Modeller:	David Lyttleton
Height:	4", 10.1 cm
Colour:	Purple, yellow and white
Issued:	1990 in a limited edition of 250
Series:	Bunnykins Royal Family
Varieties:	DB45

Back Stamp	Price			
	U.S. $	Can. $	U.K. £	Aust. $
BK-Special	500.00	600.00	250.00	500.00
Set DB91 - 95 (5 pcs.)	2,500.00	3,000.00	1,250.00	2,500.00

DB92
QUEEN SOPHIE™
Second Variation

Designer:	Harry Sales
Modeller:	David Lyttleton
Height:	4 ½", 11.4 cm
Colour:	Pink and purple
Issued:	1990 in a limited edition of 250
Series:	Bunnykins Royal Family
Varieties:	DB46

Back Stamp	Price			
	U.S. $	Can. $	U.K. £	Aust. $
BK-5	500.00	600.00	250.00	500.00

DB93
PRINCESS BEATRICE™
Second Variation

Designer:	Harry Sales
Modeller:	David Lyttleton
Height:	3 ½", 8.9 cm
Colour:	Yellow and gold
Issued:	1990 in a limited edition of 250
Series:	Bunnykins Royal Family
Varieties:	DB47

Back Stamp		Price		
	U.S. $	Can. $	U.K. £	Aust. $
BK-5	500.00	600.00	250.00	500.00

DB94
PRINCE FREDERICK™
Second Variation

Designer:	Harry Sales
Modeller:	David Lyttleton
Height:	3 ½", 8.9 cm
Colour:	Red, blue and yellow
Issued:	1990 in a limited edition of 250
Series:	Bunnykins Royal Family
Varieties:	DB48

Back Stamp		Price		
	U.S. $	Can. $	U.K. £	Aust. $
BK-5	500.00	600.00	250.00	500.00

DB95
HARRY THE HERALD™
Second Variation

Designer:	Harry Sales
Modeller:	David Lyttleton
Height:	3 ½", 8.9 cm
Colour:	Blue, red and yellow
Issued:	1990 in a limited edition of 250
Series:	Bunnykins Royal Family
Varieties:	DB49, 115

Back Stamp		Price		
	U.S. $	Can. $	U.K. £	Aust. $
BK-5	500.00	600.00	250.00	500.00

DB96
TOUCHDOWN BUNNYKINS™
Third Variation (Ohio State University)

Designer:	Harry Sales
Modeller:	David Lyttleton
Height:	3 ¼", 8.3 cm
Colour:	Grey and orange
Issued:	1990 in a limited edition of 200
Varieties:	DB 29A, 29B, 97, 98, 99, 100

Back Stamp	Price U.S. $	Can. $	U.K. £	Aust. $
BK-5	700.00	900.00	500.00	500.00
Set DB96-100 (5 pcs.)	3,500.00	4,500.00	1,500.00	2,500.00

DB97
TOUCHDOWN BUNNYKINS™
Fourth Variation (University of Michigan)

Designer:	Harry Sales
Modeller:	David Lyttleton
Height:	3 ¼", 8.3 cm
Colour:	Yellow and blue
Issued:	1990 in a limited edition of 200
Varieties:	DB 29A, 29B, 96, 98, 99, 100

Back Stamp	Price U.S. $	Can. $	U.K. £	Aust. $
BK-5	700.00	900.00	500.00	500.00

DB98
TOUCHDOWN BUNNYKINS™
Fifth Variation (Cincinnati Bengals)

Designer:	Harry Sales
Modeller:	David Lyttleton
Height:	3 ½", 8.3 cm
Colour:	Orange and black
Issued:	1990 in a limited edition of 200
Varieties:	DB 29A, 29B, 96, 97, 99, 100

Back Stamp	Price U.S. $	Can. $	U.K. £	Aust. $
BK-5	700.00	900.00	500.00	500.00

DB99
TOUCHDOWN BUNNYKINS™
Sixth Variation (Notre Dame College)

Designer:	Harry Sales
Modeller:	David Lyttleton
Height:	3 ½", 8.3 cm
Colour:	Green and yellow
Issued:	1990 in a limited edition of 200
Varieties:	DB 29A, 29B, 96, 97, 98, 100

Back Stamp	Price			
	U.S. $	Can. $	U.K. £	Aust. $
BK-5	700.00	900.00	500.00	500.00

DB100
TOUCHDOWN BUNNYKINS™
Seventh Variation (University of Indiana)

Designer:	Harry Sales
Modeller:	David Lyttleton
Height:	3 ½", 8.3 cm
Colour:	White and red
Issued:	1990 in a limited edition of 200
Varieties:	DB 29A, 29B, 96, 97, 98, 99

Back Stamp	Price			
	U.S. $	Can. $	U.K. £	Aust. $
BK-5	700.00	900.00	500.00	500.00

DB101
BRIDE BUNNYKINS™

Designer:	Graham Tongue
Modeller:	Amanda Hughes-Lubeck
Height:	4", 10.1 cm
Colour:	Cream dress, grey, blue and white train
Issued:	1991 to the present

Back Stamp	Price			
	U.S. $	Can. $	U.K. £	Aust. $
BK-5	45.00	70.00	19.00	80.00

DB102
GROOM BUNNYKINS™

Designer:	Graham Tongue
Modeller:	Martyn Alcock
Height:	4 ½", 11.4 cm
Colour:	Grey and burgundy
Issued:	1991 to the present

Back Stamp	Price U.S. $	Can. $	U.K. £	Aust. $
BK-5	45.00	70.00	19.00	80.00

DB103
BEDTIME BUNNYKINS™
Fourth Variation

Designer:	Graham Tongue
Modeller:	David Lyttleton
Height:	3 ¼", 8.3 cm
Colour:	Yellow and green striped pyjamas, brown teddy bear
Issued:	1991 - 1991
Varieties:	DB55, 63, 79

Back Stamp	Colour	Price U.S. $	Can. $	U.K. £	Aust. $
BK-Special	Pale yellow	375.00	400.00	125.00	225.00
BK-Special	Daffodil yellow	375.00	400.00	125.00	225.00

DB104
CAROL SINGER BUNNYKINS™

Designer:	Harry Sales
Modeller:	David Lyttleton
Height:	4", 10.1 cm
Colour:	Dark green, red, yellow and white
Issued:	1991 in a special edition of 1,000

Back Stamp	Price U.S. $	Can. $	U.K.£	Aust. $
BK-Special, UK Backstamp - 700	300.00	375.00	200.00	320.00
BK-Special, USA Backstamp - 300	400.00	475.00	250.00	400.00

DB105
SOUSAPHONE BUNNYKINS™
From the Oompah Band - Third Variation

Designer:	Harry Sales
Modeller:	David Lyttleton
Height:	4", 10.1 cm
Colour:	Dark green, red and yellow
Issued:	1991 in a limited edition of 200
Series:	Royal Doulton Collectors Band
Varieties:	DB 23, 86

Back	Price			
Stamp	U.S. $	Can. $	U.K. £	Aust. $
BK 5	500.00	600.00	250.00	500.00
Set DB 105 to 109 (5 pcs.)	2,500.00	3,000.00	1,250.00	2,500.00

DB106
TRUMPETER BUNNYKINS™
From the Oompah Band - Third Variation

Designer:	Harry Sales
Modeller:	David Lyttleton
Height:	3 ¾", 9.5 cm
Colour:	Dark green, red and yellow
Issued:	1991 in a limited edition of 250
Series:	Royal Doulton Collectors Band
Varieties:	DB 24, 87

Back	Price			
Stamp	U.S. $	Can. $	U.K. £	Aust. $
BK-5	500.00	600.00	250.00	500.00

DB107
CYMBALS BUNNYKINS™
From the Oompah Band - Third Variation

Designer:	Harry Sales
Modeller:	David Lyttleton
Height:	4", 10.1 cm
Colour:	Dark green, red and yellow
Issued:	1991 in a limited edition of 250
Series:	Royal Doulton Collectors Band
Varieties:	DB 25, 88

Back	Price			
Stamp	U.S. $	Can. $	U.K. £	Aust. $
BK-5	500.00	600.00	250.00	500.00

DB 108
DRUMMER BUNNYKINS™
From the Oompah Band - Fourth Variation

Designer:	Harry Sales
Modeller:	David Lyttleton
Height:	3 ½", 8.9 cm
Colour:	Dark green, red and white
Issued:	1991 in a special edition of 250
Series:	Royal Doulton Collectors Band
Varieties:	DB 26, 26A, 26B, 89

Back Stamp	Price U.S. $	Can. $	U.K. £	Aust. $
BK-Special	500.00	600.00	250.00	500.00

DB 109
DRUM-MAJOR BUNNYKINS™
From the Oompah Band - Third Variation

Designer:	Harry Sales
Modeller:	David Lyttleton
Height:	3 ½", 8.9 cm
Colour:	Dark green, red and yellow
Issued:	1991 in a limited edition of 250
Series:	Royal Doulton Collectors Band
Varieties:	DB 27, 90

Back Stamp	Price U.S. $	Can. $	U.K. £	Aust. $
BK-5	500.00	600.00	250.00	500.00

DB 110 TO DB 114 — Not issued

DB115
HARRY THE HERALD™
Third Variation

Designer:	Harry Sales
Modeller:	David Lyttleton
Height:	3 ½", 8.9 cm
Colour:	Yellow and dark blue
Issued:	1991 in a special edition of 300
Series:	Bunnykins Royal Family
Varieties:	DB 49, 95

Back Stamp	Price U.S. $	Can. $	U.K. £	Aust. $
BK-Special	1,100.00	1,200.00	600.00	950.00

DB116
GOALKEEPER BUNNYKINS™
First Variation

Designer:	Denise Andrews
Modeller:	Warren Platt
Height:	4 ½", 11.4 cm
Colour:	Green and black
Issued:	1991 in a special edition of 250
Series:	Footballers
Varieties:	DB 118, 120, 122

Back Stamp	Price U.S. $	Can. $	U.K. £	Aust. $
BK-Special	500.00	600.00	250.00	600.00

DB117
FOOTBALLER BUNNYKINS™
First Variation

Designer:	Denise Andrews
Modeller:	Warren Platt
Height:	4 ½", 11.4 cm
Colour:	Green and white
Issued:	1991 in a special edition of 250
Series:	Footballers
Varieties:	DB 119, 121; also called Soccer Player, DB123

Back Stamp	Price U.S. $	Can. $	U.K. £	Aust. $
BK-Special	500.00	600.00	250.00	600.00

DB118
GOALKEEPER BUNNYKINS™
Second Variation

Designer:	Denise Andrews
Modeller:	Warren Platt
Height:	4 ½", 11.4 cm
Colour:	Red and black
Issued:	1991 in a special edition of 250
Series:	Footballers
Varieties:	DB 116, 120, 122

Back Stamp	Price U.S. $	Can. $	U.K. £	Aust. $
BK-Special	500.00	600.00	250.00	600.00

DB119
FOOTBALLER BUNNYKINS™
Second Variation

Designer:	Denise Andrews
Modeller:	Warren Platt
Height:	4 ½", 11.4 cm
Colour:	Red
Issued:	1991 in a special edition of 250
Series:	Footballers
Varieties:	DB 117, 121; also called Soccer Player, DB123

Back Stamp	Price			
	U.S. $	Can. $	U.K. £	Aust. $
BK-Special	500.00	600.00	250.00	600.00

DB120
GOALKEEPER BUNNYKINS™
Third Variation

Designer:	Denise Andrews
Modeller:	Warren Platt
Height:	4 ½", 11.4 cm
Colour:	Yellow and black
Issued:	1991 in a special edition of 250
Series:	Footballers
Varieties:	DB 116, 118, 122

Back Stamp	Price			
	U.S. $	Can. $	U.K. £	Aust. $
BK-Special	500.00	600.00	250.00	600.00

DB121
FOOTBALLER BUNNYKINS™
Third Variation

Designer:	Denise Andrews
Modeller:	Warren Platt
Height:	4 ½", 11.4 cm
Colour:	White and blue
Issued:	1991 in a special edition of 250
Series:	Footballers
Varieties:	DB 117, 119; also called Soccer Player, DB123

Back Stamp	Price			
	U.S. $	Can. $	U.K. £	Aust. $
BK-Special	500.00	600.00	250.00	600.00

DB122
GOALKEEPER BUNNYKINS™
Fourth Variation

Designer:	Denise Andrews
Modeller:	Warren Platt
Height:	4 ½", 1.4 cm
Colour:	Grey and black
Issued:	1991 in a special edition of 250
Series:	Footballers
Varieties:	DB 118, 118, 120

Back Stamp	Price			
	U.S. $	Can. $	U.K. £	Aust. $
BK-Special	500.00	600.00	250.00	600.00

DB123
SOCCER PLAYER BUNNYKINS™

Designer:	Denise Andrews
Modeller:	Warren Platt
Height:	4 ½", 11.4 cm
Colour:	Dark blue and white
Issued:	1991 in a special edition of 250
Series:	Footballers
Varieties:	Also called Footballer Bunnykins, DB 117, 119, 121

Back Stamp	Price			
	U.S. $	Can. $	U.K. £	Aust. $
BK-Special	500.00	600.00	250.00	600.00

DB124
ROCK AND ROLL BUNNYKINS™

Designer:	Harry Sales
Modeller:	David Lyttleton
Height:	4 ½", 11.4 cm
Colour:	White, blue and red
Issued:	1991 in a limited edition of 1,000
Varieties:	Also called Mr. Bunnybeat Strumming, DB16

Back Stamp	Price			
	U.S. $	Can. $	U.K. £	Aust. $
BK-Special	500.00	700.00	300.00	525.00

DB125
MILKMAN BUNNYKINS™

Designer:	Graham Tongue
Modeller:	Amanda Hughes-Lubeck
Height:	4 ½", 11.4 cm
Colour:	White, green and grey
Issued:	1992 in a special edition of 1,000

Back Stamp		Price		
	U.S. $	Can. $	U.K. £	Aust. $
BK-Special	500.00	600.00	250.00	500.00

DB126
MAGICIAN BUNNYKINS™

Designer:	Graham Tongue
Modeller:	Warren Platt
Height:	4 ½", 11.4 cm
Colour:	Black and yellow
Issued:	1992 - 1992

Back Stamp		Price		
	U.S. $	Can. $	U.K. £	Aust. $
BK-5	400.00	500.00	250.00	350.00

DB127
GUARDSMAN BUNNYKINS™

Designer:	Denise Andrews
Modeller:	Warren Platt
Height:	4 ½", 11.4 cm
Colour:	Scarlet jacket, black trousers and bearskin hat
Issued:	1992 in a special edition of 1,000

Back Stamp		Price		
	U.S. $	Can. $	U.K. £	Aust. $
BK-Special	500.00	600.00	300.00	400.00

DB128
CLOWN BUNNYKINS™
First Variation

Designer:	Denise Andrews
Modeller:	Warren Platt
Height:	4 ¼", 10.8 cm
Colour:	White costume with black patterned costume, red square on trousers and red ruff at neck
Issued:	1992 in a special edition of 750
Varieties:	DB 129

Back Stamp	Price			
	U.S. $	Can. $	U.K. £	Aust. $
BK-Special	950.00	1,100.00	650.00	900.00

DB129
CLOWN BUNNYKINS™
Second Variation

Designer:	Denise Andrews
Modeller:	Warren Platt
Height:	4 ¼", 10.8 cm
Colour:	White costume with red patterned costume, black ruff around neck
Issued:	1992 in a special edition of 250
Varieties:	DB 128

Back Stamp	Price			
	U.S. $	Can. $	U.K. £	Aust. $
BK-Special	2,000.00	2,500.00	1,250.00	1.750.00

DB130
SWEETHEART BUNNYKINS™
First Variation

Designer:	Graham Tongue
Modeller:	Warren Platt
Height:	3 ¾", 9.5 cm
Colour:	Yellow sweater, blue trousers, red heart
Issued:	1992 - 1997
Varieties:	DB174

Back Stamp	Price			
	U.S. $	Can. $	U.K. £	Aust. $
BK-5	45.00	65.00	25.00	75.00

DB131
MASTER POTTER BUNNYKINS™

Designer:	Graham Tongue
Modeller:	Warren Platt
Height:	3 ¾", 9.3 cm
Colour:	Blue, white, green and brown
Issued:	1993 - 1993
Series:	R.D.I.C.C.

Back Stamp	Price			
	U.S. $	Can. $	U.K. £	Aust. $
BK-Special	300.00	375.00	200.00	325.00

DB132
HALLOWEEN BUNNYKINS™

Designer:	Graham Tongue
Modeller:	Martyn Alcock
Height:	3 ¼", 8.3 cm
Colour:	Orange and yellow pumpkin
Issued:	1993 - 1997

Back Stamp	Price			
	U.S. $	Can.$	U.K. £	Aust. $
BK-5	55.00	85.00	25.00	90.00

DB133
AUSSIE SURFER BUNNYKINS™

Designer:	Graham Tongue
Modeller:	Martyn Alcock
Height:	4", 10.1 cm
Colour:	Gold and green outfit, white and blue base
Issued:	1994 - 1994

Back Stamp	Price			
	U.S. $	Can. $	U.K. £	Aust. $
BK-Special	275.00	325.00	125.00	200.00

DB134
JOHN BULL BUNNYKINS™

Designer:	Denise Andrews
Modeller:	Amanda Hughes-Lubeck
Height:	4 ½", 11.0 cm
Colour:	Grey, yellow, red, white and blue Union Jack waistcoat
Issued:	1993 in a special edition of 1,000

Back Stamp	Price			
	U.S. $	Can. $	U.K. £	Aust. $
BK-Special	450.00	525.00	250.00	325.00

DB135
MOUNTIE BUNNYKINS™

Designer:	Graham Tongue
Modeller:	Warren Platt
Height:	4", 10.1 cm
Colour:	Red jacket, dark blue trousers and brown hat
Issued:	1993 in a special edition of 750

Back Stamp	Price			
	U.S. $	Can. $	U.K. £	Aust. $
BK-Special	850.00	1,000.00	650.00	1,500.00

DB136
SERGEANT MOUNTIE BUNNYKINS™

Designer:	Graham Tongue
Modeller:	Warren Platt
Height:	4", 10.1 cm
Colour:	Red jacket, yellow stripes on sleeve, dark blue trousers, brown hat
Issued:	1993 in a special edition of 250

Back Stamp	Price			
	U.S. $	Can. $	U.K. £	Aust. $
BK-Special	2,000.00	2,250.00	1,250.00	2,100.00

DB137
60th ANNIVERSARY BUNNYKINS™

Designer:	Graham Tongue
Modeller:	Martyn Alcock
Height:	4 ½", 11.0 cm
Colour:	Lemon, yellow and white
Issued:	1994 - 1994

Back Stamp		Price			
		U.S. $	Can. $	U.K. £	Aust. $
BK-5		100.00	150.00	65.00	100.00

DB142
CHEERLEADER BUNNYKINS™
First Variation

Designer:	Denise Andrews
Modeller:	Warren Platt
Height:	4 ½", 11.0 cm
Colour:	Red
Issued:	1994 in a special edition of 1,000

Back Stamp		Price			
		U.S. $	Can. $	U.K. £	Aust. $
BK-Special		300.00	375.00	125.00	200.00

DB143
CHEERLEADER BUNNYKINS™
Second Variation

Designer:	Denise Andrews
Modeller:	Warren Platt
Height:	4 ½", 11.0 cm
Colour:	Yellow
Issued:	1994 in a special edition of 1,000

Back Stamp		Price			
		U.S. $	Can. $	U.K. £	Aust. $
BK-Special		300.00	375.00	125.00	200.00

DB144
BATSMAN BUNNYKINS™

Designer:	Denise Andrews
Modeller:	Amanda Hughes-Lubeck
Height:	4", 10.1 cm
Colour:	White, beige and black
Issued:	1994 in a special edition of 1,000

Back Stamp	Price			
	U.S. $	Can. $	U.K. £	Aust. $
BK-Special	425.00	500.00	250.00	325.00

DB145
BOWLER BUNNYKINS™

Designer:	Denise Andrews
Modeller:	Warren Platt
Height:	4", 10.1 cm
Colour:	White, beige and black
Issued:	1994 in a special edition of 1,000

Back Stamp	Price			
	U.S. $	Can. $	U.K. £	Aust. $
BK-Special	425.00	500.00	250.00	325.00

DB146
CHRISTMAS SURPRISE BUNNYKINS™

Designer:	Graham Tongue
Modeller:	Warren Platt
Height:	3 ½", 8.9 cm
Colour:	Cream and red
Issued:	1994 to the present

Back Stamp	Price			
	U.S. $	Can. $	U.K. £	Aust. $
BK-5	55.00	85.00	20.00	85.00

DB147
RAINY DAY BUNNYKINS™

Designer:	Graham Tongue
Modeller:	Warren Platt
Height:	4", 10.1 cm
Colour:	Yellow coat and hat, blue trousers, black boots
Issued:	1994 - 1997

RAINY DAY
BUNNYKINS
DB 147
© 1994 ROYAL DOULTON

Back Stamp	Price			
	U.S. $	Can. $	U.K. £	Aust. $
BK-5	45.00	65.00	20.00	75.00

DB148
BATHTIME BUNNYKINS™

Designer:	Graham Tongue
Modeller:	Warren Platt
Height:	4", 10.1 cm
Colour:	White bathrobe with grey trim, yellow towel and duck
Issued:	1994 - 1997

BATHTIME BUNNYKINS
DB 148
© 1994 ROYAL DOULTON

Back Stamp	Price			
	U.S. $	Can. $	U.K. £	Aust. $
BK-5	50.00	65.00	20.00	75.00

DB149
EASTER GREETINGS BUNNYKINS™

Designer:	Graham Tongue
Modeller:	Warren Platt
Height:	4 ½", 11.4 cm
Colour:	Yellow, white and green
Issued:	1995 to the present

EASTER GREETINGS
BUNNYKINS
DB 149
© 1994 ROYAL DOULTON

Back Stamp	Price			
	U.S. $	Can. $	U.K. £	Aust. $
BK-5	55.00	80.00	19.00	85.00

DB150
WICKETKEEPER BUNNYKINS™

Designer:	Denise Andrews
Modeller:	Amanda Hughes-Lubeck
Height:	3 ½", 8.9 cm
Colour:	White, beige and black
Issued:	1995 in a special edition of 1,000

Back Stamp	Price			
	U.S. $	Can. $	U.K. £	Aust. $
BK-Special	425.00	500.00	250.00	325.00

DB151
PARTNERS IN COLLECTING™

Designer:	Walter Hayward
Modeller:	Albert Hallam
Height:	3", 7.6 cm
Colour:	Red, white and blue
Issued:	1995 - 1995
Varieties:	Also called Storytime Bunnykins, DB9, DB59

Back Stamp	Price			
	U.S. $	Can. $	U.K. £	Aust. $
BK-Special	175.00	225.00	100.00	150.00

DB152
BOY SKATER BUNNYKINS™

Designer:	Graham Tongue
Modeller:	Martyn Alcock
Height:	4 ¼", 10.8 cm
Colour:	Blue coat, brown pants, yellow hat, green boots and black skates
Issued:	1995 to the present

Back Stamp	Price			
	U.S. $	Can. $	U.K. £	Aust. $
BK-5	45.00	68.00	19.00	80.00

DB153
GIRL SKATER BUNNYKINS™

Designer:	Graham Tongue
Modeller:	Martyn Alcock
Height:	3 ½", 8.9 cm
Colour:	Green coat with white trim, pink dress, blue books, yellow skates
Issued:	1995 - 1997

Back Stamp	Price			
	U.S. $	Can. $	U.K. £	Aust. $
BK-5	50.00	70.00	20.00	80.00

GIRL SKATER
BUNNYKINS
DB 153
© 1995 ROYAL DOULTON

DB154
FATHER BUNNKINS™

Designer:	Graham Tongue
Modeller:	Martyn Alcock
Height:	4", 10.5 cm
Colour:	Red and white striped blazer, creamy yellow trousers
Issued:	1996 - 1996
Series:	Bunnykins of the Year, 1994

Back Stamp	Price			
	U.S. $	Can. $	U.K. £	Aust. $
BK-Special	75.00	100.00	25.00	75.00

DB155
MOTHER'S DAY BUNNYKINS™

Designer:	Graham Tongue
Modeller:	Shane Ridge
Height:	3 ½", 8.9 cm
Colour:	Brown and blue
Issued:	1995 to the present

Back Stamp	Price			
	U.S. $	Can. $	U.K. £	Aust. $
BK-5	55.00	80.00	20.00	80.00

MOTHER'S DAY
BUNNYKINS
DB 155
© 1995 ROYAL DOULTON

DB156
GARDENER BUNNYKINS™

Designer:	Graham Tongue
Modeller:	Warren Platt
Height:	4 ¼", 10.8 cm
Colour:	Brown jacket, white shirt, grey trousers, light green wheelbarrow
Issued:	1996 to the present

Back Stamp	Price			
	U.S. $	Can. $	U.K. £	Aust. $
BK-5	45.00	63.00	19.00	75.00

DB157
GOODNIGHT BUNNYKINS™

Designer:	Graham Tongue
Modeller:	Shane Ridge
Height:	3 ¾", 9.5 cm
Colour:	Pink nightgown, reddish brown teddy, blue and white base
Issued:	1995 to the present

Back Stamp	Price			
	U.S. $	Can. $	U.K. £	Aust. $
BK-5	45.00	68.00	17.00	70.00

DB158
NEW BABY BUNNYKINS™

Designer:	Graham Tongue
Modeller:	Graham Tongue
Height:	3 ¾", 9.5 cm
Colour:	Blue dress with white trim, white cradle, pink pillow, yellow blanket
Issued:	1995 to the present

Back Stamp	Price			
	U.S. $	Can. $	U.K. £	Aust. $
BK-5	45.00	68.00	18.00	80.00

DB160
OUT FOR A DUCK BUNNYKINS™

Designer:	Denise Andrews
Modeller:	Amanda Hughes-Lubeck
Height:	4", 10.1 cm
Colour:	White, beige and green
Issued:	1995 in a special edition of 1,250

Back Stamp	Price			
	U.S. $	Can. $	U.K. £	Aust. $
BK-Special	375.00	450.00	225.00	325.00

DB161
JESTER BUNNYKINS™

Designer:	Denise Andrews
Modeller:	Shane Ridge
Height:	4 ½", 11.9 cm
Colour:	Red, green and yellow
Issued:	1995 in a special edition of 1,500

Back Stamp	Price			
	U.S. $	Can. $	U.K. £	Aust. $
BK-Special	600.00	750.00	350.00	675.00

DB162
TRICK OR TREAT BUNNYKINS™

Designer:	Denise Andrews
Modeller:	Amanda Hughes-Lubeck
Height:	4 ½", 11.9 cm
Colour:	Red dress, black hat, shoes and cloak, white moons and stars
Issued:	1995 in a special edition of 1,500

Back Stamp	Price			
	U.S. $	Can. $	U.K. £	Aust. $
BK-Special	750.00	950.00	450.00	900.00

DB163
BEEFEATER BUNNYKINS™

Designer:	Denise Andrews
Modeller:	Unknown
Height:	4 ½", 11.9 cm
Colour:	Red, gold, black and white livery, black hat with red, blue and white band
Issued:	1996 in a special edition of 1,500

Back Stamp		Price		
	U.S. $	*Can. $*	*U.K. £*	*Aust. $*
BK-Special	500.00	675.00	250.00	600.00

DB164
JUGGLER BUNNYKINS™

Designer:	Denise Andrews
Modeller:	Warren Platt
Height:	4 ½", 11.9 cm
Colour:	Blue suit, black pompons, white ruff
Issued:	1996 in a special edition of 1,500

Back Stamp		Price		
	U.S. $	*Can. $*	*U.K. £*	*Aust. $*
BK-Special	375.00	500.00	250.00	475.00

DB165
RINGMASTER BUNNYKINS™

Designer:	Denise Andrews
Modeller:	Warren Platt
Height:	4 ½", 11.9 cm
Colour:	Black hat and trousers, red jacket, white waistcoat and shirt, black bowtie
Issued:	1996 in a special edition of 1,500

Back Stamp		Price		
	U.S. $	*Can. $*	*U.K. £*	*Aust. $*
BK-Special	500.00	600.00	225.00	500.00

DB166
SAILOR BUNNYKINS™

Designer:	Graham Tongue
Modeller:	Shane Ridge
Height:	2 ½", 6.4 cm
Colour:	White and blue
Issued:	1997 - 1997
Series:	Bunnykins of the Year, 1997

SAILOR BUNNYKINS
DB 166
BUNNYKINS OF THE YEAR 1997
© 1996 ROYAL DOULTON

Back Stamp	Price			
	U.S. $	Can. $	U.K. £	Aust. $
BK-Special	60.00	85.00	25.00	70.00

DB167
MOTHER AND BABY BUNNYKINS™

Designer:	Unknown
Modeller:	Shane Ridge
Height:	4 ½", 11.9 cm
Colour:	Brown, light pink dress, red shoes, yellow blanket
Issued:	1997 to the present

MOTHER AND
BABY BUNNYKINS
DB 167
© 1996 ROYAL DOULTON

Back Stamp	Price			
	U.S. $	Can. $	U.K. £	Aust. $
BK-5	45.00	82.00	17.50	—

DB168
WIZARD BUNNYKINS™

Designer:	Denise Andrews
Modeller:	Shane Ridge
Height:	5", 12.7 cm
Colour:	Brown rabbit, purple robes and hat
Issued:	1997 in a special edition of 1,500

Back Stamp	Price			
	U.S. $	Can. $	U.K. £	Aust. $
BK-Special	500.00	675.00	295.00	600.00

DB169
JOCKEY BUNNYKINS™

Designer:	Denise Andrews
Modeller:	Martyn Alcock
Height:	4 ½", 11.9 cm
Colour:	Green, white and yellow jockey suit, black shoes
Issued:	1997 in a special edition of 2,000

Back Stamp	Price			
	U.S. $	Can. $	U.K. £	Aust. $
BK-5	500.00	675.00	275.00	600.00

Photograph not available at press time

DB170
FISHERMAN BUNNYKINS™
Style Two

Designer:	Graham Tongue
Modeller:	Shane Ridge
Height:	4", 10.1 cm
Colour:	Blue hat and trousers, light yellow sweater, black wellingtons
Issued:	1997 to the present

Back Stamp	Price			
	U.S. $	Can. $	U.K. £	Aust. $
BK-5	55.00	80.00	20.00	—

DB171
JOKER BUNNYKINS™

Designer:	Denise Andrews
Modeller:	Martyn Alcock
Height:	5", 12.7 cm
Colour:	Yellow jacket, orange and white trousers, black hat
Issued:	1997 in a special edition of 2,500

Back Stamp	Price			
	U.S. $	Can. $	U.K. £	Aust. $
BK-Special	500.00	675.00	275.00	600.00

DB172
WELSH LADY BUNNYKINS™

Designer:	Denise Andrews	
Modeller:	Warren Platt	
Height:	5", 12.7 cm	
Colour:	Light pink and yellow dress, black hat	
Issued:	1997 in a special edition of 2,500	

Back Stamp	Price			
	U.S. $	Can. $	U.K. £	Aust. $
BK-Special	400.00	500.00	200.00	500.00

DB173
BRIDESMAID BUNNYKINS™

Designer:	Graham Tongue
Modeller:	Amanda Hughes-Lubeck
Height:	3 ¾", 9.5 cm
Colour:	Light yellow dress, darker yellow flowers
Issued:	1997 to the present

Back Stamp	Price			
	U.S. $	Can. $	U.K. £	Aust. $
BK-5	44.00	80.00	18.00	—

DB174
SWEETHEART BUNNYKINS™
Second Variation "I Love Bunnykins"

Designer:	Graham Tongue	
Modeller:	Warren Platt	
Height:	3 ¾", 9.5 cm	
Colour:	White and blue, pink heart	
Issued:	1997 in a special edition of 2,500	
Varieties:	DB130	

Back Stamp	Price			
	U.S. $	Can. $	U.K. £	Aust. $
BK-Special	500.00	675.00	250.00	600.00

DB175
UNCLE SAM BUNNYKINS™
Second Variation

Designer:	Harry Sales
Modeller:	David Lyttleton
Height:	4 ½", 11.9 cm
Colour:	Red jacket, yellow shirt, blue and white striped trousers, red white and blue hat, silver bowtie
Issued:	1997 - 1997
Varieties:	DB50

Back Stamp	Price			
	U.S. $	Can. $	U.K. £	Aust. $
BK-Special	250.00	375.00	175.00	350.00

DB176
BALLERINA BUNNYKINS™

Designer:	Graham Tongue
Modeller:	Graham Tongue
Height:	3 ½", 8.9 cm
Colour:	Pink dress, yellow footstool
Issued:	1998 to the present

Back Stamp	Price			
	U.S. $	Can. $	U.K. £	Aust. $
BK-5	55.00	80.00	20.00	—

DB177
SEASIDE BUNNYKINS

Designer:	Unknown
Modeller:	Martyn Alcock
Height:	3", 7.6 cm
Colour:	Blue bathing costume, white and blue bathing cap, yellow sandy base
Issued:	1998 - 1998
Series:	Bunnykins of the Year, 1998

Back Stamp	Price			
	U.S.	Can. $	U.K. £	Aust. $
BK-5	55.00	80.00	20.00	—

Photograph not available at press time

DB178
IRISHMAN BUNNYKINS™

Designer:	Denise Andrews
Modeller:	Unknown
Height:	5", 12.7 cm
Colour:	Green waistcoat with shamrocks, white shirt, tan hat and trousers, white socks and black shoes
Issued:	1998 in an special edition of 2,500

Back Stamp	Price			
	U.S. $	Can. $	U.K. £	Aust. $
BK-Special	—	—	58.00	—

DB179
CAVALIER BUNNYKINS™

Designer:	Unknown
Modeller:	Graham Tongue
Height:	4 ½", 11.9 cm
Colour:	Red tunic, white collar, black trousers and hat, yellow cape, light brown boots
Issued:	1998 in an special edition of 2,500

CAVALIER BUNNYKINS
DB 179
PRODUCED EXCLUSIVELY FOR
PASCOE & CO. AND SEAWAY CHINA
IN A SPECIAL EDITION OF 2,500
© 1997 ROYAL DOULTON

Back Stamp	Price			
	U.S. $	Can. $	U.K. £	Aust. $
BK-Special	150.00	—	—	—

BUNNYKINS TEAPOTS

1994-1996

D6966A
LONDON CITY GENT
BUNNYKINS TEAPOT™

Designer:	Unknown
Modeller:	Martyn Alcock
Height:	8", 20.3 cm
Colour:	Brown and black
Issued:	1994 in a special edition of 2,500
Varieties:	D6966B
Series:	Bunnykins Teapots of the World

BUNNYKINS TEAPOTS OF THE WORLD
Royal Doulton®
BUNNYKINS®
LONDON CITY GENT
D 6966
© 1994 ROYAL DOULTON
SPECIAL EDITION OF 2,500

Back Stamp	Price			
	U.S. $	Can. $	U.K. £	Aust. $
BK-Special	200.00	175.00	75.00	200.00

D6966B
U.S.A. PRESIDENT BUNNYKINS TEAPOT™

Designer:	Unknown
Modeller:	Shane Ridge
Height:	8", 20.3 cm
Colour:	Red, white and blue
Issued:	1995 in a special edition of 2,500
Varieties:	D6966A
Series:	Bunnykins Teapots of the World

BUNNYKINS TEAPOTS OF THE WORLD
Royal Doulton®
BUNNYKINS®
U.S.A. PRESIDENT
D 6996
© 1995 ROYAL DOULTON
SPECIAL EDITION OF 2,500

Back Stamp	Price			
	U.S. $	Can. $	U.K. £	Aust. $
BK-Special	200.00	185.00	65.00	200.00

D7027
AUSSIE EXPLORER BUNNYKINS TEAPOT™

Designer:	Unknown
Modeller:	Unknown
Height:	7 ¾", 19.5 cm
Colour:	Brown bunny, yellow waistcoat, green hat, orange boomerang
Issued:	1996 in a special edition of 2,500
Series:	Bunnykins Teapots of the World

BUNNYKINS TEAPOTS OF THE WORLD
Royal Doulton®
BUNNYKINS®
AUSSIE EXPLORER
D 7027
© 1996 ROYAL DOULTON
SPECIAL EDITION OF 2,500

Back Stamp	Price			
	U.S. $	Can. $	U.K. £	Aust. $
BK-Special	150.00	125.00	60.00	200.00

BUNNYKINS

RESIN SERIES — 1996-1997

DBR1
HARRY BUNNYKINS
A LITTLE BUNNY AT PLAY™

Designer:	Unknown
Modeller:	Unknown
Height:	1 ¾", 4.5 cm
Colour:	Pale blue pyjamas, red and dark blue toys
Issued:	1996 - 1997

Royal Doulton
Harry Bunnykins
"a little bunny at play"
DBR1/ **491**
© 1996 Royal Doulton
Made in China

Doulton Number	Price			
	U.S. $	Can. $	U.K. £	Aust. $
DBR1	15.00	20.00	10.00	20.00

DBR2
HARRY BUNNYKINS
PLAYTIME™

Designer:	Unknown
Modeller:	Unknown
Height:	2", 5.0 cm
Colour:	Pale blue pyjamas, yellow toy, pink, yellow and green pillow
Issued:	1996 - 1997

Royal Doulton
Harry Bunnykins
Playtime
DBR2/ **3605**
© 1996 Royal Doulton
Made in China

Doulton Number	Price			
	U.S. $	Can. $	U.K. £	Aust. $
DBR2	15.00	20.00	10.00	20.00

DBR3
REGINALD RATLEY
UP TO NO GOOD™

Designer:	Unknown
Modeller:	Unknown
Height:	2 ¼", 5.7 cm
Colour:	Black jacket, hat and shoes, yellow shirt, red tie
Issued:	1996 - 1997

Royal Doulton
Reginald Ratley
Up to no good
DBR3/ **3530**
© 1996 Royal Doulton
Made in China

Doulton Number	Price			
	U.S. $	Can. $	U.K. £	Aust. $
DBR3	15.00	20.00	10.00	20.00

DBR4
SUSAN BUNNYKINS
THE HELPER™

Designer:	Unknown
Modeller:	Unknown
Height:	3", 7.6 cm
Colour:	White and blue dress
Issued:	1996 - 1997

Doulton Number		Price		
	U.S. $	Can. $	U.K. £	Aust. $
DBR4	15.00	20.00	10.00	20.00

DBR5
WILLIAM BUNNYKINS
ASLEEP IN THE SUN™

Designer:	Unknown
Modeller:	Unknown
Height:	2 ¼" 5.7 cm
Colour:	White shirt, red jacket, brown trousers
Issued:	1996 - 1997

Royal Doulton
William Bunnykins
Asleep in the sun
DBR5/3626
© 1996 Royal Doulton
Made in China

Doulton Number		Price		
	U.S. $	Can. $	U.K. £	Aust. $
DBR5	15.00	20.00	10.00	20.00

DBR6
LADY RATLEY
HER LADYSHIP EXPLAINS™

Designer:	Unknown
Modeller:	Unknown
Height:	3 ¼", 8.3 cm
Colour:	Light and dark purple dress black shoes and handbag
Issued:	1996 - 1997

Royal Doulton
Lady Ratley
Her ladyship explains
DBR6/939
© 1996 Royal Doulton
Made in China

Doulton Number		Price		
	U.S. $	Can. $	U.K. £	Aust. $
DBR6	20.00	30.00	15.00	30.00

DBR7
MRS. BUNNYKINS
A BUSY MORNING SHOPPING™

Designer:	Unknown
Modeller:	Unknown
Height:	3 ½", 8.9 cm
Colour:	White dress with blue flowers, pale yellow apron and hat, brown basket
Issued:	1996 - 1997

Royal Doulton
Mrs Bunnykins
A busy morning
shopping
DBR7/ *186*
© 1996 Royal Doulton
Made in China

Doulton Number	Price			
	U.S. $	Can. $	U.K. £	Aust. $
DBR7	20.00	30.00	15.00	30.00

DBR8
FATHER BUNNYKINS
HOME FROM WORK™

Designer:	Unkown
Modeller:	Unknown
Height:	3 ¾", 9.5 cm
Colour:	Cream trousers, green jacket and black shoes
Issued:	1996 - 1997

Royal Doulton
Father Bunnykins
Home from work
DBR8/ *1036*
© 1996 Royal Doulton
Made in China

Doulton Number	Price			
	U.S. $	Can. $	U.K. £	Aust. $
DBR8	20.00	30.00	15.00	30.00

DBR9
WILLIAM BUNNYKINS
A BUNNY IN A HURRY™

Designer:	Unknown
Modeller:	Unknown
Height:	2 ¼", 5.7 cm
Colour:	Brown trousers, white shirt and red jacket
Issued:	1996 - 1997

Royal Doulton
William Bunnykins
A bunny in a hurry
DBR9/ *188*
© 1996 Royal Doulton
Made in China

Doulton Number	Price			
	U.S. $	Can. $	U.K. £	Aust. $
DBR9	15.00	20.00	10.00	20.00

DBR10
SUSAN BUNNYKINS
WILDLIFE SPOTTING™

Designer:	Unknown
Modeller:	Unknown
Height:	2 ¾", 7.0 cm
Colour:	White dress with blue flowers, brown basket
Issued:	1996 - 1997

Doulton Number		Price		
	U.S. $	Can. $	U.K. £	Aust. $
DBR10	15.00	20.00	10.00	20.00

DBR11
SUSAN AND HARRY BUNNYKINS
MINDING THE BABY BROTHER™

Designer:	Unknown
Modeller:	Unknown
Height:	2 ½", 6.4 cm
Colour:	Susan - white dress with blue flowers
	Harry - pale blue pyjamas, multi-coloured toys
Issued:	1996 - 1997

Doulton Number		Price		
	U.S. $	Can. $	U.K. £	Aust. $
DBR11	30.00	45.00	17.00	45.00

DBR12
FATHER BUNNYKINS AND HARRY
DECORATING THE TREE™

Designer:	Unknown
Modeller:	Unknown
Height:	4", 10.1 cm
Colour:	Father - blue trousers, white shirt and red pullover
	Harry - white pyjamas, green tree
Issued:	1996 - 1997

Doulton Number		Price		
	U.S. $	Can. $	U.K. £	Aust. $
DBR12	30.00	45.00	20.00	45.00

DBR13
MRS. BUNNYKINS AND WILLIAM
THE BIRTHDAY CAKE™

Designer:	Unknown
Modeller:	Unknown
Height:	3 ¼", 8.3 cm
Colour:	White dress with blue flowers, light yellow apron, red jacket, white shirt and brown trousers
Issued:	1996 - 1997

Royal Doulton
Mrs Bunnykins and William
The birthday cake
DBR13/ 342
© 1996 Royal Doulton
Made in China

Doulton Number		Price		
	U.S. $	Can. $	U.K. £	Aust. $
DBR13	30.00	40.00	17.00	40.00

DBR14
HAPPY CHRISTMAS FROM THE
BUNNYKINS FAMILY™

Designer:	Unknown
Modeller:	Unknown
Height:	6", 15.0 cm
Colour:	Multi-coloured
Issued:	1996 - 1997

Royal Doulton
Happy Christmas from the Bunnykins family
DBR14/ 1018
© 1996 Royal Doulton
Made in China

Doulton Number		Price		
	U.S. $	Can. $	U.K. £	Aust. $
DBR14	110.00	150.00	75.00	150.00

Note: This musical piece plays "We Wish You A Merry Christmas."

DBR15
PICNIC TIME WITH THE
BUNNYKINS FAMILY™

Designer:	Unknown
Modeller:	Unknown
Height:	5", 12.7 cm
Colour:	Multi-coloured
Issued:	1996 - 1997

Royal Doulton
Picnic time with the Bunnykins family
DBR15/ 838
© 1996 Royal Doulton
Made in China

Doulton Number		Price		
	U.S. $	Can. $	U.K. £	Aust. $
DBR15	90.00	150.00	75.00	150.00

Note: This musical piece plays "Here We Go Round the Mulberry Bush."

DBR16
BIRTHDAY GIRL™

Designer:	Unknown
Modeller:	Unknown
Height:	1 ½", 4 cm
Colour:	Pink and white dress
Issued:	1997 - 1997

Doulton Number		Price		
	U.S. $	Can. $	U.K. £	Aust. $
DBR16	15.00	20.00	10.00	20.00

DBR17
BIRTHDAY BOY™

Designer:	Unknown
Modeller:	Unknown
Height:	1 ½", 4 cm
Colour:	Blue pyjamas, white bib
Issued:	1997 - 1997

Doulton Number		Price		
	U.S. $	Can. $	U.K. £	Aust. $
DBR17	15.00	20.00	10.00	20.00

DBR18
THE NEW BABY™

Designer:	Unknown
Modeller:	Unknown
Height:	3 ½", 8.9 cm
Colour:	Mother - white, lilac and rose
	Baby - light blue
Issued:	1997 - 1997

Doulton Number		Price		
	U.S. $	Can. $	U.K. £	Aust. $
DBR18	20.00	30.00	15.00	30.00

DBR19
THE ROCKING HORSE™

Designer:	Unknown
Modeller:	Unknown
Height:	2 ¾", 7.0 cm
Colour:	Brown bunny, red and white dress, white horse
Issued:	1997 - 1997

Royal Doulton
Bunnykins
The Rocking Horse
DBR19/ *180*
©1996 Royal Doulton
Made In China

Doulton Number	Price U.S. $	Can. $	U.K. £	Aust. $
DBR19	15.00	20.00	10.00	20.00

DBR20
PHOTOGRAPH FRAME - GIRL

Designer:	Unknown
Modeller:	Unknown
Height:	5 ¼", 14 cm
Colour:	Cream and brown bunny dressed in pink
Issued:	1997 - 1997

Doulton Number	Price U.S. $	Can. $	U.K. £	Aust. $
DBR20	—	—	13.95	—

DBR21
PHOTOGRAPH FRAME - BOY

Designer:	Unknown
Modeller:	Unknown
Height:	5 ¼", 14 cm
Colour:	Cream and brown bunny dressed in blue
Issued:	1997 - 1997

Doulton Number	Price U.S. $	Can. $	U.K. £	Aust. $
DBR21	—	—	13.95	—

CAT CHORUS

CAT CHORUS

1998 to the present

CC1
PURRFECT PITCH™

Designer:	Shane Ridge
Height:	4", 10.1 cm
Colour:	White cat, black dress, red gloves and shoes, black hair
Issued:	1998 to the present

CC2
CALYPSO KITTEN™

Designer:	Shane Ridge
Height:	4", 10.1 cm
Colour:	Black cat, patterned yellow shirt, beige trousers, red and yellow drum
Issued:	1998 to the present

CC3
ONE COOL CAT™

Designer:	Shane Ridge
Height:	4", 10.1 cm
Colour:	Ginger cat, blue suit with black lapels, cuffs and pockets, white shirt, black shoes, yellow saxaphone
Issued:	1998 to the present

CC4
RATCATCHER BILK

Designer:	Shane Ridge
Height:	4", 10.1 cm
Colour:	White cat, blue shirt and hat, yellow waistcoat, black trousers and clarinet
Issued:	1998 to the present

CC5
TRADJAZZ TOM™

Designer:	Shane Ridge
Height:	4", 10.1 cm
Colour:	Grey cat, trousers and waistcoat, lemon shirt, black hat, yellow trumpet
Issued:	1998 to the present

CC6
CATWALKING BRASS™

Designer:	Shane Ridge
Height:	4", 10.1 cm
Colour:	White cat, yellow jacket, green shirt, red trousers, black hat, tan bass
Issued:	1998 to the present

CC7
FELINE FLAMENCO™

Designer:	Shane Ridge
Height:	4", 10.1 cm
Colour:	Ginger cat, lemon shirt, black waistcoat and trousers, red and white cumberbund, tan guitar
Issued:	1998 to the present

CC8
BRAVURA BRASS

Designer:	Shane Ridge
Height:	4", 10.1 cm
Colour:	Ginger cat, black suit and shoes, shite shirt, yellow french horn
Issued:	1998 to the present

Beswick Number	Name	Price			
		U.S. $	Can. $	U.K. £	Aust. $
CC1	Purrfect Pitch	—	—	25.00	—
CC2	Calypso Kitten	—	—	25.00	—
CC3	One Cool Cat	—	—	25.00	—
CC4	Ratcatcher Bilk	—	—	25.00	—
CC5	Tradjazz Tom	—	—	25.00	—
CC6	Catwalking Brass	—	—	25.00	—
CC7	Feline Flamenco	—	—	25.00	—
CC8	Bravura Brass	—	—	25.00	—

COUNTRY COUSINS

PM 2101
SWEET SUZIE
Thank You

Designer:	Unknown
Height:	2 ¾", 7.0 cm
Colour:	Brown and yellow pinafore, brown rabbit
Issued:	1994 - 1994

Back Stamp	Beswick Number	Price U.S. $	Can. $	U.K. £	Aust. $
BK-1	PM2101	35.00	50.00	20.00	55.00

PM 2102
PETER
Once Upon A Time

Designer:	Unknown
Height:	2 ½", 5.6 cm
Colour:	Blue suit, white bowtie, brown pencil
Issued:	1994 - 1994

Back Stamp	Beswick Number	Price U.S. $	Can. $	U.K. £	Aust. $
BK-1	PM2102	35.00	50.00	20.00	55.00

PM 2103
HARRY
A New Home for Fred

Designer:	Unknown
Height:	2", 5.0 cm
Colour:	Blue and white striped top, brown trousers, yellow bird
Issued:	1994 - 1994

Back Stamp	Beswick Number	Price U.S. $	Can. $	U.K. £	Aust. $
BK-1	PM2103	35.00	50.00	20.00	55.00

PM 2104
MICHAEL
Happily Ever After

Designer:	Unknown
Height:	2 ½", 6.4 cm
Colour:	Green jacket, yellow pencil, brown rabbit
Issued:	1994 - 1994

Back Stamp	Beswick Number	Price U.S. $	Can. $	U.K. £	Aust. $
BK-1	PM2104	35.00	50.00	20.00	55.00

PM 2105
BERTRAM
Ten Out of Ten

Designer:	Unknown
Height:	3", 7.6 cm
Colour:	Green and blue striped waistcoat, red bow, blue mortar board with red tassel, brown owl
Issued:	1994 - 1994

Back Stamp	Beswick Number	Price U.S. $	Can. $	U.K. £	Aust. $
BK-1	PM2105	35.00	50.00	20.00	55.00

PM 2106
LEONARDO
Practice Makes Perfect

Designer:	Unknown
Height:	2 ¾", 7.0 cm
Colour:	Brown owl, blue paintbrush, brown hat, white palette
Issued:	1994 - 1994

Back Stamp	Beswick Number	Price U.S. $	Can. $	U.K. £	Aust. $
BK-1	PM2106	35.00	50.00	20.00	55.00

PM 2107
LILY
Flowers Picked Just for You

Designer:	Unknown
Height:	3", 7.6 cm
Colour:	Brown hedgehog, pink dress with matching bonnet, yellow pinafore with white collar, white ribbon on bonnet,
Issued:	1994 - 1994

Back Stamp	Beswick Number	U.S. $	Price Can. $	U.K. £	Aust. $
BK-1	PM2107	35.00	50.00	20.00	55.00

PM 2108
PATRICK
This Ways Best

Designer:	Unknown
Height:	3", 7.6 cm
Colour:	Brown owl, blue and yellow checked waistcoat, yellow hat with red band, blue bowtie, white collar
Issued:	1994 - 1994

Back Stamp	Beswick Number	U.S. $	Price Can. $	U.K. £	Aust. $
BK-1	PM2108	35.00	50.00	20.00	55.00

PM 2109
JAMIE
Hurrying Home

Designer:	Unknown
Height:	3", 7.6 cm
Colour:	Brown hedgehog, pink sailor top with white stripes, blue trousers
Issued:	1994 - 1994

Back Stamp	Beswick Number	U.S. $	Price Can. $	U.K. £	Aust. $
BK-1	PM2109	35.00	50.00	20.00	55.00

PM 2111
MUM AND LIZZIE
Let's Get Busy

Designer:	Unknown
Height:	3 ¼", 8.3 cm
Colour:	Large rabbit - brown, blue dress with white pinafore
	Small rabbit - brown, white pinafore
Issued:	1994 - 1994

Back Stamp	Beswick Number	U.S. $	Price Can. $	U.K. £	Aust. $
BK-1	PM2111	50.00	75.00	25.00	65.00

PM 2112
MOLLY AND TIMMY
Picnic Time

Designer:	Unknown
Height:	2 ¾", 7 cm
Colour:	Large mouse - brown, pink dress, blue pinafore, yellow bonnet
	Small mouse - brown, yellow dungarees, white top, blue hat, brown teddy bear
Issued:	1994 - 1994

Back Stamp	Beswick Number	U.S. $	Price Can. $	U.K. £	Aust. $
BK-1	PM2112	50.00	75.00	25.00	65.00

PM 2113
POLLY AND SARAH
Good News!

Designer:	Unknown
Height:	3 ¼", 8.3 cm
Colour:	Rabbit - brown, blue dress, pink apron
	Hedgehog - brown, blue dress, green jacket, white pinafore, blue scarf
Issued:	1994 - 1994

Back Stamp	Beswick Number	U.S. $	Price Can. $	U.K. £	Aust. $
BK-1	PM2113	50.00	75.00	25.00	65.00

PM 2114
BILL AND TED
Working Together

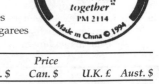

Designer:	Unknown
Height:	3 ¼", 8.3 cm
Colour:	Mouse - brown, blue dungarees
	Hedgehog - brown, green dungarees
Issued:	1994 - 1994

Back Stamp	Beswick Number	U.S. $	Price Can. $	U.K. £	Aust. $
BK-1	PM2114	50.00	75.00	25.00	60.00

PM 2115
JACK AND DAISY
How Does Your Garden Grow

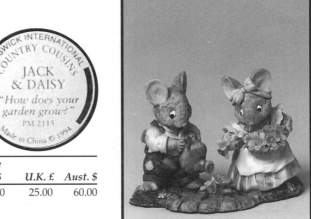

Designer:	Unknown
Height:	2 ¾", 7 cm
Colour:	Male - brown mouse, white shirt, blue dungarees
	Female - brown mouse, pink and white striped dress, white pinafore
Issued:	1994 - 1994

Back Stamp	Beswick Number	U.S. $	Price Can. $	U.K. £	Aust. $
BK-1	PM2115	50.00	75.00	25.00	60.00

PM 2116
ALISON AND DEBBIE
Friendship is Fun

Designer:	Unknown
Height:	2 ¾", 7 cm
Colour:	Rabbit - brown, pink dress, white pinafore
	Squirrel - brown, blue dress, pink apron
Issued:	1994 - 1994

Back Stamp	Beswick Number	U.S. $	Price Can. $	U.K. £	Aust. $
BK-1	PM2116	50.00	75.00	25.00	60.00

PM 2119
ROBERT AND ROSIE
Perfect Partners

Designer:	Unknown
Height:	3 ¼", 8.3 cm
Colour:	Male - brown squirrel, blue dungarees, blue hat with red band Female - brown squirrel, pink dress with white collar, yellow hat
Issued:	1994 - 1994

Back Stamp	Beswick Number	U.S. $	Price Can. $	U.K. £	Aust. $
BK-1	PM2119	50.00	75.00	25.00	60.00

PM 2120
SAMMY
Treasure Hunting

Designer:	Unknown
Height:	2 ¼", 5.7 cm
Colour:	Brown squirrel, green shirt, blue sack
Issued:	1994 - 1994

Back Stamp	Beswick Number	U.S. $	Price Can. $	U.K. £	Aust. $
BK-1	PM2120	35.00	50.00	20.00	55.00

Collect it !

Collect it! launched in response to a need - the need for a magazine for the collector in everyone!

Collect it! has already established itself in the UK as THE magazine for collectors. Covering subjects from McDonalds toys and cigarette packets, to Wade, Lilliput, Royal Doulton and Moorcroft, all in a full colour glossy magazine.

Antiques worth fortunes are out of the range of all but the very few. What people want to read about are the bargains they can find at prices they can afford and the values of the things they already have. Collect it! covers all of these, with articles on future collectables, affordable antiques and memorabilia.

Available at major newsagents in the UK, USA, Canada, Australia, New Zealand and Japan, Collect it! has become indispensable to anyone with a general interest in spotting the antiques of tomorrow.

For further information and the cost of a year's subscription,

call: +44 1344 868 280

TITLE .... FULL NAME ....

ADDRESS ....

....

....

DAYTIME TEL NO .... ZIPCODE ....

☐ I enclose a cheque for .... made payable to Collect it Ltd.

☐ Please debit £................:.................. from my ☐ Mastercard ☐ Visa

CARD NUMBER: ☐☐☐☐ ☐☐☐☐ ☐☐☐☐ ☐☐☐☐

EXPIRY DATE .... / ....

SIGNATURE .... DATE ....

Collect it Ltd, P.O. Box 3658, Bracknell, Berkshire RG12 7XZ, Great Britain.

DAVID HAND'S ANIMALAND

1148
DINKUM PLATYPUS™

Designer: Arthur Gredington
Height: 4 ¼", 10.8 cm
Colour: Brown and beige platypus, green base
Issued: 1949 - 1955

Beswick Number	Price			
	U.S. $	Can. $	U.K. £	Aust. $
1148	200.00	300.00	125.00	175.00

1150
ZIMMY LION™

Designer: Arthur Gredington
Height: 3 ¾", 9.5 cm
Colour: Brown lion with white face
Issued: 1949 - 1955

Beswick Number	Price			
	U.S. $	Can. $	U.K. £	Aust. $
1150	550.00	700.00	325.00	225.00

1151
FELIA™

Designer: Arthur Gredington
Height: 4", 10.1 cm
Colour: Green cat
Issued: 1949 - 1955

Beswick Number	Price			
	U.S. $	Can. $	U.K. £	Aust. $
1151	900.00	1,100.00	600.00	225.00

1152
GINGER NUTT™

Designer:	Arthur Gredington
Height:	4", 10.1 cm
Colour:	Brown and beige squirrel, green base
Issued:	1949 - 1955

Beswick Number	U.S. $	Price Can. $	U.K. £	Aust. $
1152	800.00	1,000.00	500.00	225.00

1153
HAZEL NUTT™

Designer:	Arthur Gredington
Height:	3 ¾", 9.5 cm
Colour:	Brown and beige squirrel, green base
Issued:	1949 - 1955

Beswick Number	U.S. $	Price Can. $	U.K. £	Aust. $
1153	900.00	1,100.00	600.00	225.00

1154
OSCAR OSTRICH™

Designer:	Arthur Gredington
Height:	3 ¾", 9.5 cm
Colour:	Beige and mauve ostrich, brown base
Issued:	1949 - 1955

Beswick Number	U.S. $	Price Can. $	U.K. £	Aust. $
1154	800.00	1,000.00	500.00	225.00

1155
DUSTY MOLE™

Designer:	Arthur Gredington
Height:	3 ½", 8.9 cm
Colour:	Blue mole, white face
Issued:	1949 - 1955

Beswick		Price		
Number	U.S. $	Can. $	U.K. £	Aust. $
1155	375.00	500.00	200.00	225.00

1156
LOOPY HARE™

Designer:	Arthur Gredington
Height:	4 ¼", 10.8 cm
Colour:	Brown and beige hare
Issued:	1949 - 1955

Beswick		Price		
Number	U.S. $	Can. $	U.K. £	Aust. $
1156	800.00	1,000.00	500.00	225.00

ENGLISH COUNTRY FOLK

ECF1
HUNTSMAN FOX™

Designer:	Amanda Hughes-Lubeck
Height:	5 ¾", 14.6 cm
Colour:	Dark green jacket and cap, blue-grey trousers, green wellingtons
Issued:	1993 to the present

ECF 1
HUNTSMAN FOX

Beswick Number	Price			
	U.S. $	Can. $	U.K. £	Aust. $
9150	70.00	93.00	29.50	110.00

ECF2
FISHERMAN OTTER™

Designer:	Warren Platt
Height:	5 ¾", 14.6 cm
Colour:	Yellow shirt and hat, dark green waistcoat, blue-grey trousers, green wellingtons
Issued:	1993 to the present

ECF 2
FISHERMAN OTTER

Beswick Number	Price			
	U.S. $	Can. $	U.K. £	Aust. $
9152	70.00	93.00	29.50	110.00

ECF3
GARDENER RABBIT™

Designer:	Warren Platt
Height:	6", 15.0 cm
Colour:	White shirt, red pullover, blue trousers, grey hat, black wellingtons
Issued:	1993 to the present

ECF 3
GARDENER RABBIT

Beswick Number	Price			
	U.S. $	Can. $	U.K. £	Aust. $
9155	70.00	93.00	29.50	100.00

ECF4
GENTLEMAN PIG™

Designer:	Amanda Hughes-Lubeck
Height:	5 ¾", 14.6 cm
Colour:	Brown suit
Issued:	1993 to the present

BESWICK
B
ECF 4
GENTLEMAN PIG

Beswick Number	Price			
	U.S. $	Can. $	U.K. £	Aust. $
9149	70.00	93.00	29.50	110.00

ECF5
SHEPHERD SHEEPDOG™

Designer:	Warren Platt
Height:	6 ¾", 17.2 cm
Colour:	Yellow smock
Issued:	1993 to the present

BESWICK
B
ECF 5
SHEPHERD SHEEPDOG

Beswick Number	Price			
	U.S. $	Can. $	U.K. £	Aust. $
9156	70.00	93.00	29.50	110.00

ECF6
HIKER BADGER™
First Variation

Designer:	Warren Platt
Height:	5 ¼", 13.3 cm
Colour:	Yellow shirt, blue waistcoat, red cap and socks
Issued:	1993 to the present
Varieties:	ECF9

BESWICK
B
ECF 6
HIKER BADGER

Beswick Number	Price			
	U.S. $	Can. $	U.K. £	Aust. $
9157	70.00	93.00	29.50	110.00

ECF7
MRS RABBIT BAKING™

Designer:	Martyn Alcock
Height:	5 ½", 14.0 cm
Colour:	Mauve dress, white apron and cap
Issued:	1994 to the present

BESWICK
B
ENGLAND
ECF 7
MRS RABBIT BAKING

Beswick Number	Price			
	U.S. $	Can. $	U.K. £	Aust. $
—	70.00	105.00	29.50	110.00

ECF8
THE LADY PIG™

Designer:	Amanda Hughes-Lubeck
Height:	5 ½", 14.0 cm
Colour:	Green jacket, skirt and hat, brown umbrella
Issued:	1995 to the present

BESWICK
B
ENGLAND
ECF 8
THE LADY PIG

Beswick Number	Price			
	U.S. $	Can. $	U.K. £	Aust. $
—	70.00	105.00	29.50	110.00

ECF9
HIKER BADGER™
Second Variation

Designer:	Warren Platt
Height:	5 ¼", 13.3 cm
Colour:	Green shirt and trousers, red jumper, hat and socks, black walking stick
Issued:	1997 in a special edition of 1,000
Varieties:	ECF6

BESWICK
B
ENGLAND
Sinclairs
China, Crystal & Luxuries
NEW COLOURWAY 1997
ECF 9
HIKER BADGER
PRODUCED EXCLUSIVELY FOR
20th CENTURY FAIRS JUNE 1997
IN A SPECIAL EDITION OF 1,000
85

Beswick Number	Price			
	U.S. $	Can. $	U.K. £	Aust. $
9157	100.00	125.00	40.00	130.00

ENID BLYTON
NODDY COLLECTION

3676
BIG EARS™

Designer: Andy Moss
Height: 5", 12.7 cm
Colour: Red and white striped shirt,
dark blue jacket, yellow buttons
and trousers, red hat
Issued: 1997 in a special edition of 1,500

Doulton Number		Price			
		U.S. $	Can. $	U.K. £	Aust. $
3676	Noddy and Big Ears (pair)	—	—	125.00	—

3678
NODDY™

Designer: Andy Moss
Height: 5", 12.7 cm
Colour: Red shirt and shoes, light blue
trousers, dark blue hat with light
brown bell
Issued: 1997 in a special edition of 1,500

Doulton Number		Price			
		U.S. $	Can. $	U.K. £	Aust. $
3678	Noddy and Big Ears (pair)	—	—	125.00	—

**Photographs not
available
at press time**

To be released in 1998

3769 MR. PLOD™ and 3770 TESSIE BEAR™

Designer: Andy Moss
Height: 5", 12.7 cm
Colour: Multi-coloured
Issued: 1998 each in a special edition of 1,500

Doulton Number		Price			
		U.S. $	Can. $	U.K. £	Aust.
3679 / 3770		—	—	125.00	—

HANNA-BARBERA

THE FLINTSTONES
TOP CAT

THE FINTSTONES

1996-1997

3577
PEBBLES™

Designer: Simon Ward
Height: 3 ½", 8.9 cm
Colour: Green dress, blue pants, red hair, light brown base
Issued: 1997 in a limited edition of 2,000

Beswick Number		Price		
	U.S. $	Can. $	U.K. £	Aust. $
3577	75.00	100.00	45.00	125.00

3579
BAMM BAMM™

Designer: Simon Ward
Height: 3", 7.6 cm
Colour: Light and dark brown pants, white hair, yellow club, light brown base
Issued: 1997 in a limited edition of 2,000

Beswick Number		Price		
	U.S. $	Can. $	U.K. £	Aust. $
3579	75.00	100.00	45.00	125.00

3583
WILMA FLINTSTONE™

Designer:	Simon Ward
Height:	4 ¾", 12.1 cm
Colour:	White dress, red hair, light brown base
Issued:	1996 in a limited edition of 2,000

Beswick Number	Price U.S. $	Can. $	U.K. £	Aust. $
3583	75.00	100.00	45.00	125.00

3584
BETTY RUBBLE™

Designer:	Simon Ward
Height:	4", 10.1 cm
Colour:	Blue dress, black hair, light brown base
Issued:	1996 in a limited edition of 2,000

Beswick Number	Price U.S. $	Can. $	U.K. £	Aust. $
3584	75.00	100.00	45.00	125.00

3587
BARNEY RUBBLE™

Designer:	Simon Ward
Height:	3 ½", 8.9 cm
Colour:	Reddish brown shirt, yellow hair, light brown base
Issued:	1996 in a limited edition of 2,000

Beswick Number	Price U.S. $	Can. $	U.K. £	Aust. $
3587	75.00	100.00	45.00	150.00

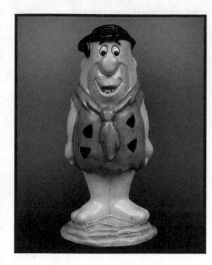

3588
FRED FLINTSTONE™

Designer:	Simon Ward
Height:	4 ¾", 12.1 cm
Colour:	Light brown shirt with dark patches, black hair, blue tie, light brown base
Issued:	1996 in a limited edition of 2,000

Beswick Number	Price			
	U.S. $	Can. $	U.K. £	Aust. $
3588	75.00	100.00	45.00	125.00

3590
DINO™

Designer:	Simon Ward
Height:	4 ¾", 12.1 cm
Colour:	Red, white and light brown
Issued:	1997 in a limited edition of 2,000

Beswick Number	Price			
	U.S. $	Can. $	U.K. £	Aust. $
3590	75.00	100.00	45.00	125.00

TOP CAT

1996-1998

3581
TOP CAT™

Designer:	Andy Moss
Height:	4 ½", 11.9 cm
Colour:	Yellow cat wearing a mauve waistcoat and hat
Issued:	1996 in a limited edition of 2,000
Series:	Top Cat

John Beswick
TOP CAT ™
© 1996 H-B PROD., INC
LICENSED BY CPL
© 1996 ROYAL DOULTON
EXCLUSIVE EDITION OF 2,000
FOR THE DOULTON &
BESWICK FAIRS IN ENGLAND

Beswick Number		*Price*			
		U.S.	Can. $	U.K. £	Aust. $
3581	Top Cat / Choo Choo (pair)	—	—	90.00	—

3586
CHOO-CHOO™

Designer:	Andy Moss
Height:	4 ½", 11.9 cm
Colour:	Pink cat wearing a white shirt
Issued:	1996 in a limited edition of 2,000
Series:	Top Cat

John Beswick
CHOO-CHOO ™
© 1996 H-B PROD., INC.
LICENSED BY CPL
© 1996 ROYAL DOULTON
EXCLUSIVE EDITION OF 2,000
FOR THE DOULTON &
BESWICK FAIRS IN ENGLAND

Beswick Number		*Price*			
		U.S. $	Can. $	U.K. £	Aust. $
3586	Top Cat / Choo Choo (pair)	—	—	90.00	—

3624
FANCY FANCY™

Designer:	Andy Moss
Height:	4 ½", 11.9 cm
Colour:	Pink cat with black tip on tail, white scarf
Issued:	1997 in a limited edition of 2,000
Series:	Top Cat

Beswick Number		Price			
		U.S. $	Can. $	U.K. £	Aust. $
3624	Fancy Fancy / Benny (pair)	—	—	85.00	—

John Beswick
FANCY FANCY ™
© 1997 H-B PROD., INC.
LICENSED BY CPL
© 1997 ROYAL DOULTON
EXCLUSIVE EDITION OF 2,000
FOR THE DOULTON &
BESWICK FAIRS IN ENGLAND

3627
BENNY™

Designer:	Andy Moss
Height:	3 ¾", 8.5 cm
Colour:	Lilac cat wearing a white jacket
Issued:	1997 in a limited edition of 2,000
Series:	Top Cat

John Beswick
BENNY ™
© 1997 H-B PROD., INC.
LICENSED BY CPL
© 1997 ROYAL DOULTON
EXCLUSIVE EDITION OF 2,000
FOR THE DOULTON &
BESWICK FAIRS IN ENGLAND

Beswick Number		Price			
		U.S. $	Can. $	U.K. £	Aust. $
3627	Fancy Fancy / Benny (pair)	—	—	85.00	—

3671
OFFICER DIBBLE™

Designer:	Andy Moss
Height:	6 ¾", 17.5 cm
Colour:	Dark blue police uniform
Issued:	1998 in a limited edition of 2,000
Series:	Top Cat

Beswick Number		Price			
		U.S. $	Can. $	U.K. £	Aust. $
3671		—	—	65.00	—

3673
SPOOK

Designer:	Andy Moss
Height:	4 ½", 11.9 cm
Colour:	Beige cat with black tie
Issued:	1998 in a limited edition of 2,000
Series:	Top Cat

Beswick Number		Price U.S. $	Can. $	U.K. £	Aust. $
3673	Spook and Brain (pair)	—	—	85.00	—

3674
BRAIN™

Designer:	Andy Moss
Height:	4", 10.1 cm
Colour:	Yellow cat wearing a purple shirt
Issued:	1998 in a limited edition of 2,000
Series:	Top Cat

Beswick Number		Price U.S. $	Can. $	U.K. £	Aust. $
3674	Spook and Brain (pair)	—	—	85.00	—

JANE HISSEY
OLD BEAR

> *Photograph not available at press time*

OB4601
OLD BEAR™

Designer:	Unknown
Modeller:	Paul Gurney
Height:	Unknown
Colour:	Unknown
Issued:	1997 to the present

Beswick Number		Price		
	U.S. $	Can. $	U.K. £	Aust. $
OB4601	—	—	9.95	—

OB4602
TIME FOR BED™

Designer:	Unknown
Modeller:	Paul Gurney
Height:	4", 10.1 cm
Colour:	Golden brown giraffe, light brown bear wearing blue and white striped pyjamas, yellow toothbrush
Issued:	1997 to the present

Beswick Number		Price		
	U.S. $	Can. $	U.K. £	Aust. $
OB4602	—	—	14.95	—

OB4603
BRAMWELL BROWN HAD A GOOD IDEA™

Designer:	Unknown
Modeller:	Paul Gurney
Height:	Unknown
Colour:	Unknown
Issued:	1997 to the present

Beswick Number		Price		
	U.S. $	Can. $	U.K. £	Aust. $
OB4603	—	—	13.95	—

> *Photograph not available at press time*

OB4604
DONT WORRY RABBIT™

Designer:	Unknown
Modeller:	Paul Gurney
Height:	Unknown
Colour:	Unknown
Issued:	1997 to the present

Beswick		Price		
Number	U.S. $	Can. $	U.K. £	Aust. $
OB4604	—	—	13.95	—

Photograph not available at press time

OB4605
THE LONG RED SCARF™

Designer:	Unknown
Modeller:	Paul Gurney
Height:	4", 10.1 cm
Colour:	Golden brown giraffe wearing long red scarf, dark brown bear
Issued:	1997 to the present

Beswick		Price		
Number	U.S. $	Can. $	U.K. £	Aust. $
OB4605	—	—	19.95	—

OB4606
WAITING FOR SNOW™

Designer:	Unknown
Modeller:	Paul Gurney
Height:	4", 10.1 cm
Colour:	Golden brown giraffe, light brown bear, white duck with brown beak
Issued:	1997 to the present

Beswick		Price		
Number	U.S. $	Can. $	U.K. £	Aust. $
OB4606	—	—	16.95	—

OB4607
THE SNOWFLAKE BISCUITS™

Designer:	Unknown
Modeller:	Paul Gurney
Height:	4", 10.1 cm
Colour:	Golden brown giraffe wearing red scarf, light brown bear wearing red dungarees, white donkey with black stripes, brown biscuits
Issued:	1997 to the present

Beswick Number		Price		
	U.S. $	Can. $	U.K. £	Aust. $
OB4607	—	—	19.95	—

OB4608
WELCOME HOME, OLD BEAR™

Designer:	Unknown
Modeller:	Paul Gurney
Height:	4", 10.1 cm
Colour:	Brown bear with two light brown bears and a white duck
Issued:	1997 to the present

Beswick Number		Price		
	U.S. $	Can. $	U.K. £	Aust. $
OB4608	—	—	13.95	—

OB4609
RUFF'S PRIZE™

Designer:	Unknown
Modeller:	Paul Gurney
Height:	2 ½", 6.5 cm
Colour:	Light brown dog wearing a dark brown coat, light brown bear wearing red dungarees
Issued:	1997 to the present

Beswick Number		Price		
	U.S. $	Can. $	U.K. £	Aust. $
OB4609	—	—	13.95	—

OB4610
TIME FOR A CUDDLE ME TIGHT™

Designer:	Unknown
Modeller:	Paul Gurney
Height:	3 ½", 8.9 cm
Colour:	Golden brown bear, light brown bear wearing blue and white striped pyjamas
Issued:	1997 to the present

Beswick Number	U.S. $	Price Can. $	U.K. £	Aust. $
OB4610	—	—	13.95	—

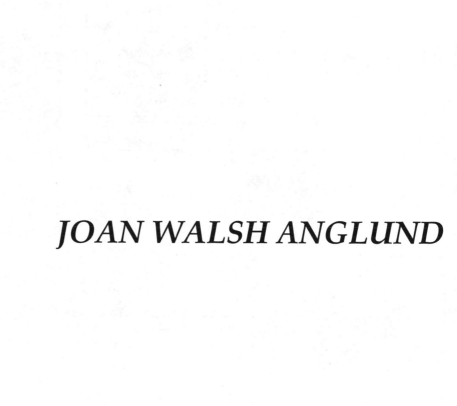

JOAN WALSH ANGLUND

2272
ANGLUND BOY™

Designer:	Albert Hallam
Height:	4 ½", 11.9 cm
Colour:	Green dungarees, brown hat
Issued:	1970 - 1971

Beswick Number	Price U.S. $	Can. $	U.K. £	Aust. $
2272	250.00	325.00	150.00	325.00

2293
ANGLUND GIRL WITH DOLL™

Designer:	Albert Hallam
Height:	4 ½", 11.9 cm
Colour:	Green dress and bow, white apron
Issued:	1970 - 1971

Beswick Number	Price U.S. $	Can. $	U.K. £	Aust. $
2293	250.00	325.00	150.00	325.00

2317
ANGLUND GIRL WITH FLOWERS™

Designer:	Albert Hallam
Height:	4 ¾", 12.1 cm
Colour:	White dress, blue leggings, straw hat with blue ribbon
Issued:	1971 - 1971

Beswick Number	Price U.S. $	Can. $	U.K. £	Aust. $
2317	250.00	325.00	150.00	325.00

KITTY MACBRIDE

2526
A FAMILY MOUSE™

Designer:	Graham Tongue
Height:	3 ½", 8.9 cm
Colour:	Brown, mauve and turquoise, light and dark green base
Issued:	1975 - 1983

Beswick		Price		
Number	U.S. $	Can. $	U.K. £	Aust. $
2526	225.00	275.00	150.00	150.00

2527
A DOUBLE ACT™

Designer:	Graham Tongue
Height:	3 ½", 8.9 cm
Colour:	Yellow, orange, brown, green and blue
Issued:	1975 - 1983

Beswick		Price		
Number	U.S. $	Can. $	U.K. £	Aust. $
2527	150.00	200.00	110.00	150.00

2528
THE RACEGOER™

Designer:	David Lyttleton
Height:	3 ½", 8.9 cm
Colour:	Brown and yellow, light and dark green base
Issued:	1975 - 1983

Beswick		Price		
Number	U.S. $	Can. $	U.K. £	Aust. $
2528	100.00	150.00	75.00	150.00

2529
A GOOD READ™

Designer:	David Lyttleton
Height:	2 ½", 6.4 cm
Colour:	Yellow, blue, brown and white
Issued:	1975 - 1983

Beswick	Price			
Number	U.S. $	Can. $	U.K. £	Aust. $
2529	475.00	575.00	285.00	350.00

2530
LAZYBONES™

Designer:	David Lyttleton
Height:	1 ½", 3.8 cm
Colour:	Blue, black and brown, green and white base
Issued:	1975 - 1983

Beswick	Price			
Number	U.S. $	Can. $	U.K. £	Aust. $
2530	175.00	200.00	110.00	150.00

2531
A SNACK™

Designer:	David Lyttleton
Height:	3 ¼", 8.3 cm
Colour:	Brown, blue and yellow, green base
Issued:	1975 - 1983

Beswick	Price			
Number	U.S. $	Can. $	U.K. £	Aust. $
2531	100.00	150.00	75.00	150.00

2532
STRAINED RELATIONS™

Designer:	David Lyttleton
Height:	3", 7.6 cm
Colour:	Brown, blue and green
Issued:	1975 - 1983

Beswick	Price			
Number	U.S. $	Can. $	U.K. £	Aust. $
2532	100.00	175.00	65.00	150.00

2533
JUST GOOD FRIENDS™

Designer:	David Lyttleton
Height:	3", 7.6 cm
Colour:	Brown, yellow, blue, red and green
Issued:	1975 - 1983

Beswick	Price			
Number	U.S. $	Can. $	U.K. £	Aust. $
2533	200.00	250.00	125.00	150.00

2565
THE RING™

Designer:	David Lyttleton
Height:	3 ¼", 8.3 cm
Colour:	Brown, white, purple and yellow
Issued:	1976 - 1983

Beswick	Price			
Number	U.S. $	Can. $	U.K. £	Aust. $
2565	200.00	250.00	130.00	175.00

2566
GUILTY SWEETHEARTS™

Designer:	David Lyttleton
Height:	2 ¼", 5.7 cm
Colour:	Brown, yellow, green and white
Issued:	1976 - 1983

Beswick	Price			
Number	U.S. $	Can. $	U.K. £	Aust. $
2566	200.00	250.00	115.00	150.00

2589
ALL I DO IS THINK OF YOU™

Designer:	David Lyttleton
Height:	2 ½", 6.4 cm
Colour:	Brown, yellow and white
Issued:	1976 - 1983

Beswick	Price			
Number	U.S. $	Can. $	U.K. £	Aust. $
2589	350.00	400.00	250.00	250.00

LITTLE LIKABLES

LL1
FAMILY GATHERING™
(Hen and Two Chicks)

Designer:	Diane Griffiths
Height:	4 ½", 11.9 cm
Colour:	White hen and chicks with yellow beaks and gold comb on hen
Issued:	1985 - 1987

Beswick Number	Price U.S. $	Can. $	U.K. £	Aust. $
LL1	70.00	95.00	40.00	95.00

LL2
WATCHING THE WORLD GO BY™
(Frog)

Designer:	Robert Tabbenor
Height:	3 ¾", 9.5 cm
Colour:	White frog, black and green eyes
Issued:	1985 - 1987

Beswick Number	Price U.S. $	Can. $	U.K. £	Aust. $
LL2	110.00	155.00	65.00	160.00

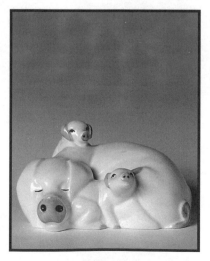

LL3
HIDE AND SEEK™
(Pig and Two Piglets)

Designer:	Robert Tabbenor
Height:	3 ¼", 8.3 cm
Colour:	White pigs with pink noses, ears and tails
Issued:	1985 - 1987

Beswick Number	Price U.S. $	Can. $	U.K. £	Aust. $
LL3	70.00	95.00	40.00	85.00

LL4
MY PONY™
(Pony)

Designer:	Diane Griffiths
Height:	7 ¼", 18.4 cm
Colour:	White pony with blue highlights in mane and tail
Issued:	1985 - 1987

Beswick Number	Price			
	U.S. $	Can. $	U.K. £	Aust. $
LL4	95.00	130.00	55.00	125.00

LL5
ON TOP OF THE WORLD™
(Elephant)

Designer:	Diane Griffiths
Height:	3 ¾", 9.5 cm
Colour:	White elephant with black eyes and gold nails
Issued:	1985 - 1987

Beswick Number	Price			
	U.S. $	Can. $	U.K. £	Aust. $
LL5	70.00	95.00	40.00	90.00

LL6
TREAT ME GENTLY™
(Fawn)

Designer:	Diane Griffiths
Height:	4 ½", 11.9 cm
Colour:	White fawn with black and brown eyes, black nose and gold hoof
Issued:	1985 - 1987

Beswick Number	Price			
	U.S. $	Can. $	U.K. £	Aust. $
LL6	70.00	95.00	40.00	85.00

LL7
OUT AT LAST™
(Duckling)

Designer:	Robert Tabbenor
Height:	3 ¼", 8.3 cm
Colour:	White duck with black and brown eyes and gold beak
Issued:	1985 - 1987

Beswick		Price			
Number			U.S. $	Can. $	U.K. £	Aust. $
LL7			70.00	95.00	40.00	85.00

LL8
CATS CHORUS™
(Cats)

Designer:	Robert Tabbenor
Height:	4 ¾", 12.1 cm
Colour:	Two white cats with black and green eyes, black nose, pink ears and mouth
Issued:	1985 - 1987

Beswick		Price			
Number		U.S. $	Can. $	U.K. £	Aust. $
LL8		70.00	95.00	40.00	95.00

LITTLE LOVABLES

LL1
HAPPY BIRTHDAY™

Designer:	Amanda Hughes-Lubeck
Height:	4 ½", 11.9 cm
Colour:	White, pink and orange (gloss)
Issued:	1992 - 1994
Varieties:	LL8; LL15; also unnamed LL22

Model		Price		
No.	U.S. $	Can. $	U.K. £	Aust. $
3328	40.00	50.00	25.00	60.00

LL2
I LOVE YOU™

Designer:	Amanda Hughes-Lubeck
Height:	4 ½", 11.9 cm
Colour:	White, green and pink (gloss)
Issued:	1992 - 1994
Varieties:	LL9, LL16; also unnamed LL23

Model		Price		
No.	U.S. $	Can. $	U.K. £	Aust. $
3320	40.00	50.00	25.00	70.00

LL3
GOD LOVES ME™

Designer:	Amanda Hughes-Lubeck
Height:	3 ¾", 9.5 cm
Colour:	White, green and turquoise (gloss)
Issued:	1992 - 1993
Varieties:	LL10, LL17; also called Please, LL33, LL34; also unnamed LL24

Model		Price		
No.	U.S. $	Can. $	U.K. £	Aust. $
3336	150.00	250.00	100.00	75.00

LL4
JUST FOR YOU™

Designer:	Warren Platt
Height:	4 ½", 11.9 cm
Colour:	White, pink and blue (gloss)
Issued:	1992 - 1994
Varieties:	LL11, LL18; also unnamed LL25

Model No.	Price			
	U.S. $	Can. $	U.K. £	Aust. $
3361	60.00	80.00	25.00	60.00

LL5
TO MOTHER™

Designer:	Amanda Hughes-Lubeck
Height:	4 ½", 11.9 cm
Colour:	White, blue and purple (gloss)
Issued:	1992 - 1994
Varieties:	LL12, LL19; also called To Daddy, also unnamed LL26

Model No.	Price			
	U.S. $	Can. $	U.K. £	Aust. $
3331	40.00	50.00	25.00	60.00

LL6
CONGRATULATIONS™

Designer:	Warren Platt
Height:	4 ½", 11.9 cm
Colour:	White, green and pink (gloss)
Issued:	1992 - 1994
Varieties:	LL13, LL20; also unnamed LL27

Model No.	Price			
	U.S. $	Can. $	U.K. £	Aust. $
3340	40.00	50.00	25.00	60.00

LL7
PASSED™

Designer:	Amanda Hughes-Lubeck
Height:	3", 7.6 cm
Colour:	White, lilac and pink (gloss)
Issued:	1992 - 1994
Varieties:	LL14, LL21; also unnamed LL28

Model	Price			
No.	U.S. $	Can. $	U.K. £	Aust. $
3334	60.00	80.00	35.00	60.00

LL8
HAPPY BIRTHDAY™

Designer:	Amanda Hughes-Lubeck
Height:	4 ½", 11.9 cm
Colour:	White, yellow and green (gloss)
Issued:	1992 - 1994
Varieties:	LL1, LL15; also unnamed LL22

Model	Price			
No.	U.S. $	Can. $	U.K. £	Aust. $
3328	40.00	50.00	25.00	60.00

LL9
I LOVE YOU™

Designer:	Amanda Hughes-Lubeck
Height:	4 ½", 11.9 cm
Colour:	White, blue and orange (gloss)
Issued:	1992 - 1994
Varieties:	LL2, LL16; also unnamed LL23

Model	Price			
No.	U.S. $	Can. $	U.K. £	Aust. $
3320	40.00	50.00	25.00	60.00

LL10
GOD LOVES ME™

Designer:	Amanda Hughes-Lubeck
Height:	3 ¾", 9.5 cm
Colour:	White, gold and blue (gloss)
Issued:	1992 - 1993
Varieties:	LL3, LL17; also called Please, LL33, LL34; also unnamed LL24

Model No.	Price			
	U.S. $	Can. $	U.K. £	Aust. $
3336	150.00	250.00	100.00	90.00

LL11
JUST FOR YOU™

Designer:	Warren Platt
Height:	4 ½", 11.9 cm
Colour:	White, yellow and pale green (gloss)
Issued:	1992 - 1994
Varieties:	LL4, LL18; also unnamed LL25

Model No.	Price			
	U.S. $	Can. $	U.K. £	Aust. $
3361	40.00	50.00	25.00	60.00

LL12
TO MOTHER™

Designer:	Amanda Hughes-Lubeck
Height:	4 ½", 11.9 cm
Colour:	White, yellow and pink (gloss)
Issued:	1992 - 1994
Varieties:	LL5, LL19; also called To Daddy, LL29; also unnamed LL26

Model No.	Price			
	U.S. $	Can. $	U.K. £	Aust. $
3331	40.00	50.00	25.00	60.00

LL13
CONGRATULATIONS™

Designer:	Warren Platt
Height:	4 ½", 11.9 cm
Colour:	White, pale blue and yellow (gloss)
Issued:	1992 - 1994
Varieties:	LL6, LL20; also unnamed LL27

Model	Price			
No.	U.S. $	Can. $	U.K. £	Aust. $
3340	40.00	50.00	25.00	85.00

LL14
PASSED™

Designer:	Amanda Hughes-Lubeck
Height:	3", 7.6 cm
Colour:	White, light blue and orange (gloss)
Issued:	1992 - 1994
Varieties:	LL7, LL21; also unnamed LL28

Model	Price			
No.	U.S. $	Can. $	U.K. £	Aust. $
3334	60.00	85.00	35.00	60.00

LL15
HAPPY BIRTHDAY™

Designer:	Amanda Hughes-Lubeck
Height:	4 ½", 11.9cm
Colour:	White, salmon and green (matt)
Issued:	1992 - 1993
Varieties:	LL8, LL15; also unnamed LL22

Model	Price			
No.	U.S. $	Can. $	U.K. £	Aust. $
3407	175.00	275.00	100.00	75.00

LL16
I LOVE YOU™

Designer:	Amanda Hughes-Lubeck
Height:	4 ½", 11.9 cm
Colour:	White, green and yellow (matt)
Issued:	1992 - 1993
Varieties:	LL2, LL9; also unnamed LL23

Model	Price			
No.	U.S. $	Can. $	U.K. £	Aust. $
3406	175.00	275.00	100.00	70.00

LL17
GOD LOVES ME™

Designer:	Amanda Hughes-Lubeck
Height:	3 ¾", 9.5 cm
Colour:	White, purple and yellow (matt)
Issued:	1992 - 1993
Varieties:	LL3, LL10; also called Please, LL33, LL34; also unnamed LL24

Model	Price			
No.	U.S. $	Can. $	U.K. £	Aust.
3410	200.00	250.00	125.00	95.00

LL18
JUST FOR YOU™

Designer:	Warren Platt
Height:	4 ½", 11.9 cm
Colour:	White, yellow and dark blue (matt)
Issued:	1992 - 1993
Varieties:	LL4, LL11; also unnamed LL25

Model	Price			
No.	U.S. $	Can. $	U.K. £	Aust. $
3412	175.00	275.00	100.00	70.00

LL19
TO MOTHER™

Designer:	Amanda Hughes-Lubeck
Height:	4 ½", 11.9 cm
Colour:	White, green and orange (matt)
Issued:	1992 - 1993
Varieties:	LL5, LL12; also called To Daddy, LL29; also unnamed LL26

Model No.	Price			
	U.S. $	Can. $	U.K. £	Aust. $
3408	175.00	275.00	100.00	75.00

LL20
CONGRATULATIONS™

Designer:	Warren Platt
Height:	4 ½", 11.9 cm
Colour:	White, blue and red (matt)
Issued:	1992 - 1993
Varieties:	LL6, LL13; also unnamed LL27

Model No.	Price			
	U.S. $	Can. $	U.K. £	Aust. $
3411	175.00	275.00	100.00	70.00

LL21
PASSED™

Designer:	Amanda Hughes-Lubeck
Height:	3", 7.6 cm
Colour:	White, blue and orange (matt)
Issued:	1992 - 1993
Varieties:	LL7, LL14; also unnamed LL28

Model No.	Price			
	U.S. $	Can. $	U.K. £	Aust. $
3409	175.00	275.00	110.00	75.00

LL22
(No Name)

Designer:	Unknown
Height:	4 ½", 11.9 cm
Colour:	White, pink and orange (gloss)
Issued:	1993 - 1993
Varieties:	Also called Happy Birthday, LL1, LL8, LL15

Model No.	Price			
	U.S. $	Can. $	U.K. £	Aust. $
3329	100.00	125.00	65.00	60.00

LL23
(No Name)

Designer:	Amanda Hughes-Lubeck
Height:	4 ½", 11.9 cm
Colour:	White, green and pink (gloss)
Issued:	1993 - 1993
Varieties:	Also called I Love You, LL2, LL9, LL16

Model No.	Price			
	U.S. $	Can. $	U.K. £	Aust. $
3320	100.00	125.00	65.00	60.00

LL24
(No Name)

Designer:	Amanda Hughes-Lubeck
Height:	3 ¾", 9.5 cm
Colour:	White, green and turquoise (gloss)
Issued:	1993 - 1993
Varieties:	Also called God Loves Me, LL3, LL10, LL17; also called Please, LL33, LL34

Model No.	Price			
	U.S. $	Can. $	U.K. £	Aust. $
3336	125.00	175.00	100.00	60.00

LL25
(No Name)

Designer:	Warren Platt
Height:	4 ½", 11.9 cm
Colour:	White, pink and blue (gloss)
Issued:	1993 - 1993
Varieties:	Also called Just For You, LL4, LL11, LL18

Model	Price			
No.	U.S. $	Can. $	U.K. £	Aust. $
3361	100.00	125.00	65.00	70.00

LL26
(No Name)

Designer:	Amanda Hughes-Lubeck
Height:	4 ¼", 10.8 cm
Colour:	White, blue and purple (gloss)
Issued:	1993 - 1993
Varieties:	Also called To Mother, LL5, LL12, LL19; also called To Daddy, LL29

Model	Price			
No.	U.S. $	Can. $	U.K. £	Aust. $
3331	100.00	125.00	65.00	65.00

LL27
(No Name)

Designer:	Warren Platt
Height:	4 ½", 11.9 cm
Colour:	White, green and pink (gloss)
Issued:	1993 - 1993
Varieties:	Also called Congratulations, LL6, LL13, LL20

Model	Price			
No.	U.S. $	Can. $	U.K. £	Aust. $
3340	100.00	125.00	65.00	70.00

LL28
(No Name)

Designer:	Amanda Hughes-Lubeck
Height:	3", 7.6 cm
Colour:	White, lilac and pink (gloss)
Issued:	1993 - 1993
Varieties:	Also called Passed, LL7, LL14, LL21

Model	Price			
No.	U.S. $	Can. $	U.K. £	Aust. $
3334	100.00	125.00	75.00	60.00

LL29
TO DADDY™

Designer:	Amanda Hughes-Lubeck
Height:	4 ½", 11.9 cm
Colour:	White, light blue and green (gloss)
Issued:	1994 - 1994
Varieties:	Also called To Mother, LL5, LL12, LL19; also unnamed LL26

Model	Price			
No.	U.S. $	Can. $	U.K. £	Aust. $
3331	60.00	75.00	40.00	90.00

LL30
MERRY CHRISTMAS™

Designer:	Amanda Hughes-Lubeck
Height:	4", 10.1 cm
Colour:	White, red and green (gloss)
Issued:	1993 - 1994

Model	Price			
No.	U.S. $	Can. $	U.K. £	Aust. $
3389	100.00	150.00	60.00	90.00

BESWICK
(B)
ENGLAND
LL 30

LL31
GOOD LUCK™

Designer:	Amanda Hughes-Lubeck
Height:	4 ¼", 10.8 cm
Colour:	White, pink and green (gloss)
Issued:	1993 - 1994

| Model | Price | | | |
No.	U.S. $	Can. $	U.K. £	Aust. $
3388	90.00	150.00	60.00	90.00

LL32
GET WELL SOON™

Designer:	Amanda Hughes-Lubeck
Height:	4 ¼", 10.8 cm
Colour:	White, green and purple (gloss)
Issued:	1994 - 1994

| Model | Price | | | |
No.	U.S. $	Can. $	U.K. £	Aust. $
3390	125.00	165.00	75.00	90.00

LL33
PLEASE™

Designer:	Amanda Hughes-Lubeck
Height:	3 ¾", 9.5 cm
Colour:	White, green and blue (gloss)
Issued:	1993 - 1994
Varieties:	LL34; also called God Loves Me, LL3, LL10, LL17; also unnamed LL24

| Model | Price | | | |
No.	U.S. $	Can. $	U.K. £	Aust. $
3336	60.00	75.00	35.00	90.00

LL34
PLEASE™

Designer:	Amanda Hughes-Lubeck
Height:	3 ¾", 9.5 cm
Colour:	White, gold and light blue (gloss)
Issued:	1993 - 1994
Varieties:	LL33; also called God Loves Me, LL3, LL10, LL17; also unnamed LL24

Model No.	Price U.S. $	Can. $	U.K. £	Aust. $
3336	60.00	75.00	35.00	90.00

LL35 is the prototype for "I Love Beswick." Colourway not issued.

LL36
I LOVE BESWICK™

Designer:	Amanda Hughes-Lubeck
Height:	4 ½", 11.9 cm
Colour:	White, green and pink (gloss)
Issued:	1995 - 1995
Varieties:	Also called I Love You, LL2, LL9, LL16; also unamed LL23

Model No.	Price U.S. $	Can. $	U.K. £	Aust. $
3320	275.00	325.00	150.00	185.00

Note: This piece was specially commissioned for the 10th Anniversary of the Beswick Collectors Circle.

NORMAN THELWELL

EARTHENWARE SERIES

RESIN STUDIO SCULPTURES

NORMAN THELWELL

EARTHENWARE SERIES 1981-1989

2704A
AN ANGEL ON HORSEBACK™
First Variation

Designer: Harry Sales
Modeller: David Lyttleton
Height: 4 ½", 11.4 cm
Colour: Grey horse, rider wears brown
              jumper, yellow pants
Issued: 1981 - 1989
Varieties: 2704B

Beswick Number	Price U.S. $	Can. $	U.K. £	Aust. $
2704A	250.00	350.00	120.00	190.00

2704B
AN ANGEL ON HORSEBACK™
Second Variation

Designer: Harry Sales
Modeller: David Lyttleton
Height: 4 ½", 11.4 cm
Colour: Bay horse, rider wears
              red jumper, yellow pants
Issued: 1981 - 1989
Varieties: 2704A

Beswick Number	Price U.S. $	Can. $	U.K. £	Aust. $
2704B	250.00	350.00	120.00	190.00

2769A
KICK-START™
First Variation

Designer: Harry Sales
Modeller: David Lyttleton
Height: 3 ½", 8.9 cm
Colour: Grey horse, rider wears
              red jersey and yellow
              pants
Issued: 1982 - 1989
Varieties: 2769B

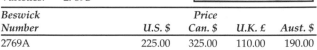

Beswick Number	Price U.S. $	Can. $	U.K. £	Aust. $
2769A	225.00	325.00	110.00	190.00

2769B
KICK-START™
Second Variation

Designer:	Harry Sales
Modeller:	David Lyttleton
Height:	3 ½", 8.9 cm
Colour:	Bay horse, rider wears red jersey and yellow pants
Issued:	1982 - 1989
Varieties:	2769B

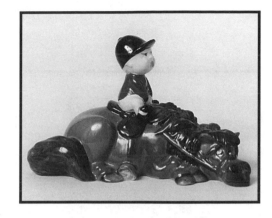

Beswick Number	Price			
	U.S. $	Can. $	U.K. £	Aust. $
2769B	225.00	300.00	100.00	225.00

2789A
PONY EXPRESS™
First Variation

Designer:	Harry Sales
Modeller:	David Lyttleton
Height:	4 ½", 11.4 cm
Colour:	Grey horse, rider wears green jersey and yellow trousers
Issued:	1982 - 1989
Varieties:	2789B

Beswick Number	Price			
	U.S. $	Can. $	U.K. £	Aust. $
2789A	225.00	325.00	110.00	185.00

2789B
PONY EXPRESS™
Second Variation

Designer:	Harry Sales
Modeller:	David Lyttleton
Height:	4 ½", 11.4 cm
Colour:	Bay horse, rider wears red jersey and yellow pants
Issued:	1982 - 1989
Varieties:	2789A

Beswick Number	Price			
	U.S. $	Can. $	U.K. £	Aust. $
2789B	200.00	300.00	100.00	225.00

NORMAN THEWELL

RESIN STUDIO SCULPTURES — 1985-1985

SS7A
I FORGIVE YOU™
First Variation

Designer:	Harry Sales
Modeller:	David Lyttleton
Height:	4", 10.1 cm
Colour:	Grey horse, rider wears red jacket and yellow pants
Issued:	1985 - 1985
Series:	Studio Sculptures
Varieties:	SS7B

Beswick	Price			
Number	U.S. $	Can. $	U.K. £	Aust. $
SS7A	225.00	325.00	135.00	200.00

SS7B
I FORGIVE YOU™
Second Variation

Designer:	Harry Sales
Modeller:	David Lyttleton
Height:	4", 10.1 cm
Colour:	Bay horse, rider wears red jacket and yellow pants
Issued:	1985 - 1985
Series:	Studio Sculptures
Varieties:	SS7A

Beswick	Price			
Number	U.S. $	Can. $	U.K. £	Aust. $
SS7B	200.00	325.00	115.00	200.00

SS12A
EARLY BATH™
First Variation

Designer:	Harry Sales
Modeller:	David Lyttleton
Height:	4 ¾", 12.1 cm
Colour:	Grey horse, rider wears red jacket and yellow pants
Issued:	1985 - 1985
Series:	Studio Sculptures
Varieties:	SS12B

Beswick	Price			
Number	U.S. $	Can. $	U.K. £	Aust. $
SS12A	250.00	325.00	150.00	250.00

SS12B
EARLY BATH™
Second Variation

Designer:	Harry Sales
Height:	4 ¾", 12.1 cm
Colour:	Bay horse, rider wears red jacket and yellow pants
Issued:	1985 - 1985
Series:	Studio Sculptures
Varieties:	SS12A

Beswick Number	Price			
	U.S. $	Can. $	U.K. £	Aust. $
SS12B	250.00	325.00	150.00	325.00

PADDINGTON BEAR CO. LTD.

PB1
PADDINGTON AT THE STATION™

Designer:	Zoe Annand
Height:	4 ¼", 11.0 cm
Colour:	Brown bear, blue coat, yellow hat, brown cobbled base
Issued:	1996 to the present

Doulton		Price		
Number	U.S. $	Can. $	U.K. £	Aust. $
PB1	—	—	12.95	—

Note: This set is exclusive to the U.K.

PB2
PADDINGTON BAKES A CAKE™

Designer:	Zoe Annand
Height:	4 ¼", 10.1 cm
Colour:	Red jacket, black hat, multi-coloured cake, blue and white striped bowl
Issued:	1996 to the present

Doulton		Price		
Number	U.S. $	Can. $	U.K. £	Aust. $
PB2	—	—	12.95	—

PB3
PADDINGTON DECORATING™

Designer:	Zoe Annand
Height:	4 ¾", 12.0 cm
Colour:	Blue coat, red hat, silver bucket, cream paint
Issued:	1996 to the present

Doulton		Price		
Number	U.S. $	Can. $	U.K. £	Aust. $
PB3	—	—	12.95	—

PB4
PADDINGTON SURFING™

Designer:	Zoe Annand
Height:	4", 10.1 cm
Colour:	Multi-coloured shorts, blue hat, yellow surfboard, red rubber ring, brown suitcase
Issued:	1996 to the present

Royal Doulton
Paddington ™
"Surfing"
PB4
© Paddington & Co. Ltd. 1996
Licensed by ©OPYRIGHTS

Doulton Number	Price			
	U.S. $	Can. $	U.K. £	Aust. $
PB4	—	—	12.95	—

PB5
PADDINGTON GARDENING™

Designer:	Zoe Annand
Height:	4", 10.1 cm
Colour:	Blue jacket, red hat, green watering can, yellow and red bucket and spade
Issued:	1996 to the present

Royal Doulton
Paddington ™
"Gardening"
PB5
© Paddington & Co. Ltd. 1996
Licensed by ©OPYRIGHTS

Doulton Number	Price			
	U.S. $	Can. $	U.K. £	Aust. $
PB5	—	—	12.95	—

PB6
PADDINGTON BATHTIME™

Designer:	Zoe Annand
Height:	3 ¼", 8.5 cm
Colour:	Blue coat, yellow hat, brown scrubbing brush, yellow duck, pink soap
Issued:	1996 to the present

Royal Doulton
Paddington ™
"Bathtime"
PB6
© Paddington & Co. Ltd. 1996
Licensed by ©OPYRIGHTS

Doulton Number	Price			
	U.S. $	Can. $	U.K. £	Aust. $
PB6	—	—	12.95	—

PB7
PADDINGTON THE GOLFER™

Designer:	Zoe Annand
Height:	3 ¾", 9.5 cm
Colour:	White top, red and yellow sweater, red hat, green trousers, white shoes
Issued:	1996 to the present

Royal Doulton
Paddington ™
"The Golfer"
PB7
© Paddington & Co. Ltd. 1996
Licensed by ©COPYRIGHTS

Doulton Number		Price			
	U.S. $	Can. $	U.K. £	Aust. $
PB7	—	—	12.95	—

PB8
PADDINGTON THE MUSICIAN™

Designer:	Zoe Annand
Height:	3 ¾", 9.5 cm
Colour:	Black jacket, red waistcoat, brown trousers, brown violin, brass trumpet
Issued:	1996 to the present

Royal Doulton
Paddington ™
"The Musician"
PB8
© Paddington & Co. Ltd. 1996
Licensed by ©COPYRIGHTS

Doulton Number		Price			
	U.S. $	Can. $	U.K. £	Aust. $
PB8	—	—	12.95	—

PB9
PADDINGTON AT CHRISTMAS TIME™

Designer:	Zoe Annand
Height:	3 ½", 8.9 cm
Colour:	Red coat, blue boots, yellow sleigh
Issued:	1996 to the present

Royal Doulton
Paddington ™
"At Christmas Time"
PB9
© Paddington & Co. Ltd. 1996
Licensed by ©COPYRIGHTS

Doulton		Price			
	U.S. $	Can. $	U.K. £	Aust. $
PB9	—	—	12.95	—

PB10
PADDINGTON MARMALADE SANDWICHES™

Designer:	Zoe Annand
Height:	3 ½", 8.9 cm
Colour:	Dark blue coat, yellow hat, green book, orange and white sandwiches
Issued:	1997 to the present

Doulton Number	Price U.S. $	Can. $	U.K. £	Aust. $
PB10	—	—	12.95	—

PB11
PADDINGTON GOING TO BED™

Designer:	Zoe Annand
Height:	3 ¾", 9.5 cm
Colour:	Turquoise, red and yellow pyjamas, red hat
Issued:	1997 to the present

Doulton Number	Price U.S. $	Can. $	U.K. £	Aust. $
PB11	—	—	12.95	—

PB12
PADDINGTON THE FISHERMAN™

Designer:	Zoe Annand
Modeller:	Andrew Hull
Height:	3 ½", 8.9 cm
Colour:	Dark blue hat and wellingtons, red jacket with yellow buttons
Issued:	1997 to the present

Doulton Number	Price U.S. $	Can. $	U.K. £	Aust. $
PB12	—	—	12.95	—

THE PIG PROMENADE

PP 1
JOHN THE CONDUCTOR™
(Vietnamese Pot Bellied Pig)

Designer:	Martyn Alcock
Height:	4 ¾", 12.1 cm
Colour:	Black jacket, black bowtie
Issued:	1993 - 1996

Beswick Ware
JOHN
PP 1

Back Stamp	Price			
	U.S. $	Can. $	U.K. £	Aust. $
PP 1	80.00	125.00	40.00	110.00

PP 2
MATTHEW THE TRUMPET PLAYER™
(Large White Pig)

Designer:	Amanda Hughes-Lubeck
Height:	5", 12.7 cm
Colour:	Light red waistcoat, black bowtie
Issued:	1993 - 1996

Beswick Ware
MATTHEW
PP 2

Back Stamp	Price			
	U.S. $	Can. $	U.K. £	Aust. $
PP 2	80.00	125.00	40.00	110.00

PP 3
DAVID THE FLUTE PLAYER™
(Tamworth Pig)

Designer:	Amanda Hughes-Lubeck
Height:	5 ¼", 13.3 cm
Colour:	Dark green waistcoat, black bowtie
Issued:	1993 - 1996

Beswick Ware
DAVID
PP 3

Back Stamp	Price			
	U.S. $	Can. $	U.K. £	Aust. $
PP 3	80.00	125.00	40.00	110.00

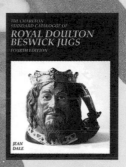

PP 4
ANDREW THE CYMBAL PLAYER™
(Gloucester Old Spotted Pig)

Designer:	Martyn Alcock
Height:	4 ¾", 12.1 cm
Colour:	Blue waistcoat, yellow cymbals, black bowtie
Issued:	1993 - 1996
Varieties:	Also called George, PP10

Beswick Ware
ANDREW
PP 4

Back Stamp	U.S. $	Price Can. $	U.K. £	Aust. $
PP 4	80.00	125.00	40.00	110.00

PP 5
DANIEL THE VIOLINIST™
(Saddleback Pig)

Designer:	Amanda Hughes-Lubeck
Height:	5 ¼", 13.3 cm
Colour:	Pale blue waistcoat, brown violin
Issued:	1993 - 1996

Beswick Ware
DANIEL
PP 5

Back Stamp	U.S. $	Price Can. $	U.K. £	Aust. $
PP 5	80.00	125.00	40.00	110.00

PP 6
MICHAEL THE BASS DRUM PLAYER™
(Large Black Pig)

Designer:	Martyn Alcock
Height:	4 ¾", 12.1 cm
Colour:	Yellow waistcoat, red and white drum
Issued:	1993 - 1996

Beswick Ware
MICHAEL
PP 6

Back Stamp	U.S. $	Price Can. $	U.K. £	Aust. $
PP 6	80.00	125.00	40.00	110.00

PP 7
JAMES THE TRIANGLE PLAYER™
(Tamworth Piglet)

Designer:	Warren Platt
Height:	4", 10.1 cm
Colour:	Tan, purple waistcoat; black bowtie
Issued:	1995 - 1996

Back Stamp	Price U.S. $	Can. $	U.K. £	Aust. $
PP 7	100.00	125.00	50.00	110.00

PP 8
RICHARD THE FRENCH HORN PLAYER™

Designer:	Shane Ridge
Height:	5", 12.7 cm
Colour:	Pale pink with dark grey spots, tan and beige waistcoat
Issued:	1996 - 1996
Varieties:	Also called Benjamin, PP12

Back Stamp	Price U.S. $	Can. $	U.K. £	Aust. $
PP 8	100.00	125.00	50.00	110.00

PP 9
CHRISTOPHER THE GUITAR PLAYER™

Designer:	Warren Platt
Height:	5 ½", 13.3 cm
Colour:	Dark grey, yellow and cream waistcoat, black bowtie
Issued:	1996 - 1996
Varieties:	Also called Thomas, PP11

Back Stamp	Price U.S.$	Can. $	U.K. £	Aust. $
PP 9	100.00	125.00	50.00	110.00

PP 10
GEORGE™

Designer:	Martyn Alcock
Height:	4 ¾", 12.1 cm
Colour:	Dark green waistcoat, yellow cymbals, black bowtie
Issued:	1996 in a limited edition of 2,000
Varieties:	Also called Andrew, PP4

Back Stamp	Price			
	U.S.$	Can. $	U.K. £	Aust. $
PP 10	80.00	125.00	50.00	110.00

PP 11
THOMAS™

Designer:	Warren Platt
Height:	5", 12.7 cm
Colour:	Black pig with green jacket, yellow bowtie, white guitar
Issued:	1997 in a limited edition of 2,000
Varieties:	Also called Christopher the Guitar Player, PP9

Back Stamp	Price			
	U.S.$	Can. $	U.K. £	Aust. $
PP 11	80.00	125.00	50.00	110.00

PP 12
BENJAMIN™

Designer:	Shane Ridge
Height:	5", 12.7 cm
Colour:	White and black pig, orange bowtie, gold french horn
Issued:	1997 in a limited edition of 2,000
Varieties:	Also called Richard the French Horn Player, PP8

Back Stamp	Price			
	U.S.$	Can. $	U.K. £	Aust. $
PP 12	80.00	125.00	50.00	110.00

RUPERT BEAR

2694
RUPERT BEAR™

Designer:	Harry Sales
Height:	4 ¼", 10.8 cm
Colour:	Red sweater, yellow check trousers and scarf
Issued:	1980 - 1986

Beswick		*Price*		
Number	*U.S. $*	*Can. $*	*U.K. £*	*Aust. $*
2694	475.00	600.00	300.00	475.00

2710
ALGY PUG™

Designer:	Harry Sales
Height:	4", 10.1 cm
Colour:	Grey jacket, yellow waistcoat, brown trousers
Issued:	1981 - 1986

Beswick		*Price*		
Number	*U.S. $*	*Can. $*	*U.K. £*	*Aust. $*
2710	350.00	475.00	200.00	250.00

2711
PONG PING™

Designer:	Harry Sales
Height:	4 ¼", 10.8
Colour:	Dark green jacket, gold trousers
Issued:	1981 - 1986

Beswick		*Price*		
Number	*U.S. $*	*Can. $*	*U.K. £*	*Aust. $*
2711	350.00	475.00	225.00	250.00

2720
BILL BADGER™

Designer:	Harry Sales
Height:	2 ¾", 7.0 cm
Colour:	Dark grey jacket, light grey trousers and red bowtie
Issued:	1981 - 1986

Beswick		Price		
Number	U.S. $	Can. $	U.K. £	Aust. $
2720	350.00	475.00	200.00	250.00

2779
RUPERT BEAR SNOWBALLING™

Designer:	Harry Sales
Height:	4 ¼", 10.8 cm
Colour:	Red coat, yellow with brown striped trousers and scarf
Issued:	1982 - 1986

Beswick		Price		
Number	U.S. $	Can. $	U.K. £	Aust. $
2779	550.00	675.00	375.00	575.00

ST. TIGGYWINKLES

TW1
HENRY HEDGEHOG™
(Standing)

Designer:	Unknown
Modeller:	Amanda Hughes-Lubeck
Height:	3 ½", 8.5 cm
Colour:	Light and dark brown hedgehog wearing a purple shirt
Issued:	1997 to the present
Series:	The Wildlife Hospital Trust

Doulton		Price		
Number	U.S. $	Can. $	U.K. £	Aust. $
TW1	—	—	13.95	—

Note: This set is exclusive to the U.K.

TW2
HARRY HEDGEHOG™
(Sitting)

Designer:	Unknown
Modeller:	Amanda Hughes-Lubeck
Height:	3 ½", 8.9 cm
Colour:	Light and dark brown hedgehog wearing a purple shirt and red cap
Issued:	1997 to the present
Series:	The Wildlife Hospital Trust

Doulton		Price		
Number	U.S. $	Can. $	U.K. £	Aust. $
TW2	—	—	13.95	—

TW3
FRED FOX™

Designer:	Unknown
Modeller:	Warren Platt
Height:	4", 10.1 cm
Colour:	Light brown fox wearing light blue overalls, pink shirt, white bandage around his head and tail
Issued:	1997 to the present
Series:	The Wildlife Hospital Trust

Royal Doulton
St. Tiggywinkles®
Fred Fox
TW3/ 1094
© St.Tiggywinkles 1996
Made in Thailand

Doulton		Price		
Number	U.S. $	Can. $	U.K. £	Aust. $
TW3	—	—	13.95	—

TW4
BOB BADGER™

Designer:	Unknown
Modeller:	Amanda Hughes-Lubeck
Height:	3 ¾", 9.5 cm
Colour:	Brown, black and white badger wearing a yellow jumper and brown scarf, beige crutch
Issued:	1997 to the present
Series:	The Wildlife Hospital Trust

Doulton Number	U.S. $	Price Can. $	U.K. £	Aust. $
TW4	—	—	13.95	—

TW5
ROSIE RABBIT™

Designer:	Unknown
Modeller:	Amanda Hughes-Lubeck
Height:	3 ½", 8.9 cm
Colour:	Grey rabbit wearing a light blue dress and rose pinafore
Issued:	1997 to the present
Series:	The Wildlife Hospital Trust

Doulton Number	U.S. $	Price Can. $	U.K. £	Aust. $
TW5	—	—	13.95	—

TW6
SARAH SQUIRREL™

Designer:	Unknown
Modeller:	Amanda Hughes-Lubeck
Height:	3 ¼", 8.3 cm
Colour:	Brown squirrel wearing a pink and white dress
Issued:	1997 to the present
Series:	The Wildlife Hospital Trust

Doulton Number	U.S. $	Price Can. $	U.K. £	Aust. $
TW6	—	—	13.95	—

TW7
DANIEL DUCK™

Designer:	Unknown
Modeller:	Shane Ridge
Height:	3 ½", 8.5 cm
Colour:	Yellow duck, white and red bandage, brown satchel
Issued:	1997 to the present
Series:	The Wildlife Hospital Trust

Doulton Number	Price			
	U.S. $	Can. $	U.K. £	Aust. $
TW7	—	—	13.95	—

TW8
OLIVER OWL™

Designer:	Unknown
Modeller:	Warren Platt
Height:	4", 10.1 cm
Colour:	Dark and light brown owl, white arm sling, red book
Issued:	1997 to the present
Series:	The Wildlife Hospital Trust

Doulton Number	Price			
	U.S. $	Can. $	U.K. £	Aust. $
TW8	—	—	13.95	—

TW9
FRIENDS™

Designer:	Unknown
Modeller:	Amanda Hughes-Lubeck
Height:	4", 10.1 cm
Colour:	Brown hedgehog with green and yellow jacket, red hat, yellow ducks with blue scarf, white bandages
Issued:	1997 to the present
Series	The Wildlife Hospital Trust

Royal Doulton
St. Tiggywinkles
Friends
TW9/ 1430
© St.Tiggywinkles 1996
Made in Thailand

Doulton Number	Price			
	U.S. $	Can. $	U.K. £	Aust. $
TW9	—	—	19.95	—

TW10
A HELPING HAND™

Designer:	Unknown
Modeller:	Amanda Hughes-Lubeck
Height:	4", 10.1 cm
Colour:	Light and dark brown hedgehogs, white and grey rabbits, blue, yellow, pink and red clothing
Issued:	1997 to the present
Series:	The Wildlife Hospital Trust

Doulton Number	U.S. $	Can. $	Price U.K. £	Aust. $
TW10	—	—	29.95	—

TW11
DEBORAH DORMOUSE

Designer:	Unknown
Modeller:	Rob Simpson
Height:	3 ¼", 8.3 cm
Colour:	Brown dormouse wearing a pink dress, white apron, carrying a brown basket
Issued:	1998 to the present
Series:	The Wildlife Hospital Trust

Doulton Number	U.S. $	Can. $	Price U.K. £	Aust. $
TW11	—	—	13.95	—

TW12
MONTY MOLE

Designer:	Unknown
Modeller:	Rob Simpson
Height:	3 ½", 8.5 cm
Colour:	Dark brown mole wearing a blue jacket, yellow hat, white arm sling
Issued:	1998 to the present
Series:	The Wildlife Hospital Trust

Doulton Number	U.S. $	Can. $	Price U.K. £	Aust. $
TW12	—	—	13.95	—

TW13
FRANCHESCA FAWN

Designer:	Unknown
Modeller:	Rob Simpson
Height:	3", 7.6 cm
Colour:	Pale brown fawn, white bandages
Issued:	1998 to the present
Series:	The Wildlife Hospital Trust

Doulton Number	Price			
	U.S. $	Can. $	U.K. £	Aust. $
TW13	—	—	13.95	—

THE SNOWMAN
GIFT COLLECTION

DS1
JAMES™

Designer:	Harry Sales
Modeller:	David Lyttleton
Height:	3 ¾", 9.5 cm
Colour:	Blue and white striped pyjamas, brown dressing gown
Issued:	1985 - 1993

Doulton Number	Price			
	U.S. $	Can. $	U.K. £	Aust. $
DS1	200.00	275.00	80.00	175.00

DS2
THE SNOWMAN™

Designer:	Harry Sales
Modeller:	David Lyttleton
Height:	5", 12.7 cm
Colour:	White snowman wearing a green hat and scarf
Issued:	1985 - 1994

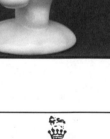

Doulton Number	Price			
	U.S. $	Can. $	U.K. £	Aust. $
DS2	140.00	200.00	50.00	150.00

DS3
STYLISH SNOWMAN™

Designer:	Harry Sales
Modeller:	David Lyttleton
Height:	5", 12.7 cm
Colour:	White snowman wearing blue trousers, lilac braces, grey hat, yellow tie with red stripes
Issued:	1985 - 1993

Doulton Number	Price			
	U.S. $	Can. $	U.K. £	Aust. $
DS3	350.00	450.00	145.00	200.00

DS4
THANK YOU SNOWMAN™

Designer:	Harry Sales
Modeller:	David Lyttleton
Height:	5", 12.7 cm
Colour:	Snowman - green hat and scarf
	James - brown dressing gown
Issued:	1985 - 1994

Doulton	Price			
Number	U.S. $	Can. $	U.K. £	Aust. $
DS4	200.00	225.00	70.00	185.00

DS5
SNOWMAN MAGIC MUSIC BOX™

Designer:	Harry Sales
Modeller:	David Lyttleton
Height:	8", 20.3 cm
Colour:	White snowman wearing a green hat and scarf, cream music box with blue, green and pink balloon design
Issued:	1985 - 1994
Tune:	Walking in the Air

Doulton		Price		
Number	U.S. $	Can. $	U.K. £	Aust. $
DS5	400.00	475.00	110.00	250.00

DS6
COWBOY SNOWMAN™

Designer:	Harry Sales
Modeller:	David Lyttleton
Height:	5", 12.7 cm
Colour:	White snowman wearing a brown hat and holster belt
Issued:	1986 - 1992

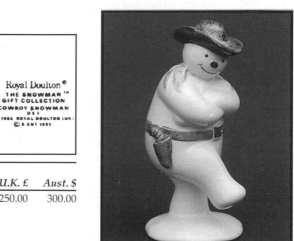

Doulton	Price			
Number	U.S. $	Can. $	U.K. £	Aust. $
DS6	500.00	525.00	250.00	300.00

DS7
HIGHLAND SNOWMAN™

Designer:	Harry Sales
Modeller:	David Lyttleton
Height:	5 ¼", 13.3 cm
Colour:	White snowman wearing a red, blue and white kilt
Issued:	1987 - 1993

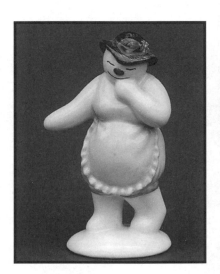

Royal Doulton®
THE SNOWMAN™
GIFT COLLECTION
HIGHLAND SNOWMAN
DS7
© 1985 ROYAL DOULTON (UK)
© S ENT 1985

Doulton Number	Price			
	U.S. $	Can. $	U.K. £	Aust. $
DS7	325.00	400.00	150.00	225.00

DS8
LADY SNOWMAN™

Designer:	Harry Sales
Modeller:	David Lyttleton
Height:	5", 12.7 cm
Colour:	White snowman wearing a pink apron and blue hat
Issued:	1987 - 1992

Royal Doulton®
THE SNOWMAN™
GIFT COLLECTION
LADY SNOWMAN
DS8
© 1985 ROYAL DOULTON (UK)
© S ENT 1985

Doulton Number	Price			
	U.S. $	Can. $	U.K. £	Aust. $
DS8	500.00	575.00	225.00	300.00

DS9
BASS DRUMMER SNOWMAN™

Designer:	Graham Tongue
Modeller:	Warren Platt
Height:	5 ¼", 13.3 cm
Colour:	White snowman with pale blue hat; pink and yellow drum, pale brown straps
Issued:	1987 - 1993

Royal Doulton®
THE SNOWMAN™
GIFT COLLECTION
BASS DRUMMER SNOWMAN
DS9
© 1987 ROYAL DOULTON
© S ENT 1987

Doulton Number	Price			
	U.S. $	Can. $	U.K. £	Aust. $
DS9	450.00	500.00	150.00	300.00

DS10
FLAUTIST SNOWMAN™

Designer:	Graham Tongue
Modeller:	Warren Platt
Height:	5 ½", 14.0 cm
Colour:	White snowman wearing a yellow and red cap and a brown tie
Issued:	1987 - 1993

Doulton Number	Price U.S. $	Can. $	U.K. £	Aust. $
DS10	275.00	325.00	150.00	300.00

DS11
VIOLINIST SNOWMAN™

Designer:	Graham Tongue
Modeller:	Warren Platt
Height:	5 ¼", 13.3 cm
Colour:	White snowman wearing a green waistcoat with yellow collar, blue bowtie, brown cap, playing a violin
Issued:	1987 - 1994

Doulton Number	Price U.S. $	Can. $	U.K. £	Aust. $
DS11	125.00	200.00	60.00	175.00

DS12
PIANIST SNOWMAN™

Designer:	Graham Tongue
Modeller:	Warren Platt
Height:	5", 12.7 cm
Colour:	White snowman wearing a blue crown and orange tie
Issued:	1987 - 1994

Doulton Number	Price U.S. $	Can. $	U.K. £	Aust. $
DS12	150.00	200.00	60.00	190.00

DS13
SNOWMAN'S PIANO™

Designer:	Graham Tongue
Modeller:	Warren Platt
Height:	5¼", 13.3 cm
Colour:	White piano
Issued:	1987 - 1994

Doulton	*Price*			
Number	*U.S. $*	*Can. $*	*U.K. £*	*Aust. $*
DS13	100.00	200.00	35.00	115.00

DS14
CYMBAL PLAYER SNOWMAN™

Designer:	Graham Tongue
Modeller:	Warren Platt
Height:	5 ¼", 13.3 cm
Colour:	White snowman wearing a brown waistcoat, green cap and bowtie, playing yellow cymbals
Issued:	1988 - 1993

Doulton	*Price*			
Number	*U.S. $*	*Can. $*	*U.K. £*	*Aust. $*
DS14	325.00	400.00	150.00	170.00

DS15
DRUMMER SNOWMAN™

Designer:	Graham Tongue
Modeller:	Warren Platt
Height:	5 ¾", 14.6 cm
Colour:	White snowman wearing a red and black hat, purple bowtie, playing pink and yellow drum
Issued:	1988 - 1994

Doulton	*Price*			
Number	*U.S. $*	*Can. $*	*U.K. £*	*Aust. $*
DS15	200.00	200.00	50.00	170.00

DS16
TRUMPETER SNOWMAN™

Designer:	Graham Tongue
Modeller:	Warren Platt
Height:	5", 12.7 cm
Colour:	White snowman wearing a pink hat playing a yellow trumpet
Issued:	1988 - 1993

Royal Doulton ®
THE SNOWMAN ™
GIFT COLLECTION
UMPETER SNOWMAN
DS 16
1988 ROYAL DOULTON
© S ENT 1988

Doulton Number	Price			
	U.S. $	Can. $	U.K. £	Aust. $
DS16	300.00	350.00	145.00	190.00

DS17
CELLIST SNOWMAN™

Designer:	Graham Tongue
Modeller:	Warren Platt
Height:	5 ¼", 13.3 cm
Colour:	White snowman wearing a green waistcoat with yellow collar, blue bowtie, playing a brown cello
Issued:	1988 - 1993

Royal Doulton ®
THE SNOWMAN ™
GIFT COLLECTION
CELLIST SNOWMAN
DS 17
© 1988 ROYAL DOULTON
© S ENT 1988

Doulton Number	Price			
	U.S. $	Can. $	U.K. £	Aust. $
DS17	175.00	200.00	60.00	150.00

DS18
SNOWMAN MUSICAL BOX™

Designer:	Unknown
Height:	8", 22.5 cm
Colour:	White snowman wearing a red, blue and white kilt; green, pink and blue balloons on box
Issued:	1988 - 1990
Tune:	Blue Bells of Scotland

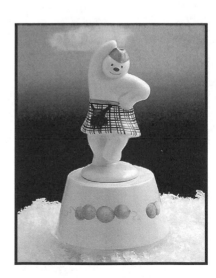

Doulton Numbers	Price			
	U.S. $	Can. $	U.K. £	Aust. $
DS18	300.00	400.00	150.00	300.00

DS19
SNOWMAN MONEY BOX™

Designer:	Graham Tongue
Modeller:	Warren Platt
Height:	8 ½", 21.6 cm
Colour:	White snowman wearing a green hat with grey band and green scarf
Issued:	1990 - 1994

Doulton		Price		
Number	U.S. $	Can. $	U.K. £	Aust. $
DS19	300.00	325.00	100.00	250.00

DS20
THE SNOWMAN TOBOGGANING™

Designer:	Graham Tongue
Modeller:	Warren Platt
Height:	5", 12.7 cm
Colour:	White snowman wearing a green hat and scarf, rose-pink toboggan
Issued:	1990 - 1994

Doulton		Price		
Number	U.S. $	Can. $	U.K. £	Aust. $
DS20	225.00	300.00	50.00	250.00

Royal Doulton ®
THE SNOWMAN ™
GIFT COLLECTION
THE SNOWMAN
TOBOGGANING
DS 20
© 1990 ROYAL DOULTON
© S. ENT 1990

DS21
THE SNOWMAN SKIING™

Designer:	Graham Tongue
Modeller:	Warren Platt
Height:	5", 12.7 cm
Colour:	White snowman wearing a green hat and scarf, yellow and black goggles
Issued:	1990 - 1992

Royal Doulton ®
THE SNOWMAN ™
GIFT COLLECTION
THE SNOWMAN
SKIING
DS 21
© 1990 ROYAL DOULTON
© S. ENT 1990

Doulton		Price		
Number	U.S. $	Can. $	U.K. £	Aust. $
DS21	1,500.00	1,500.00	650.00	525.00

DS22
THE SNOWBALLING SNOWMAN™

Designer:	Graham Tongue
Modeller:	Warren Platt
Height:	5", 12.7 cm
Colour:	White snowman wearing a green hat and scarf, brown tree stump
Issued:	1990 - 1994

Doulton Number	Price			
	U.S. $	Can. $	U.K. £	Aust. $
DS22	150.00	225.00	60.00	200.00

DS23
BUILDING THE SNOWMAN™

Designer:	Graham Tongue
Modeller:	Warren Platt
Height:	4", 10.1 cm
Colour:	White snowman wearing a green hat and scarf
Issued:	1990 - 1994

Doulton Number	Price			
	U.S. $	Can. $	U.K. £	Aust. $
DS23	175.00	250.00	60.00	150.00

D6972
SNOWMAN MINIATURE CHARACTER JUG™

Designer:	Graham Tongue
Modeller:	Martyn Alcock
Height:	2 ¾", 7.0 cm
Colour:	White snowman wearing a black hat, green scarf forms the handle
Issued:	1994 - 1994

Doulton Number	Price			
	U.S. $	Can. $	U.K. £	Aust. $
D6972	160.00	200.00	75.00	200.00

THUNDERBIRDS

3337
LADY PENELOPE™

Designer:	William K. Harper
Height:	4", 10.1 cm
Colour:	Pink hat and coat, blonde hair
Issued:	1992 in a limited edition of 2,500

Beswick Number		Price U.S. $	Can. $	U.K. £	Aust. $
3337	(For complete set)	950.00	1,500.00	500.00	1,200.00

3339
BRAINS™

Designer:	William K. Harper
Height:	4", 10.1 cm
Colour:	Black and blue uniform, blue glasses, black hair
Issued:	1992 in a limited edition of 2,500

Beswick Number		Price U.S. $	Can. $	U.K. £	Aust. $
3339	(For complete set)	950.00	1,500.00	500.00	1,200.00

3344
SCOTT TRACY™

Designer:	William K. Harper
Height:	4", 10.1 cm
Colour:	Blue uniform, light blue band
Issued:	1992 in a limited edition of 2,500

Beswick Number		Price U.S. $	Can. $	U.K. £	Aust. $
3344	(For complete set)	950.00	1,500.00	500.00	1,200.00

3345
VIRGIL TRACY™

Designer: William K. Harper
Height: 4", 10.1 cm
Colour: Blue uniform, yellow band
Issued: 1992 in a limited edition of 2,500

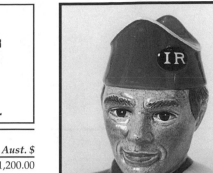

Beswick Number		Price			
		U.S. $	Can. $	U.K. £	Aust. $
3345	(For complete set)	950.00	1,500.00	500.00	1,200.00

3346
PARKER™

Designer: William K. Harper
Height: 4", 10.1 cm
Colour: Blue-grey uniform
Issued: 1992 in a limited edition of 2,500

Beswick Number		Price			
		U.S. $	Can. $	U.K. £	Aust. $
3346	(For complete set)	950.00	1,500.00	500.00	1,200.00

3348
THE HOOD™

Designer: William K. Harper
Height: 4", 10.1 cm
Colour: Browns
Issued: 1992 in a limited edition of 2,500

Beswick Number		Price			
		U.S. $	Can. $	U.K. £	Aust. $
3348	(For complete set)	950.00	1,500.00	500.00	1,200.00

TURNER ENTERTAINMENT

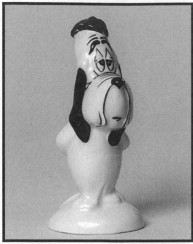

3547
DROOPY™

Designer:	Simon Ward
Height:	4 ½", 11.4 cm
Colour:	White dog with black ears, red cap
Issued:	1995 in a special edition of 2,000

Beswick Number	Price U.S. $	Can. $	U.K. £	Aust. $
3547	100.00	150.00	65.00	100.00

3549
JERRY™

Designer:	Simon Ward
Height:	3", 7.6 cm
Colour:	Red-brown and cream mouse, white base
Issued:	1995 in special edition of 2,000

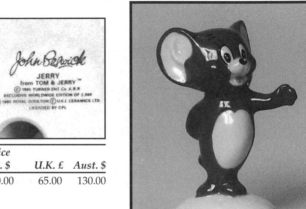

Beswick Number	Price U.S. $	Can. $	U.K. £	Aust. $
3549	100.00	150.00	65.00	130.00

3552
TOM™

Designer:	Simon Ward
Height:	4 ½", 11.4 cm
Colour:	Grey-blue and pink cat, white base
Issued:	1995 in a special edition of 2,000

Beswick Number	Price U.S. $	Can. $	U.K. £	Aust. $
3552	75.00	100.00	40.00	130.00

WALT DISNEY

101 DALMATIANS

1997 to the present

DM1
CRUELLA de VIL™
Style One

Designer: Martyn Alcock
Height: 6 ¼", 15.9 cm
Colour: Black dress, pale yellow coat with
             red lining and gloves
Issued: 1997 to the present
Series: 101 Dalmatians Collection

Doulton Number	Price U.S. $	Can. $	U.K. £	Aust. $
DM1	—	—	80.00	—

DM2
PENNY™

Designer: Unknown
Modeller: Shane Ridge
Height: 2 ¾", 7.0 cm
Colour: White and black dalmatian,
             red collar
Issued: 1997 to the present
Series: 101 Dalmatians Collection

Doulton Number	Price U.S. $	Can. $	U.K. £	Aust. $
DM2	—	—	18.00	—

DM3
PENNY AND FRECKLES™

Designer: Unknown
Modeller: Martyn Alcock
Height: 2 ¼", 5.5 cm
Colour: Two white and black
             dalmatians with red collars
Issued: 1997 to the presemt
Series: 101 Dalmatians Collections

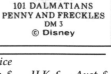

Doulton Number	Price U.S. $	Can. $	U.K. £	Aust. $
DM3	—	—	22.50	—

DM4
ROLLY™

Designer:	Unknown
Modeller:	Shane Ridge
Height:	2 ¾", 7.0 cm
Colour:	White and black dalmatian, red collar, black base
Issued:	1997 to the present
Series:	101 Dalmatians Collections

Doulton			*Price*	
Number	*U.S. $*	*Can. $*	*UK. £*	*Aust. $*
DM4	—	—	18.00	—

DM5
PATCH, ROLLY AND FRECKLES™

Designer:	Unknown
Modeller:	Shane Ridge
Height:	3 ¾", 9.5 cm
Length:	7 ½", 19 cm
Colour:	Three white and black dalmatians with red collars
Issued:	1997 in a limited edition of 3,500
Series:	101 Dalmatians Collection

Doulton			*Price*	
Number	*U.S. $*	*Can. $*	*U.K. £*	*Aust. $*
DM5	600.00	900.00	375.00	900.00

DM6
PONGO™

Designer:	Unknown
Modeller:	Martyn Alcock
Height:	4 ½", 11.9 cm
Colour:	White and black dalmatian, red collar
Issued:	1997 to the present
Series:	101 Dalmatians Collection

Doulton			*Price*	
Number	*U.S. $*	*Can. $*	*U.K. £*	*Aust. $*
DM6	—	—	25.00	—

DM7
PERDITA™

Designer:	Unknown
Modeller:	Martyn Alcock
Height:	2 ½", 6.4 cm
Colour:	White and black dalmatian dark turquoise collar and blanket
Issued:	1997 to the present
Series:	101 Dalmatians Collections

Hand made and hand decorated
Royal Doulton®
DISNEY'S
101 DALMATIANS
PERDITA
DM 7
© Disney

Doulton	Price			
Number	U.S. $	Can. $	U.K. £	Aust. $
DM7	—	—	22.50	—

DM8
LUCKY™

Designer:	Unknown
Modeller:	Martyn Alcock
Height:	2 ¾", 7.0 cm
Colour:	White and black dalmatian, red collar
Issued:	1997 to the present
Series:	101 Dalmatians Collections

Hand made and hand decorated
Royal Doulton
DISNEY'S
101 DALMATIANS
LUCKY DM 8
© Disney

Doulton	Price			
Number	U.S. $	Can. $	U.K. £	Aust. $
DM8	—	—	18.00	—

DISNEY CHARACTERS

1952-1965

1278
MICKEY MOUSE™

Designer:	Jan Granoska
Height:	4", 10.1 cm
Colour:	Black, white and red
Issued:	1952 - 1965

Back Stamp	Beswick Number	Price			
		U.S. $	*Can. $*	*U.K.£*	*Aust. $*
Beswick Gold	1278	650.00	825.00	425.00	400.00

1279
JIMINY CRICKET™

Designer:	Jan Granoska
Height:	4", 10.1 cm
Colour:	Black, white, beige and blue
Issued:	1952 - 1965

Back Stamp	Beswick Number	Price			
		U.S. $	*Can. $*	*U.K. £*	*Aust. $*
Beswick Gold	1279	625.00	775.00	375.00	400.00

1280
PLUTO™

Designer:	Jan Granoska
Height:	3 ½", 8.9 cm
Colour:	Brown dog with red collar
Issued:	1953 - 1965

Back Stamp	Beswick Number	Price			
		U.S. $	*Can. $*	*U.K. £*	*Aust. $*
Beswick Gold	1280	625.00	775.00	375.00	350.00

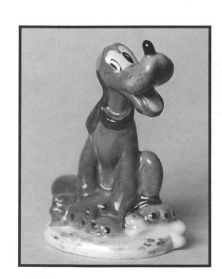

1281
GOOFY™

Designer:	Jan Granoska
Height:	4 ¼", 10.8 cm
Colour:	Red jersey, blue trousers, black suspenders, white gloves, brown and black hat, brown boots
Issued:	1953 - 1965

Back Stamp	Beswick Number	Price U.S. $	Can. $	U.K. £	Aust. $
Beswick Gold	1281	625.00	775.00	375.00	350.00

1282
PINOCCHIO™

Designer:	Jan Granoska
Height:	4", 10.1 cm
Colour:	White and yellow jacket, red trousers, blue bowtie and shoes, brown cap
Issued:	1953 - 1965

Back Stamp	Beswick Number	Price U.S. $	Can. $	U.K. £	Aust. $
Beswick Gold	1282	675.00	875.00	450.00	450.00

1283
DONALD DUCK™

Designer:	Jan Granoska
Height:	4", 10.1 cm
Colour:	White duck, blue sailors jacket, red bow, blue and black hat
Issued:	1953 - 1965

Back Stamp	Beswick Number	Price U.S. $	Can. $	U.K. £	Aust. $
Beswick Gold	1283	650.00	875.00	425.00	450.00

1289
MINNIE MOUSE™

Designer:	Jan Granoska
Height:	4", 10.1 cm
Colour:	Black and white mouse wearing a yellow top and red skirt with white spots, white gloves and hair bow, brown shoes
Issued:	1953 - 1965

Back Stamp	Beswick Number	Price U.S. $	Can. $	U.K. £	Aust. $
Beswick Gold	1289	650.00	800.00	425.00	425.00

1291
THUMPER™

Designer:	Jan Granoska
Height:	3 ¾", 9.5 cm
Colour:	Grey and white rabbit, yellow, red and pink flowers on brown base
Issued:	1953 - 1965

Back Stamp	Beswick Number	Price U.S. $	Can. $	U.K. £	Aust. $
Beswick Gold	1291	625.00	775.00	400.00	550.00

PETER PAN

1953-1965

1301
NANA™

Designer:	Jan Granoska
Height:	3 ¼", 8.3 cm
Colour:	Brown dog, white frilled cap with blue ribbon
Issued:	1953 - 1965
Series:	Peter Pan

Back Stamp	Beswick Number	Price U.S. $	Can. $	U.K. £	Aust. $
Beswick Gold	1301	575.00	700.00	425.00	350.00

1302
SMEE™

Designer:	Jan Granoska
Height:	4 ¼", 10.8 cm
Colour:	Blue and white shirt, blue pants, red cap, green bottle
Issued:	1953 - 1965
Series:	Peter Pan

Back Stamp	Beswick Number	Price U.S. $	Can. $	U.K. £	Aust. $
Beswick Gold	1302	600.00	750.00	250.00	350.00

1307
PETER PAN™

Designer:	Jan Granoska
Height:	5", 12.7 cm
Colour:	Light green tunic, dark green pants, brown shoes, red and green cap
Issued:	1953 - 1965
Series:	Peter Pan

Back Stamp	Beswick Number	Price			
		U.S. $	Can. $	U.K. £	Aust. $
Beswick Gold	1307	750.00	900.00	425.00	500.00

1312
TINKER BELL™

Designer:	Jan Granoska
Height:	5", 12.7 cm
Colour:	Light green dress, dark green wings and shoes
Issued:	1953 - 1965
Series:	Peter Pan

Back Stamp	Beswick Number	Price			
		U.S. $	Can. $	U.K. £	Aust. $
Beswick Gold	1312			Rare	

THE DISNEY PRINCESS COLLECTION

1995-1996

HN 3677
CINDERELLA™

Designer:	Pauline Parsons
Height:	8", 20.3 cm
Colour:	Blue and white dress, yellow hair
Issued:	1995 in a limited edition of 2,000
Series:	The Disney Princess Collection

Back Stamp	Doulton Number	U.S. $	Price Can. $	U.K.£	Aust. $
Doulton	HN 3677	650.00	850.00	225.00	500.00

HN 3678
SNOW WHITE™
Style Two

Designer:	Pauline Parsons
Height:	8 ¼", 21.0 cm
Colour:	Yellow, blue and white dress, royal blue and red cape, black hair
Issued:	1995 in a limited edition of 2,000
Series:	The Disney Princess Collection

Back Stamp	Doulton Number	U.S. $	Price Can. $	U.K. £	Aust. $
Doulton	HN 3678	750.00	1,250.00	250.00	550.00

HN 3830
BELLE™

Designer:	Pauline Parsons
Height:	8", 20.3 cm
Colour:	Yellow dress and gloves, brown hair
Issued:	1996 in a limited edition of 2,000
Series:	The Disney Princess Collection

Back Stamp	Doulton Number	U.S. $	Price Can. $	U.K. £	Aust. $
Doulton	HN3830	650.00	850.00	200.00	400.00

HN 3831
ARIEL™

Designer:	Pauline Parsons
Height:	8 ¼", 21.0 cm
Colour:	White dress and veil, red hair
Issued:	1996 in a limited edition of 2,000
Series:	The Disney Princess Collection

Back Stamp	Doulton Number	Price U.S. $	Can. $	U.K. £	Aust. $
Doulton	HN 3831	650.00	750.00	200.00	400.00

HN3832
JASMINE™

Designer:	Pauline Parsons
Height:	7 ½", 19.1 cm
Colour:	Lilac dress
Issued:	1996 in a limited edition of 2,000
Series:	The Disney Princess Collection

Back Stamp	Doulton Number	Price U.S. $	Can. $	U.K. £	Aust. $
Doulton	HN 3832	600.00	750.00	175.00	350.00

HN3833
AURORA™

Designer:	Pauline Parsons
Height:	7 ½", 19.1 cm
Colour:	Light and dark blue dress with white trim
Issued:	1996 in a limited edition of 2,000
Series:	The Disney Princess Collection

Back Stamp	Doulton Number	Price U.S. $	Can. $	U.K. £	Aust. $
Doulton	HN 3833	600.00	750.00	175.00	350.00

DISNEY VILLAINS COLLECTIONS

1997 to the present

Photograph not
available
at press time

HN3839
CRUELLA de VIL™
Style Two

Designer:	Pauline Parsons
Height:	8", 20.3 cm
Colour:	Black dress, white fur coat, red gloves
Issued:	1997 in a limited edition of 2,000
Series:	The Disney Villains Collection

Back Stamp	Doulton Number	U.S. $	Can. $	U.K. £	Aust. $
Doulton	HN 3839	—	—	150.00	—

HN3840
MALEFICENT™

Designer:	Pauline Parsons
Height:	8", 20.3 cm
Colour:	Black and purple
Issued:	1997 in a limited edition of 2,000
Series:	The Disney Villains Collection

Back Stamp	Doulton Number	U.S. $	Can. $	U.K. £	Aust. $
Doulton	HN 3840	—	—	150.00	—

SNOW WHITE AND THE SEVEN DWARFS

FIRST SERIES 1954-1967

1325
DOPEY™
Style One

Designer:	Arthur Gredington
Height:	3 ½", 8.9 cm
Colour:	Green coat, maroon cap, grey shoes
Issued:	1954 - 1967
Series:	Snow White and the Seven Dwarfs (Style One)

Back Stamp	Beswick Number	Price			
		U.S. $	Can. $	U.K. £	Aust. $
Beswick Gold	1325	425.00	550.00	175.00	350.00

1326
HAPPY™
Style One

Designer:	Arthur Gredington
Height:	3 ½", 8.9 cm
Colour:	Purple tunic, light blue trousers, light brown cap, brown shoes
Issued:	1954 - 1967
Series:	Snow White and the Seven Dwarfs (Style One)

Back Stamp	Beswick Number	Price			
		U.S. $	Can. $	U.K. £	Aust. $
Beswick Gold	1326	425.00	550.00	175.00	350.00

1327
BASHFUL™
Style One

Designer:	Arthur Gredington
Height:	3 ½", 8.9 cm
Colour:	Brown tunic, purple trousers, grey cap, brown shoes
Issued:	1954 - 1967
Series:	Snow White and the Seven Dwarfs (Style One)

Back Stamp	Beswick Number	Price			
		U.S. $	Can. $	U.K. £	Aust. $
Beswick Gold	1327	425.00	550.00	175.00	350.00

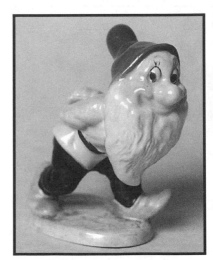

1328
SNEEZY™
Style One

Designer:	Arthur Gredington
Height:	3 ½", 8.9 cm
Colour:	Green tunic, purple trousers, brown cap and shoes
Issued:	1954 - 1967
Series:	Snow White and the Seven Dwarfs (Style One)

Back Stamp	*Beswick Number*	*U.S. $*	*Price Can. $*	*U.K. £*	*Aust. $*
Beswick Gold	1328	425.00	550.00	175.00	350.00

1329
DOC™
Style One

Designer:	Arthur Gredington
Height:	3 ½", 8.9 cm
Colour:	Brown tunic, blue trousers, yellow cap, brown shoes
Issued:	1954 - 1967
Series:	Snow White and the Seven Dwarfs (Style One)

Back Stamp	*Beswick Number*	*U.S. $*	*Price Can. $*	*U.K. £*	*Aust. $*
Beswick Gold	1329	425.00	550.00	200.00	400.00

1330
GRUMPY™
Style One

Designer:	Arthur Gredington
Height:	3 ¾", 9.5 cm
Colour:	Purple tunic, red trousers, blue cap, brown shoes
Issued:	1954 - 1967
Series:	Snow White and the Seven Dwarfs (Style One)

Back Stamp	*Beswick Number*	*U.S. $*	*Price Can. $*	*U.K. £*	*Aust. $*
Beswick Gold	1330	425.00	550.00	175.00	300.00

1331
SLEEPY™
Style One

Designer:	Arthur Gredington
Height:	3 ½", 8.9 cm
Colour:	Tan tunic, red trousers, green hat, grey shoes
Issued:	1954 - 1967
Series:	Snow White and the Seven Dwarfs (Style One)

Sleepy
COPYRIGHT
WALT DISNEY LTD
BESWICK
ENGLAND

Back Stamp	Beswick Number	U.S. $	Price Can. $	U.K. £	Aust. $
Beswick Gold	1331	425.00	550.00	175.00	375.00

1332A
SNOW WHITE™
Style One
First Version (Hair in Flounces)

Designer:	Arthur Gredington
Height:	5 ½", 14.0 cm
Colour:	Yellow and purple dress, red cape, white collar
Issued:	1954 - 1955

Back Stamp	Beswick Number	U.S. $	Price Can. $	U.K. £	Aust. $
Beswick Gold	1332A		Very rare		

1332B
SNOW WHITE™
Style One
Second Version (Hair Flat to Head)

Designer:	Arthur Gredington
Height:	5 ½", 14.0 cm
Colour:	Yellow and purple dress, red cape, white collar
Issued:	1955 - 1967
Series:	Snow White and the Seven Dwarfs (Style One)

Snowhite
COPYRIGHT
WALT DISNEY LTD
BESWICK
ENGLAND

Back Stamp	Beswick Number	U.S. $	Price Can. $	U.K. £	Aust. $
Beswick Gold	1332B	800.00	975.00	400.00	550.00

SNOW WHITE AND THE SEVEN DWARFS

SECOND SERIES 1997 to the present

SW1/SW9
SNOW WHITE
Style Three

Designer:	Amanda Hughes-Lubeck
Height:	5 ¾", 14.6 cm
Colour:	Yellow and blue dress, red cape, white collar
Issued:	SW1 1997 in a limited edition of 2,000
	SW9 1998 to the present
Series:	Snow White and the Seven Dwarfs (Style Two)

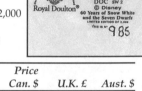

Back Stamp	Beswick Number	Price U.S. $	Can. $	U.K. £	Aust. $
Doulton/Disney 60th	SW1	300.00	450.00	150.00	450.00
Doulton/Disney	SW9	—	—	80.00	—

SW2/SW10
DOC
Style Two

Designer:	Amanda Hughes-Lubeck
Height:	3 ¼", 8.3 cm
Colour:	Red jacket, brown trousers, yellow hat, green book
Issued:	SW2 1997 in a limited edition of 2,000
	SW10 1998 to the present
Series:	Snow White and the Seven Dwarfs (Style Two)

Back Stamp	Beswick Number	Price U.S. $	Can. $	U.K. £	Aust. $
Doulton/Disney 60th	SW2	200.00	300.00	100.00	200.00
Doulton/Disney	SW10	—	—	22.50	—

SW3/SW11
GRUMPY
Style Two

Designer:	Shane Ridge
Height:	3 ½", 8.9 cm
Colour:	Dark rust coat and trousers, brown hat, light brown basket
Issued:	SW3 1997 in a limited edition of 2,000
	SW11 1998 to the present
Series:	Snow White and the Seven Dwarfs (Style Two)

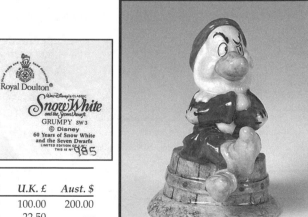

Back Stamp	Beswick Number	Price U.S. $	Can. $	U.K. £	Aust. $
Doulton/Disney 60th	SW3	200.00	300.00	100.00	200.00
Doulton/Disney	SW11	—	—	22.50	—

SW4/SW12
HAPPY
Style Two

Designer:	Amanda Hughes-Lubeck
Height:	3 ½", 8.9 cm
Colour:	Brown vest, orange shirt, light blue trousers with black belt and a yellow hat
Issued:	SW4 1997 in a limited edition of 2,000
	SW12 1998 to the present
Series:	Snow White and the Seven Dwarfs (Style Two)

Back Stamp	Beswick Number	Price			
		U.S. $	Can. $	U.K. £	Aust. $
Doulton/Disney 60th	SW4	200.00	300.00	100.00	300.00
Doulton/Disney	SW12	—	—	22.50	—

SW5/SW13
DOPEY
Style Two

Designer:	Shane Ridge
Height:	3 ½", 8.9 cm
Colour:	Yellow shirt and trousers, purple hat, black belt
Issued:	SW5 1997 in a limited edition of 2,000
	SW13 1998 to the present
Series:	Snow White and the Seven Dwarfs (Style Two)

Back Stamp	Beswick Number	Price			
		U.S. $	Can. $	U.K. £	Aust. $
Doulton/Disney 60th	SW5	200.00	300.00	100.00	300.00
Doulton/Disney	SW13	—	—	22.50	—

SW6/SW14
SNEEZY
Style Two

Designer:	Warren Platt
Height:	3 ½", 8.9 cm
Colour:	Light brown jacket, dark brown trousers, black belt
Issued:	SW6 1997 in a limited edition of 2,000
	SW14 1998 to the present
Series:	Snow White and the Seven Dwarfs (Style Two)

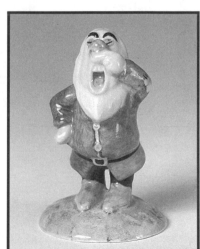

Back Stamp	Beswick Number	Price			
		U.S. $	Can. $	U.K. £	Aust. $
Doulton/Disney 60th	SW6	200.00	300.00	100.00	300.00
Doulton/Disney	SW14	—	—	22.50	—

SW7/SW15
SLEEPY
Style Two

Deisgner:	Warren Platt
Height:	3 ½", 8.9 cm
Colour:	Beige jacket, dark brown trousers, green hat and a yellow bottle
Issued:	SW7 1997 in a limited edition of 2,000
	SW15 1998 to the present
Series:	Snow White and the Seven Dwarfs (Style Two)

Back Stamp	Beswick Number	Price U.S. $	Can. $	U.K. £	Aust. $
Doulton/Disney 60th	SW7	200.00	300.00	100.00	300.00
Doulton/Disney	SW15	—	—	22.50	—

SW8/SW16
BASHFUL
Style Two

Designer:	Amanda Hughes-Lubeck
Height:	3 ½", 8.9 cm
Colour:	Dark yellow jacket, light brown trousers, green hat
Issued:	SW8 1997 in a limited edition of 2,000
	SW16 1998 to the present
Series:	Snow White and the Seven Dwarfs (Style Two)

Back Stamp	Beswick Number	Price U.S. $	Can. $	U.K. £	Aust. $
Doulton/Disney 60th	SW8	200.00	300.00	100.00	200.00
Doulton/Disney	SW16	—	—	22.50	—

WINNIE THE POOH

FIRST SERIES 1968-1990

2193
WINNIE THE POOH™

Designer:	Albert Hallam
Height:	2 ½", 6.4 cm
Colour:	Golden brown and red
Issued:	1968 - 1990
Series:	Winnie The Pooh

Back Stamp	Beswick Number	Price U.S. $	Can. $	U.K. £	Aust. $
Beswick Gold	2193	250.00	350.00	175.00	225.00
Beswick Brown	2193	225.00	300.00	85.00	225.00

2196
EEYORE™

Designer:	Albert Hallam
Height:	2" 5.0 cm
Colour:	Grey with black markings
Issued:	1968 - 1990
Series:	Winnie The Pooh

Back Stamp	Beswick Number	Price U.S. $	Can. $	U.K. £	Aust. $
Beswick Gold	2196	250.00	350.00	115.00	140.00
Beswick Brown	2196	225.00	300.00	85.00	140.00

2214
PIGLET™

Designer:	Albert Hallam
Height:	2 ¾", 7.0 cm
Colour:	Pink and red
Issued:	1968 - 1990
Series:	Winnie The Pooh

Back Stamp	Beswick Number	Price U.S. $	Can. $	U.K. £	Aust. $
Beswick Gold	2214	250.00	325.00	115.00	175.00
Beswick Brown	2214	225.00	300.00	85.00	175.00

2215
RABBIT™

Designer:	Albert Hallam
Height:	3 ¼", 8.3 cm
Colour:	Brown and beige
Issued:	1968 - 1990
Series:	Winnie The Pooh

Back Stamp	Beswick Number	Price U.S. $	Can. $	U.K. £	Aust. $
Beswick Gold	2215	275.00	350.00	115.00	200.00
Beswick Brown	2215	250.00	300.00	85.00	200.00

2216
OWL™

Designer:	Albert Hallam
Height:	3", 7.6 cm
Colour:	Brown, white and black
Issued:	1968 - 1990
Series:	Winnie The Pooh

Back Stamp	Beswick Number	Price U.S. $	Can. $	U.K. £	Aust. $
Beswick Gold	2216	175.00	225.00	110.00	150.00
Beswick Brown	2216	150.00	200.00	80.00	150.00

2217
KANGA™

Designer:	Albert Hallam
Height:	3 ¼", 8.3 cm
Colour:	Dark and light brown
Issued:	1968 - 1990
Series:	Winnie The Pooh

Back Stamp	Beswick Number	Price U.S. $	Can. $	U.K. £	Aust. $
Beswick Gold	2217	250.00	325.00	115.00	150.00
Beswick Brown	2217	225.00	300.00	85.00	150.00

2394
TIGGER™

Designer:	Graham Tongue
Height:	3", 7.6 cm
Colour:	Yellow with black stripes
Issued:	1971 - 1990
Series:	Winnie The Pooh

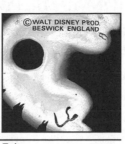

Back Stamp	Beswick Number	Price			
		U.S. $	Can. $	U.K. £	Aust. $
Beswick Gold	2394	300.00	400.00	160.00	300.00
Beswick Brown	2394	275.00	350.00	125.00	300.00

2395
CHRISTOPHER ROBIN™
Style One

Designer:	Graham Tongue
Height:	4 ¾", 12.1 cm
Colour:	Yellow, blue and white
Issued:	1971 - 1990
Series:	Winnie The Pooh

Back Stamp	Beswick Number	Price			
		U.S. $	Can. $	U.K. £	Aust. $
Beswick Gold	2395	400.00	500.00	200.00	400.00
Beswick Brown	2395	375.00	475.00	175.00	400.00

WINNIE THE POOH

SECOND SERIES 1996 to the present

WP1
WINNIE THE POOH AND THE HONEY POT™

Designer:	Warren Platt	
Height:	2 ½", 6.5 cm	
Colour:	Yellow bear, red jersey, red-brown honey pot	
Issued:	1996 to the present	
Series:	Winnie the Pooh and Friends from the One Hundred Acre Wood	

Back Stamp	Doulton Number	U.S. $	Price Can. $	U.K. £	Aust. $
BK-1	WP1	150.00	200.00	70.00	200.00
BK-2	WP1	—	70.00	22.50	79.00

WP2
POOH AND PIGLET THE WINDY DAY™

Designer:	Martyn Alcock
Height:	3 ¼", 8 cm
Colour:	Yellow bear, pink piglet with green suit, light brown base
Issued:	1996 to the present
Series:	Winnie the Pooh and Friends from the One Hundred Acre Wood

Back Stamp	Doulton Number	U.S. $	Price Can. $	U.K. £	Aust. $
BK-1	WP2	75.00	100.00	45.00	100.00
BK-2	WP2	—	75.00	30.00	79.00

WP3
WINNIE THE POOH AND THE PAW-MARKS™

Designer:	Warren Platt
Height:	2 ¾", 7.0 cm
Colour:	Yellow bear, red jersey
Issued:	1996 - 1997
Series:	Winnie the Pooh and Friends from the One Hundred Acre Wood

Back Stamp	Doulton Number	U.S. $	Price Can. $	U.K. £	Aust. $
BK-1	WP3	100.00	125.00	55.00	125.00
BK-2	WP3	75.00	90.00	40.00	90.00

WP4
WINNIE THE POOH IN THE ARMCHAIR™

Designer:	Shane Ridge
Height:	3 ¼", 8 cm
Colour:	Yellow bear, pink armchair
Issued:	1996 to the present
Series:	Winnie the Pooh and Friends from the One Hundred Acre Wood

Back Stamp	Doulton Number	U.S. $	Can. $	U.K. £	Aust. $
BK-1	WP4	100.00	125.00	55.00	125.00
BK-2	WP4	—	70.00	20.00	79.00

WP5
PIGLET AND BALLOON™

Designer:	Warren Platt
Height:	2 ¾", 7.0 cm
Colour:	Pink piglet, green suit, blue balloon, light brown base
Issued:	1996 to the present
Series:	Winnie the Pooh and Friends from the One Hundred Acre Wood

Back Stamp	Doulton Number	U.S. $	Can. $	U.K. £	Aust. $
BK-1	WP5	75.00	100.00	45.00	100.00
BK-2	WP5	—	63.00	20.00	79.00

WP6
TIGGER SIGNS THE RISSOLUTION™

Designer:	Martyn Alcock
Height:	1 ¾", 4.5 cm
Colour:	Yellow tiger with black stripes
Issued:	1996 to the present
Series:	Winnie the Pooh and Friends from the One Hundred Acre Wood

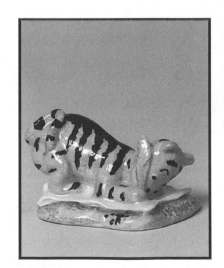

Back Stamp	Doulton Number	U.S. $	Can. $	U.K. £	Aust. $
BK-1	WP6	85.00	120.00	50.00	120.00
BK-2	WP6	—	70.00	20.00	79.00

WP7
EEYORE'S TAIL™

Designer:	Shane Ridge
Height:	3 ½", 8.9 cm
Colour:	Grey donkey with black markings, pink bow
Issued:	1996 to the present
Series:	Winnie the Pooh and Friends from the One Hundred Acre Wood

Back Stamp	Doulton Number	Price			
		U.S. $	Can. $	U.K. £	Aust. $
BK-1	WP7	75.00	100.00	45.00	100.00
BK-2	WP7	—	70.00	20.00	79.00

WP8
KANGA AND ROO™

Designer:	Martyn Alcock
Height:	3 ½", 8.9 cm
Colour:	Dark and light brown kangaroos
Issued:	1996 to the present
Series:	Winnie the Pooh and Friends from the One Hundred Acre Wood

Back Stamp	Doulton Number	Price			
		U.S. $	Can. $	U.K. £	Aust. $
BK-1	WP8	75.00	1000.00	45.00	100.00
BK-2	WP8	—	70.00	20.00	79.00

WP9
CHRISTOPHER ROBIN™
Style One

Designer:	Shane Ridge
Height:	5 ½", 14.0 cm
Colour:	White and blue checkered shirt, blue shorts, black wellingtons, red-brown hair
Issued:	1996 to the present
Series:	Winnie the Pooh and Friends from the One Hundred Acre Wood

Back Stamp	Doulton Number	Price			
		U.S. $	Can. $	U.K. £	Aust. $
BK-1	WP9	100.00	150.00	55.00	150.00
BK-2	WP9	—	95.00	25.00	110.00

WP10
CHRISTOPHER ROBIN AND POOH™

Designer:	Shane Ridge
Height:	3 ¼", 8.5 cm
Colour:	Light blue shirt and shorts, black boots, reddish brown hair, yellow bear
Issued:	1996 - 1997
Series:	Winnie the Pooh and Friends from the One Hundred Acre Wood

Back Stamp	Doulton Number	Price U.S.$	Can. $	U.K. £	Aust. $
BK-1	WP10	125.00	195.00	75.00	225.00
BK-2	WP10	100.00	160.00	55.00	185.00

WP11
POOH LIGHTS THE CANDLE™

Designer:	Graham Tongue
Height:	3 ½", 8.9 cm
Colour:	Yellow bear with white candle and hat
Issued:	1997 to the present
Series:	Winnie the Pooh and friends from the One Hundred Acre Woods

Back Stamp	Doulton Number	Price U.S.$	Can. $	U.K. £	Aust. $
BK-1	WP11	75.00	100.00	45.00	100.00
BK-2	WP11	—	70.00	20.00	79.00

WP12
POOH COUNTING THE HONEYPOTS™

Designer:	Martyn Alcock
Height:	3 ½", 8.9 cm
Colour:	Yellow bear, brown honeypots
Issued:	1997 to the present
Series:	Winnie the Pooh and friends from the One Hundred Acre Woods

Back Stamp	Doulton Number	Price U.S.$	Can. $	U.K. £	Aust. $
BK-1	WP12	125.00	175.00	65.00	175.00
BK-2	WP12	—	70.00	20.00	79.00

WP13
PIGLET PICKING THE VIOLETS™

Designer:	Graham Tongue
Height:	2 ½", 6.4 cm
Colour:	Pink, light and dark greens
Issued:	1997 to the present
Series:	Winnie the Pooh and Friends from the One Hundred Acre Wood

Back Stamp	Doulton Number	U.S. $	Price Can. $	U.K. £	Aust.
BK-2	WP13	—	70.00	20.00	79.00

WP14
EEYORE'S BIRTHDAY™

Designer:	Martyn Alcock
Height:	2 ¾", 7.0 cm
Colour:	Grey and black
Issued:	1997 to the present
Series:	Winnie the Pooh and Friends from the One Hundred Acre Wood

Back Stamp	Doulton Number	U.S. $	Price Can. $	U.K. £	Aust. $
BK-2	WP14	—	70.00	20.00	79.00

WP15
EEYORE LOSES A TAIL™

Designer:	Martyn Alcock
Height:	4", 10.1 cm
Colour:	Pink, yellow, lilac, green and brown
Issued:	1997 in a limited edition of 5,000
Series:	Winnie the Pooh and Friends from the One Hundred Acre Wood

Back Stamp	Doulton Number	U.S. $	Price Can. $	U.K. £	Aust. $
Doulton	WP15	500.00	700.00	300.00	600.00

WP16
POOH'S BLUE BALLOON
MONEY BOX™

Designer:	Shane Ridge
Height:	4 ¼", 10.8 cm
Colour:	Yellow bear, pink pig wearing green jumper, white balloon with dark blue rope
Issued:	1997 to the present
Series:	Winnie the Pooh and Friends from the One Hundred Acre Wood

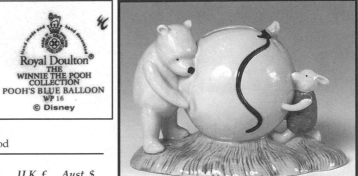

Back Stamp	Doulton Number	U.S. $	Price Can. $	U.K. £	Aust. $
Doulton	WP16	49.99	—	30.00	—

WIND IN THE WILLOWS

2939
MOLE™

Designer:	Harry Sales
Modeller:	David Lyttleton
Height:	3", 7.6 cm
Colour:	Dark grey mole, brown dressing gown
Issued:	1987 - 1989

Beswick Number		Price		
	U.S. $	Can. $	U.K. £	Aust. $
2939	85.00	200.00	70.00	125.00

2940
BADGER™

Designer:	Harry Sales
Modeller:	David Lyttleton
Height:	3", 7.6 cm
Colour:	Black and white badger, salmon dressing gown
Issued:	1987 - 1989

Beswick Number		Price		
	U.S. $	Can. $	U.K. £	Aust. $
2940	85.00	200.00	65.00	125.00

2941
RATTY™

Designer:	Harry Sales
Modeller:	David Lyttleton
Height:	3 ½", 8.9 cm
Colour:	Blue dungarees, white shirt
Issued:	1987 - 1989

Beswick Number		Price		
	U.S. $	Can. $	U.K. £	Aust. $
2941	85.00	200.00	55.00	125.00

2942
TOAD™

Designer:	Harry Sales
Modeller:	David Lyttleton
Height:	3 ½", 8.9 cm
Colour:	Green toad, yellow waistcoat and trousers, white shirt, red bowtie
Issued:	1987 - 1989

Beswick Number	Price U.S. $	Can. $	U.K. £	Aust. $
2942	130.00	200.00	65.00	125.00

3065
PORTLY™
(Otter)

Designer:	Unknown
Modeller:	Alan Maslankowski
Height:	2 ¾", 7.0 cm
Colour:	Brown otter, blue dungarees, green and yellow jumper, green shoes
Issued:	1988 - 1989

Beswick Number	Price U.S. $	Can. $	U.K. £	Aust. $
3065	225.00	300.00	150.00	200.00

3076
WEASEL GAMEKEEPER™

Designer:	Unknown
Modeller:	Alan Maslankowski
Height:	4", 10.1 cm
Colour:	Brown weasel, green jacket, trousers and cap, yellow waistcoat
Issued:	1988 - 1989

Beswick Number	Price U.S. $	Can. $	U.K. £	Aust. $
3076	225.00	300.00	150.00	200.00

INDICES

ALPHABETICAL INDEX

NUMERICAL INDEX

BEATRIX POTTER STUDIO SCULPTURES

BEDTIME CHORUS

BESWICK BEARS

ROYAL DOULTON BRAMBLY HEDGE

ROYAL DOULTON BUNNYKINS

DB35 Astro Bunnykins Rocket Man Music Box
DB36 Happy Birthday Bunnykins Music Box
DB37 Jogging Bunnykins Music Box
DB38 Mr. Bunnybeat Strumming Music Box
DB39 Mrs. Bunnykins at the Easter Parade Music Box
DB40 Aerobic Bunnykins
DB41 Freefall Bunnykins
DB42 Ace Bunnykins
DB43 Home Run Bunnykins
DB44 Not Issued
DB45 King John, First Variation
DB46 Queen Sophie, First Variation
DB47 Princess Beatrice, First Variation
DB48 Prince Frederick, First Variation
DB49 Harry the Herald, First Variation
DB50 Uncle Sam Bunnykins, First Variation
DB51 Mr. Bunnykins at the Easter Parade, Second Variation
DB52 Mrs. Bunnykins at the Easter Parade, Second Variation
DB53 Carol Singer Music Box
DB54 Collector Bunnykins
DB55 Bedtime Bunnykins, First Variation
DB56 Be Prepared Bunnykins
DB57 School Days Bunnykins
DB58 Australian Bunnykins
DB59 Storytime Bunnykins, Second Variation
DB60 Schoolmaster Bunnykins
DB61 Brownie Bunnykins
DB62 Santa Bunnykins Happy Christmas
          Christmas Tree Ornament
DB63 Bedtime Bunnykins, Second Variation
DB64 Policeman Bunnykins
DB65 Lollipopman Bunnykins
DB66 Schoolboy Bunnykins
DB67 Family Photograph Bunnykins, Second Variation
DB68 Father, Mother and Victoria Bunnykins
DB69 William Bunnykins
DB70 Susan Bunnykins
DB71 Polly Bunnykins
DB72 Tom Bunnykins
DB73 Harry Bunnykins
DB74A Nurse Bunnykins, First Variation
DB74B Nurse Bunnykins, Second Variation
DB75 Fireman Bunnykins
DB76 Postman Bunnykins
DB77 Paperboy Bunnykins
DB78 Tally Ho! Bunnykins, Second Variation
DB79 Bedtime Bunnykins, Third Variation
DB80 Dollie Bunnykins Playtime, Second Variation
DB81 Billie and Buntie Bunnykins Sleigh Ride,
          Second Variation
DB82 Ice Cream Bunnykins
DB83 Susan Bunnykins as Queen of the May
DB84 Fisherman Bunnykins, Style One
DB85 Cook Bunnykins
DB86 Sousaphone Bunnykins, Second Variation
DB87 Trumpeter Bunnykins, Second Variation
DB88 Cymbals Bunnykins, Second Variation
DB89 Drummer Bunnykins, Third Variation
DB90 Drum-major Bunnykins, Second Variation
DB91 King John, Second Variation
DB92 Queen Sophie, Second Variation
DB93 Princess Beatrice, Second Variation
DB94 Prince Frederick, Second Variation
DB95 Harry the Herald, Second Variation
DB96 Touchdown Bunnykins, Third Variation
DB97 Touchdown Bunnykins, Fourth Variation
DB98 Touchdown Bunnykins, Fifth Variation
DB99 Touchdown Bunnykins, Sixth Variation
DB100 Touchdown Bunnykins, Seventh Variation
DB101 Bride Bunnykins
DB102 Groom Bunnykins
DB103 Bedtime Bunnykins, Fourth Variation
DB104 Carol Singer Bunnykins
DB105 Sousaphone Bunnykins, Third Variation
DB106 Trumpeter Bunnykins, Third Variation
DB107 Cymbals Bunnykins, Third Variation
DB108 Drummer Bunnykins, Fourth Variation

DB109 Drum-major Bunnykins, Third Variation
DB110 to DB114 Not issued
DB115 Harry the Herald, Third Variation
DB116 Goalkeeper Bunnykins, First Variation
DB117 Footballer Bunnykins, First Variation
DB118 Goalkeeper Bunnykins, Second Variation
DB119 Footballer Bunnykins, Second Variation
DB120 Goalkeeper Bunnykins, Third Variation
DB121 Footballer Bunnykins, Third Variation
DB122 Goalkeeper Bunnykins (4th Variation
DB123 Soccer Player Bunnykins
DB124 Rock and Roll Bunnykins
DB125 Milkman Bunnykins
DB126 Magician Bunnykins
DB127 Guardsman Bunnykins
DB128 Clown Bunnykins, First Variation
DB129 Clown Bunnykins, Second Variation
DB130 Sweetheart Bunnykins, First Variation
DB131 Master Potter Bunnykins
DB132 Halloween Bunnykins
DB133 Aussie Surfer Bunnykins
DB134 John Bull Bunnykins
DB135 Mountie Bunnykins
DB136 Sergeant Mountie Bunnykins
DB137 60th Anniversary Bunnykins
DB142 Cheerleader Bunnykins, First Variation
DB143 Cheerleader Bunnykins, Second Variation
DB144 Batsman Bunnykins
DB145 Bowler Bunnykins
DB146 Christmas Surprise Bunnykins
DB147 Rainy Day Bunnykins
DB148 Bathtime Bunnykins
DB149 Easter Greetings Bunnykins
DB150 Wicketkeeper Bunnykins
DB151 Partners in Collecting
DB152 Boy Skater Bunnykins
DB153 Girl Skater Bunnykins
DB154 Father Bunnykins
DB155 Mother's Day Bunnykins
DB156 Gardener Bunnykins
DB157 Goodnight Bunnykins
DB158 New Baby Bunnykins
DB160 Out For a Duck
DB161 Jester Bunnykins
DB162 Trick or Treat Bunnykins
DB163 Beefeater Bunnykins
DB164 Juggler Bunnykins
DB165 Ringmaster Bunnykins
DB166 Sailor Bunnykins
DB167 Mother and Baby Bunnykins
DB168 Wizard Bunnykins
DB169 Jockey Bunnykins
DB170 Fisherman Bunnykins, Style Two
DB171 Joker Bunnykins
DB172 Welsh Lady Bunnykins
DB173 Bridesmaid Bunnykins
DB174 Sweetheart Bunnykins, Second Variation
BD175 Uncle Sam Bunnykins, Second Variation
DB176 Ballerina Bunnykins
DB177 Seaside Bunnykins
DB178 Irishman Bunnykins
DB179 Cavalier Bunnykins

BUNNYKINS RESIN SERIES

DBR1 Harry Bunnykins A Little Bunny At Play
DBR2 Harry Bunnykins Playtime
DBR3 Reginald Ratley Up To No Good
DBR4 Susan Bunnykins The Helper
DBR5 William Bunnykins Asleep In The Sun
DBR6 Lady Ratley Her Ladyship Explains
DBR7 Mrs. BunnykinsA Busy Morning Shopping
DBR8 Father Bunnykins Home From Work
DBR9 William Bunnykins A Bunny In A Hurry
DBR10 Susan Bunnykins Wildlife Spotting
DBR11 Susan and Harry Bunnykins Minding The Baby Brother

DBR12 Father Bunnykins and Harry Decorating The Tree
DBR13 Mrs. Bunnykins and William The Birthday Cake
DBR14 Happy Christmas From the Bunnykins Family
DBR15 Picnic Time With the Bunnykins Family
DBR16 Birthday Girl
DBR17 Birthday Boy
DBR18 The New Baby
DBR19 The Rocking Horse
DBR20 Photograph Frame - Girl
DBR21 Photograph Frame - Boy

CAT CHORUS

CC1 Purrfect Pitch
CC2 Calypso Kitten
CC3 One Cool Cat
CC4 Ratcatcher Bilk
CC5 Tradjazz Tom
CC6 Catwalking Brass
CC7 Feline Flamenco
CC8 Bravura Brass

COUNTRY COUSINS

PM2101 Sweet Suzie Thank You
PM2102 Peter Once Upon A Time
PM2103 Harry A New Home for Fred
PM2104 Michael Happily Ever After
PM2105 Bertram Ten Out of Ten
PM2106 Leonardo Practice Makes Perfect
PM2107 Lily Flowers Picked Just For You
PM2108 Patrick This Ways Best
PM2109 Jamie Hurrying Home
PM2111 Mum and Lizzie Let's Get Busy
PM2112 Molly and Timmy Picnic Time
PM2113 Polly and Sarah Good News!
PM2114 Bill and Ted Working Together
PM2115 Jack and Daisy How Does Your Garden Grow
PM2116 Alison and Debbie Friendship is Fun
PM2119 Robert and Rosie Perfect Partners
PM2120 Sammy Treasure Hunting

DAVID HAND'S ANIMALAND

1148 Dinkum Platypus
1150 Zimmy Lion
1151 Felia
1152 Ginger Nutt
1153 Hazel Nutt
1154 Oscar Ostrich
1155 Dusty Mole
1156 Loopy Hare

ENGLISH COUNTRY FOLK

ECF1 Huntsman Fox
ECF2 Fisherman Otter
ECF3 Gardener Rabbit
ECF4 Gentleman Pig
ECF5 Shepherd Sheepdog
ECF6 Hiker Badger, First Variation
ECF7 Mrs Rabbit Baking
ECF8 The Lady Pig
ECF Hiker Badger, Second Variation

ENID BLYTON

3676 Big Ears
3678 Noddy
3679 Mr. Plod
3770 Tessie Bear

HANNA-BARBERA

3577 Pebbles
3579 Bamm Bamm
3581 Top Cat
3583 Wilma Flintstone
3584 Betty Rubble
3586 Choo-Choo
3587 Barney Rubble
3588 Fred Flintstone
3590 Dino
3624 Fancy Fancy
3627 Benny
3671 Officer Dibble
3673 Spook
3674 Brain

JANE HISSEY
OLD BEAR

OB4601 Old Bear
OB4602 Time For Bed
OB4603 Bramwell Brown Had A Good Idea
OB4604 Don't Worry Rabbit
OB4605 The Long Red Scarf
OB4606 Waiting For Snow
OB4607 The Snowflake Biscuits
OB4608 Welcome Home, Old Bear
OB4609 Ruff's Prize
OB4610 Time For A Cuddle Me Tight

JOAN WALSH ANGLUND

2272 Anglund Boy
2293 Anglund Girl with Doll
2317 Anglund Girl with Flowers

KITTY MACBRIDE

2526 A Family Mouse
2527 A Double Act
2528 The Racegoer
2529 A Good Read
2530 Lazybones
2531 A Snack
2532 Strained Relations
2533 Just Good Friends
2565 The Ring
2566 Guilty Sweethearts
2589 All I Do is Think of You

LITTLE LIKABLES

LL1 Family Gathering (Hen and Two Chicks)
LL2 Watching the World Go By (Frog)
LL3 Hide and Seek (Pig and Two Piglets)
LL4 My Pony (Pony)
LL5 On Top of the World (Elephant)
LL6 Treat Me Gently (Fawn
LL7 Out at Last (Duckling)
LL8 Cats Chorus (Cats)

LITTLE LOVABLES

LL1 Happy Birthday
LL2 I Love You
LL3 God Loves Me
LL4 Just For You
LL5 To Mother
LL6 Congratulations
LL7 Passed
LL8 Happy Birthday
LL9 I Love You
LL10 God Loves Me

LL11	Just For You
LL12	To Mother
LL13	Congratulations
LL14	Passed
LL15	Happy Birthday
LL16	I Love You
LL17	God Loves Me
LL18	Just For You
LL19	To Mother
LL20	Congratulations
LL21	Passed
LL22	(No Name)
LL23	(No Name)
LL24	(No Name)
LL25	(No Name)
LL26	(No Name)
LL27	(No Name)
LL28	(No Name)
LL29	To Daddy
LL30	Merry Christmas
LL31	Good Luck
LL32	Get Well Soon
LL33	Please
LL34	Please
LL35	Prototype for I Love Beswick
LL36	I Love Beswick

NORMAN THELWELL

2704A	An Angel on Horseback, First Variation
2704B	An Angel on Horseback, Second Variation
2769A	Kick-Start, First Variation
2769B	Kick-Start, Second Variation
2789A	Pony Express, First Variation
2789B	Pony Express, Second Variation
SS7A	I Forgive You, First Variation
SS7B	I Forgive You, Second Variation
SS12A	Early Bath, First Variation
SS12B	Early Bath, Second Variation

PADDINGTON BEAR CO. LTD.

PB1	Paddington at the Station
PB2	Paddington Bakes a Cake
PB3	Paddington Decorating
PB4	Paddington Surfing
PB5	Paddington Gardening
PB6	Paddington Bathtime
PB7	Paddington the Golfer
PB8	Paddington the Musician
PB9	Paddington at Christmas Time
PB10	Paddington Marmalade Sandwiches
PB11	Paddington Going to Bed
PB12	Paddington the Fisherman

THE PIG PROMENADE

PP1	John the Conductor (Vietnamese Pot Bellied Pig)
PP2	Matthew the Trumpet Player (Large White Pig)
PP3	David the Flute Player (Tamworth Pig)
PP4	Andrew the Cymbal Player (Gloucester Old Spotted Pig)
PP5	Daniel the Violinist (Saddleback Pig)
PP6	Michael the Bass Drum Player (Large Black Pig)
PP7	James The Triangle Player (Tamworth Piglet)
PP8	Richard the French Horn Player
PP9	Christopher the Guitar Player
PP10	George
PP11	Thomas
PP12	Benjamin

RUPERT BEAR

2694	Rupert Bear
2710	Algy Pug
2711	Pong Ping

2720	Bill Badger
2779	Rupert Bear Snowballing

ST. TIGGYWINKLE

TW1	Henry Hedgehog
TW2	Harry Hedgehog
TW3	Fred Fox
TW4	Bob Badger
TW5	Rosie Rabbit
TW6	Sarah Squirrel
TW7	Daniel Duck
TW8	Oliver Owl
TW9	Friends
TW10	A Helping Hand
TW11	Deborah Dormouse
TW12	Monty Mole
TW13	Franchesca Fawn

THE SNOWMAN GIFT COLLECTION

D6972	Snowman Miniature Character Jug
DS1	James
DS2	The Snowman
DS3	Stylish Snowman
DS4	Thank You Snowman
DS5	Snowman Magic Music Box
DS6	Cowboy Snowman
DS7	Highland Snowman
DS8	Lady Snowman
DS9	Bass Drummer Snowman
DS10	Flautist Snowman
DS11	Violinist Snowman
DS12	Pianist Snowman
DS13	Snowman's Piano
DS14	Cymbal Player Snowman
DS15	Drummer Snowman
DS16	Trumpeter Snowman
DS17	Cellist Snowman
DS18	Snowman Musical Box
DS19	Snowman Money Box
DS20	The Snowman Tobogganing
DS21	The Snowman Skiing
DS22	The Snowballing Snowman
DS23	Building the Snowman

THUNDERBIRDS

3337	Lady Penelope
3339	Brains
3344	Scott Tracy
3345	Virgil Tracy
3346	Parker
3348	The Hood

TURNER ENTERTAINMENT

3547	Droopy
3549	Jerry
3552	Tom

WALT DISNEY CHARACTERS

1278	Mickey Mouse
1279	Jiminy Cricket
1280	Pluto
1281	Goofy
1282	Pinocchio
1283	Donald Duck
1289	Minnie Mouse
1291	Thumper
1301	Nana
1302	Smee
1307	Peter Pan

WIND IN THE WILLOWS

314

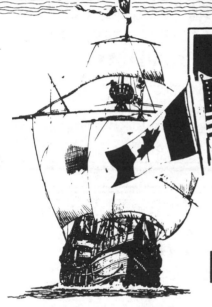

Colonial House of Collectibles & Santa's North Pole World

ROYAL DOULTON IS OUR SPECIALITY!

We Buy ✦ We Sell ✦ We Appraise

Colonial House Features the Largest Selection of Current and Discontinued Items in the Following Lines:

- ✦ OLD & NEW ROYAL DOULTON FIGURES & CHARACTER JUGS
- ✦ HUMMELS
- ✦ DAVID WINTER COTTAGES
- ✦ DEPT. 56 COTTAGES AND SNOWBABIES

- ✦ ROYAL WORCESTER
- ✦ WEE FOREST FOLK
- ✦ WALT DISNEY CLASSICS
- ✦ SWAROVSKI CRYSTAL
- ✦ LLADRO
- ✦ LILLIPUT LANE

Send for our latest product catalogue!

Colonial House Of Collectibles

We carry Current & Discontinued Beanie Babies!

WE DO MAIL ORDER

Monday to Saturday
10 am to 5 pm
or by appointment

182 Front Street, Berea, OH 44017
Tel: (440) 826-4169 or (800) 344-9299
Fax: (440) 826-0839
E-mail: yworrey@aol.com

320